Annexation Law IN NORTH CAROLINA

VOLUME 1

General Topics

Second Edition

David M. Lawrence

UNC
SCHOOL OF GOVERNMENT

THE UNIVERSITY
of NORTH CAROLINA
at CHAPEL HILL

School of Government
The University of North Carolina at Chapel Hill

The School of Government at the University of North Carolina at Chapel Hill works to improve the lives of North Carolinians by engaging in practical scholarship that helps public officials and citizens understand and strengthen state and local government. The core components of the School are the Institute of Government, established in 1931 to provide educational, advisory, and research services for state and local governments, and the two-year Master of Public Administration Program, which prepares graduates for leadership careers in public service. The School also sponsors centers focused on information technology, environmental finance, and civic education for youth.

The Institute of Government is the largest university-based local government training, advisory, and research organization in the United States, offering up to 200 classes, seminars, schools, and specialized conferences for more than 12,000 public officials each year. In addition, faculty members annually publish approximately fifty books, periodicals, and other reference works related to state and local government. Each day that the General Assembly is in session, the Institute's *Daily Bulletin*, available in electronic format, reports on the day's activities for members of the legislature and others who need to follow the course of legislation.

Operating support for the School of Government's programs and activities comes from many sources, including state appropriations, local government membership dues, private contributions, publication sales, course fees, and service contracts. Visit www.sog.unc.edu or call 919.966.5381 for more information on the School's courses, publications, programs, and services.

First edition 2002. Second edition 2007

11 10 09 08 07

ISBN 978-1-56011-555-7

To Robert A. Lawrence
1911–2002

Contents

(each chapter is internally paginated)

Introduction

This is the first of three volumes on North Carolina annexation law. It addresses topics that are relevant regardless of the statutory annexation procedure a city uses. The second volume addresses voluntary annexation, while the third considers involuntary annexation. Each volume has been issued in loose-leaf format, and it is my plan to issue replacement pages or chapters as needed, inasmuch as there is a good bit of appellate decision making on annexation topics as well as somewhat less frequent statutory changes. This second edition of volume 1 includes two rewritten chapters plus updated tables of local modifications in Chapter 1.

I have attempted to organize the chapters in this volume in a rough chronological order, as a city might work through an annexation. Chapter 1 discusses the General Assembly's authority over and role in annexation law. Chapters 2 through 4 discuss matters that condition a city's power to annex—the effect of political boundaries on annexation powers, the factors determining which of two competing cities will be permitted to annex a particular tract, and a city's authority to enter into contracts with property owners concerning possible future annexations. Chapter 5 reviews the rules for voting on annexation ordinances. Chapter 6 summarizes the requirements for filing maps of completed annexations. Chapter 7 discusses the standing of various parties to challenge a completed annexation. Chapters 8 through 12 consider the effect of an annexation on existing services and service providers—first in general terms and then with special attention to rural fire departments, private solid waste collection firms, private electric or natural gas utilities, and rural water and sewer systems financed by the U.S. Department of Agriculture. Chapter 13 considers the effect of annexation on various election matters. Chapter 14 reviews the effect of annexation on city revenues and spells out the steps a city should take to ensure receipt of revenues. Chapter 15 closes the volume by discussing a city's authority to repeal an annexation ordinance.

Two colleagues—Jake Wicker and Bill Thornton—read the entire manuscript of the first edition, while a third colleague—Bob Joyce—read the chapter on election effects. In addition, Jep Rose, city attorney for Rocky Mount, read the chapter on electric and natural gas utilities. I appreciate very much the help of each of them. Finally, I have spent more than ten years—since the first retirement of Jake Wicker—teaching and consulting on annexation for the Institute of Government, and the scope of this volume (and of the two that follow it) has been deeply influenced by the questions I've received both in teaching and in consulting. I'm grateful to all who have played a part in the making of this book.

My father died as I was completing the manuscript of the first edition of this book, and his death caused me to understand two (of the many) important influences he had on my life. First, by example he showed me the importance of giving your best effort to your work, both for personal fulfillment and as the consideration that supports your salary. Second, by equal example, he taught me the parallel importance of separating your work from the rest of your life and of making sure you remember that your family is the most important part of your life. In gratitude for those lessons, and many others, I continue to dedicate this volume to him.

David M. Lawrence
William Rand Kenan Jr. Professor of Public Law and Government
February 2007

1

General Assembly Actions Concerning Annexation

1

General Assembly Actions Concerning Annexation

Section 1.01. Introduction

The North Carolina General Assembly has enacted four statutes that authorize cities to undertake annexations; most of this series of books is an explanation of those four statutes. Before any of the statutes were enacted, however, the General Assembly itself annexed property to cities by local act, and it retains the constitutional authority to do so.[1] In addition, it may undo annexations by removing territory from a city, and it may modify the statutory procedures as they apply to a particular city. This chapter discusses these various powers retained by the General Assembly.

Section 1.02. Annexation by Legislative Act

[a] No standards bind the General Assembly

As noted above, in delegating to cities the authority to annex, the General Assembly did not forfeit its own constitutional authority to expand city boundaries. Indeed, in almost every legislative session the General Assembly enacts one or more local acts annexing territory to particular cities.[2]

When the General Assembly annexes territory to a city, it is not bound by any of the standards or procedures that bind cities undertaking statutory annexations. The area being annexed by local act need not be developed for urban purposes or be contiguous to the existing city. The General Assembly need not prepare any sort of report supporting the annexation. It need not obtain the consent of the property owners.

1. *See* N.C. Const., art. VII, § 1.

2. Article II, § 23 of the North Carolina constitution requires that any law authorizing a local government to impose a tax on its citizens be read in each house of the General Assembly on three separate days. In Lutterloh v. City of Fayetteville, 149 N.C. 65, 62 S.E. 758 (1908), the North Carolina supreme court held that this requirement did not apply to a local act annexing territory to an existing city.

By and large, those who attempt to challenge a legislative annexation find the courts unwilling to second-guess the legislature's decision about whether to annex or which properties to annex. Only if those being annexed can demonstrate an unconstitutional motive behind the annexation as a whole or in the specific boundaries of the annexation—such as to deprive persons of the right to vote on account of their race—will a court intervene.[3]

More than ninety years ago, the North Carolina supreme court made clear the legislature's primary authority in a case challenging an annexation to Fayetteville. The court wrote that

> [T]he enlargement of the municipal boundaries by the annexation of new territory, and the consequent extension of their corporate jurisdiction, including that of levying taxes, are legitimate subjects of legislation. In the absence of constitutional restriction, the extent to which such legislation shall be enacted, both with respect to the terms and circumstances under which the annexation may be had, and the manner in which it may be made, rests entirely in the discretion of the Legislature. With its wisdom, propriety or justice we have naught to do.[4]

Two more recent cases from the North Carolina court of appeals illustrate the General Assembly's authority and the unwillingness of courts to investigate into or overturn legislative judgments about city boundaries. The case of *Jones v. Jeanette*[5] involved a challenge to the legislatively established boundaries of the town of Mesic in Pamlico County. The General Assembly incorporated the town in 1971, including an area of some 4,800 acres in the new municipality. Three years later, a second legislative act added another 707 acres to the town. All of the area annexed in 1974 and much of the original town was made up of woodland and marshland, and some of the landowners refused to pay town taxes on this property. When the town initiated proceedings to collect the taxes by foreclosure, the landowners brought an action challenging, among other things, the constitutionality of the original incorporation act and the later act expanding the town. They argued that the two legislative acts were constitutionally unreasonable, given the

3. *See* Gomillion v. Lightfoot, 364 U.S. 339 (1960), in which the Supreme Court invalidated a redefinition of a city's boundaries that was found to be racially motivated.

4. Lutterloh v. City of Fayetteville, 149 N.C. at 69, 62 S.E. at 760.

5. 34 N.C. App. 526, 239 S.E.2d 293 (1977).

extent and nature of the property included in the town. The state court of appeals affirmed the trial court's dismissal of this claim. The court held that the fixing of city boundaries is a matter of legislative discretion and that "[o]rdinarily, the courts have no authority to inquire into the motives" of the General Assembly's decision to incorporate or annex territory to a city.[6]

In *Abbott v. Town of Highlands*,[7] the town had been unsuccessful in annexing an area pursuant to statute—because it could not provide the sewer services the statute required. The town had then turned to the General Assembly, which annexed the same area to the town by local act. This legislative annexation did not, however, include a golf course in the middle of the area; as a result, the golf course became an unincorporated island surrounded by the town. Residents of the annexed area brought a lawsuit challenging the annexation, in part because it excluded the golf course. The court of appeals rejected their challenge, writing that "unless contiguous areas are excluded for constitutionally impermissible reasons, we cannot substitute our judgment for that of the legislature."[8]

[b] Recording requirements

G.S. 160A-29 requires a city that has annexed an area pursuant to any of the annexation statutes to record a map of each annexation in the offices of the local register of deeds and the Secretary of State. Although this requirement does not extend to legislative annexations, a city should record maps of such annexations as well, in order to maintain a complete history of the city's growth in both offices. G.S. 163-288.1 also requires a city that has annexed an area to deliver a map of the annexation to the local board of elections. This statutory requirement applies specifically to legislative as well as statutory annexations.

Section 1.03. Deannexation

6. *Id.* at 532, 293 S.E. 2d at 296. Before the case was finally decided, the General Assembly revisited the boundaries of Mesic and enacted a third local act, this time significantly reducing the size of the town. 1977 N.C. Sess. Laws ch. 533.

7. 52 N.C. App. 69, 277 S.E.2d 820 (1981).

8. *Id.* at 78, 277 S.E.2d at 826. *See also*, Piedmont Ford Truck Sale, Inc. v. City of Greensboro, 324 N.C. 499, 380 S.E.2d 107 (1985), in which the supreme court denied an equal protection challenge to a legislative annexation in which owners of annexed property complained that similar property was not annexed.

9. 157 N.C. 515, 73 S.E. 195 (1911).

(or Removal of Territory from a City)

North Carolina has no statutory procedure by which territory may be removed from a city; therefore, such an action can only be taken by act of the General Assembly. The preceding account of the General Assembly's constitutional authority to add territory to a city also supports and applies to its authority to remove territory. In addition, two early twentieth-century cases offer indirect support to this legislative authority. In 1911, in *Commissioners of Cumberland County v. Commissioners of Harnett County,*[9] the supreme court upheld the legislature's detachment of six square miles from Cumberland County and the addition of that territory to Harnett County. And in 1932, in *Town of Highlands v. City of Hickory,*[10] the court upheld a legislative act that, subject to a single referendum held simultaneously in the three cities affected, abolished the towns of Highlands and West Hickory and annexed their territories to the city of Hickory.[11]

Deannexation is a relatively rare event. In the past thirty years it has not occurred more than twelve to fifteen times. Normally, the General Assembly removes territory from a city only if both the property owners and the city agree to the removal, although, as *Highlands v. Hickory* demonstrates, that local agreement is not constitutionally necessary.[12]

Section 1.04. Local Modification of Statutory Procedures

[a] In general

In addition to local acts that annex territory to a city or remove territory from a city, the General Assembly sometimes enacts local acts that modify the applicability of one or more annexation statutes to a particular city. The most notable example of such local modifications involved the two statutory procedures for involuntary annexation. When those statutes were enacted in 1959, their sponsors, in order to secure passage of the legislation, agreed to provisions that excluded from the procedures

10. 202 N.C. 167, 162 S.E. 471 (1932).

11. A state legislature's inherent authority to detach territory from a city is recognized nationally. 2 Eugene McQuillin, The Law of Municipal Corporations § 7.24 (3d. ed. 1996).

12. Two much more recent examples of deannexation without local agreement took place in 1998. In that year the General Assembly incorporated two new towns in Union County; in both cases the territory of the new town included land that had recently been annexed to or was in the process of being annexed to an existing city or town. The incorporation acts specifically provided that the recently annexed territories

the cities in a few specified counties. That is, while the exclusions remained in force, cities in those counties could not annex pursuant to the 1959 legislation; they either had to rely on voluntary annexations or use the pre-1959 procedure, which usually required voter approval by residents of the area being annexed. Initially, the provisions barred the cities in thirteen counties from utilizing either or both of the two involuntary statutes.[13] Over the ensuing years, this number was reduced, and all the remaining general exclusions were repealed in 1983.[14]

Since then, however, the General Assembly has enacted a few additional exclusions from one or more of the statutory annexation procedures. Usually these exclusions have been attached to the charter of a newly incorporated town, a price the town had to pay in order to garner the political support necessary to incorporation. Examples include Dobbins Heights and Sugar Mountain, which are barred from undertaking involuntary annexations; Lewisville and Pleasant Garden, which are barred from annexations in certain directions; and Oak Ridge, which is denied the power to annex any land at all until 2018.

The General Assembly has also enacted local acts that facilitate annexations by particular cities. Most commonly, these acts modify one or more of the standards governing satellite (i.e., noncontiguous) annexations. For example, under the general law, the total area of a city's satellites may not, exceed 10 percent of the area of the main body of the city. Almost three dozen cities have received legislative exceptions to the 10 percent limit—some permanent, some temporary. (Table 1.1 lists by

---

were no longer in the existing city or town but were to be part of the new towns. SL 1998-43 (Wesley Chapel) and -143 (Hemby Bridge).

In Novato Fire Protection Dist. v. United States, 181 F.3d 1135 (9th Cir. 1999), a federal court of appeals held that a deannexation of federal property violated the federal constitution. A fire district had been charging the Air Force a fee to provide fire protection to a federal military base within the district. The district became concerned that charging a fee in those circumstances might be considered taxation of federal property and therefore arranged to deannex the military base. The Air Force continued to pay for fire protection, but some years later it refused to do so any longer. When the parties litigated the effect of the deannexation, the court of appeals held that the base was entitled to fire district services without payment of a fee as long as it was in the district. Therefore, the court reasoned, to deannex the property solely in order to charge a fee violated the federal government's right to intergovernmental tax immunity.

13. 1959 N.C. Sess. Laws chs. 1009 and 1010. The original thirteen counties were Allegheny, Columbus, Cumberland, Edgecombe, Franklin, Halifax, Harnett, Iredell, Nash, Pender, Perquimans, Person, and Randolph; Allegheny was excepted only from the statute for cities of under 5,000, Columbus was excepted only from the statute for larger cities, and the other eleven counties were excepted from both. About sixty cities and towns were affected by these original exceptions.

14. 1983 N.C. Sess. Laws ch. 636.

15. *In re* Annexation Ordinances, 253 N.C. 637, 117 S.E.2d 795 (1961); *in re* Durham Annexation Ordinance, 69 N.C. App. 77, 316 S.E.2d 649 (1984). The court of

subject matter the significant local act modifications to the annexation laws currently in force, while Table 1.2 lists the same acts by city.)

There is no question that such local modifications to the annexation statutes are constitutional. The North Carolina supreme court upheld the original enactment of the involuntary annexation statute for larger cities despite the exclusion of twelve counties from its terms, and the court of appeals reaffirmed this holding some twenty years later.[15] In addition, a federal court upheld the exclusion against an equal protection attack mounted by landowners in a nonexcluded county who were being involuntarily annexed.[16]

[b] Legislative ratification of flawed annexations

Although no examples of legislative ratification have been found in the North Carolina session laws, it is clear that the General Assembly may ratify or cure an annexation that a city has carried out improperly. The national rule in such cases is that ratification is an appropriate legislative action.[17] After all, the legislature may annex property directly to a city, and the legislature has established the procedures under which cities may undertake their own annexations. Therefore, the legislature may absolve a city from errors the city has committed in attempting a statutory annexation. Although there is apparently no North Carolina case law on ratification of annexations, there are numerous cases supporting the legislative ratification of other local government proceedings. For example, in several cases the courts have ratified special assessments levied by local governments when the assessments would otherwise have been subject to attack because statutory procedures were not followed.[18]

appeals decision was necessary because of the revision of the state constitution in the late 1960s.

16. Thompson v. Whitley, 344 F. Supp. 480 (E.D.N.C. 1972). *See also* Barefoot v. City of Wilmington, 306 F.3d 113 (4th Cir. 2002).

17. 2 McQuillin, *supra* note 11, § 7.45.

18. *E.g.,* City of High Point v. Clark, 211 N.C. 607, 191 S.E. 318 (1937) (assessment project outside of city limits); Crutchfield v. City of Thomasville, 205 N.C. 709, 172 S.E. 366 (1934) (assessment project undertaken without petition when statute required petition); Gallimore v. Town of Thomasville, 191 N.C. 648, 132 S.E. 657 (1926) (insufficient number of signatures on petition).

19. Tables do not list local acts that were superseded by general laws. The two main categories of such local acts are those that (1) authorized cities within specific counties to

Table 1.1

Significant Local Acts Modifying the Annexation Statutes (through 2006)[1]

Acts Limiting Use of the Statutory Procedures		
Bethania	1995 N.C. Sess. Laws ch. 74	City may annex only those areas within its sphere of influence under annexation agreement with Winston-Salem.
Currituck County	SL 2003-27	No city located outside Currituck County may annex territory within the county.
Dobbins Heights	1983 N.C. Sess. Laws ch. 658	City may not annex, except upon receipt of petition from owners of contiguous property pursuant to G.S. 160A-31.
Fletcher	1989 N.C. Sess. Laws ch. 44	City may not annex property in Buncombe County.
Lewisville	1991 N.C. Sess. Laws ch. 116	City may not annex to the east except by agreement with Winston-Salem; city may not annex to the south except by agreement with Clemmons.
Lincoln County	SL 2006-22	No city located outside Lincoln County may annex territory within that county.
Midway	SL 2006-37	City may not annex into Forsyth County and may not annex in Davidson County west and north of specified lines without agreement of Winston-Salem.
New Bern	1993(94) N.C. Sess. Laws ch. 605	City may not undertake involuntary annexation across the Trent River.
North Topsail Beach	1995 N.C. Sess. Laws ch. 489	City may not annex territory on the mainland.
Oak Ridge	SL 1998-113	City may not annex until after July 1, 2018.
Pleasant Garden	SL 1997-344	City may only annex toward the south, within a specifically described area, and may not undertake involuntary annexations at all.

1. Tables do not list local acts that were superseded by general laws. The two main categories of such local acts are those that (1) authorized cities within specific counties to enter into annexation agreements (replaced by N.C. Gen. Stat. Chapter 160A, Article 4A, Part 6 (hereinafter G.S.)) and (2) authorized specific cities to annex satellite areas closer to another city if the satellite area was within the annexing city's exclusive sphere of influence (replaced by G.S. 160A-58.1(b1)).

Table 1.1 *(continued)*

Reidsville	SL 1997-360	City may not annex west of a described line.
Sedalia	SL 1997-444	City may not annex until after July 1, 2017.
Sugar Mountain	1985 N.C. Sess. Laws ch. 395	City may not annex using involuntary procedure. Voluntary annexations are permitted.
Swepsonville	SL 1997-448	City may not annex northeast of State Highway 54 until after August 26, 2017.
Wallburg	SL 2004-37	City may not annex into Forsyth County and may not annex in Davidson County east of line set out in act.
Wentworth	SL 1997-322	City may not annex east of a described line.
Whitsett	1991 N.C. Sess. Laws ch. 684	City may not annex to south, east, or north except by annexation agreement with Gibsonville.
Acts Establishing Requirement or Possibility of Referendum before Annexation		
Bermuda Run	SL 1999-94	City may not undertake any annexation without "vote or consent" of a majority of residents of the annexation area.
Holden Beach	1991 N.C. Sess. Laws ch. 638	City may not complete any annexation without approval from city's voters if (a) town commissioners call referendum or (b) 40 percent of town's registered voters sign petition for referendum within twenty days after adoption of annexation ordinance.
River Bend	SL 1997-363	City may not undertake involuntary annexation without approval from voters in annexation area if 25 percent of registered voters who own real property in the annexation area sign petition for referendum by date of public hearing on annexation.
Wentworth	SL 1997-322	City may not undertake involuntary annexation without approval from voters in annexation area.
Unincorporated Areas That May Not Be Annexed		
Cabarrus County industrial area	SL 2000-7, SL 2003-326	Property described in the act may not be involuntarily annexed before June 30, 2010.

Table 1.1 *(continued)*

Campbell College	SL 1998-143	Any annexation of a described tract must annex the entire tract or none of it; partial annexations of the tract are not permitted.
Eden industrial area	SL 2002-74, SL 2003-316	Authorizes City of Eden to contract not to annex described industrial sites before 2013.
Johnston County industrial area	SL 2003-418	Property described in act may not be involuntarily annexed.
Lyons Station Sanitary District	SL 2006-4	Prohibits annexation of any part of named sanitary district as long as annexation of territory within Camp Butner requires approval of secretary of health and human services.
Morganton–Lenoir Airport	SL 2001-306	Establishes the Special Airport District for Burke and Caldwell counties and prohibits annexation of property within the district.
New Hanover Airport	SL 1997-415	The airport property or properties designated for expansion of the airport may not be annexed without approval of the airport's governing board.
Piedmont Triad Airport property	1985(86) Sess. Laws ch. 818, SL 2003-202	Property described in act may not be annexed; second act allows airport authority and Greensboro to adjust limits of area off-limits to annexation.
Research Triangle Park	1985 N.C. Sess. Laws ch. 435	No part of the Research Triangle Park is subject to involuntary annexation.
R.J. Reynolds facility at Tobaccoville	1991 N.C. Sess. Laws chs. 232 and 233	Property owned by R.J. Reynolds Tobacco Company and described in the legislation may not be annexed by Tobaccoville or King for forty years.
Rock Barn community	1989 N.C. Sess. Laws ch. 27	Any involuntary annexation of a described tract of land in Catawba County must annex the entire tract or none of it; partial involuntary annexations of tract are not permitted.
Modifications to the Procedure for Voluntary Contiguous Annexations		
Durham	1993 N.C. Sess. Laws ch. 342	City may make annexation undertaken pursuant to G.S. 160A-31 effective up to three years after ordinance is adopted. City may change the effective date or repeal annexation ordinance adopted

Table 1.1 *(continued)*

		pursuant to G.S. 160A-31 at any time before it becomes effective. In annexation undertaken pursuant to G.S. 160A-31, petition need not be signed by owners of tax-exempt property or by railroad companies, public utilities, or electric or telephone membership corporations.
Durham	SL 1997-452	Any action brought to challenge a voluntary contiguous annexation must be brought within thirty days after the ordinance is adopted.
Huntersville	SL 1999-19	If property annexed pursuant to G.S. 160A-31 is subject to use-value taxation, the effective date of the annexation is delayed in the same manner as if it were an involuntary annexation.
Modifications to the Procedure for Voluntary Noncontiguous Annexations		
Modifications to Annexation Standards—Distance from City		
Beaufort	SL 2003-204	Three-mile criterion replaced by described line, and city may satellite annex any area to east of line.
Canton	1983 N.C. Sess. Laws ch. 301	City may annex satellite areas that are up to five miles from city.
Cornelius	SL 1999-103	Three-mile limit does not apply to any satellite area within city's sphere of influence under an intercity annexation agreement.
Davidson	SL 1999-85	Three-mile limit does not apply to any satellite area within city's sphere of influence under an intercity annexation agreement.
Henderson	1996 (2d extra sess.) N.C. Sess. Laws ch. 3	City may annex satellite areas that are up to five miles from city.
Huntersville	SL 1999-24	Three-mile limit does not apply to any satellite area within city's sphere of influence under an intercity annexation agreement.
Union County cities	SL 2003-321	Three-mile limit reduced to two miles or to an area contiguous to an existing satellite area.

Table 1.1 *(continued)*

Modifications to Annexation Standards—Area Closer to Another City		
Banner Elk	SL 1998-77	City may annex area closer to Sugar Mountain if area within Banner Elk's extraterritorial jurisdiction (ETJ).
Beaufort	SL 2003-204	City may annex any satellite area to east of described line, even if closer to another city.
Greensboro	SL 1997-344	City may annex satellite area closer to Pleasant Garden.
Greensboro	SL 1997-444	City may annex satellite area closer to Sedalia.
Greensboro	SL 1998-113	City may annex satellite area closer to Oak Ridge.
Henderson	1996 (2d extra sess.) N.C. Sess. Laws ch. 3	City may annex satellite area closer to another city if the other city consents.
Kernersville	SL 1998-113, SL 2004-37	City may annex satellite area closer to Oak Ridge; city may also annex satellite area closer to Wallburg.
Morehead City	SL 1997219	City may annex satellite area closer to Newport if within Morehead City's ETJ.
New Bern	N.C. Sess. Laws 1989 ch. 382	City may annex satellite area even if closer to Trent Woods.
Newport	SL 1997-219	City may annex satellite area closer to Morehead City if within Newport's ETJ.
Trent Woods	1989 N.C. Sess. Laws ch. 382	City may annex satellite area even if closer to New Bern.
Union County cities	SL 2003-321	City may annex area closer to another city if area is contiguous to an existing satellite area.
Winston-Salem	SL 2004-37	City may annex satellite area closer to Wallburg.
Modifications to Annexation Standards—Annexation of Subdivision		
Maggie Valley	SL 2005-79	Subdivision requirement is inapplicable.
Rockingham	1995(96) N.C. Sess. Laws ch. 654	City need not annex entire subdivision if area developed for commercial or industrial use.
Union County cities	SL 2003-321	Subdivision requirement is inapplicable.

Table 1.1 *(continued)*

Modifications to Annexation Standards—Cumulative Size of Satellite Areas

For the following cities, there is no limit on the cumulative size of satellite areas:

Angier	SL 2004-99
Ayden	SL 2005-71
Beaufort	SL 2003-204
Benson	SL 2006-122
Bladenboro	SL 2003-30
Burgaw	SL 2006-122
Calabash	SL 2001-37
Catawba	SL 1997-2; SL 2001-37
Claremont	SL 2002-121
Clayton	SL 2006-122
Columbia	SL 2005-433
Concord	SL 2002-121
Conover	SL 2002-121
Creswell	SL 2004-57
Dallas	SL 2001-37
Dobson	SL 2006-122
Elizabeth City	SL 2005-71
Fuquay-Varina	SL 2004-57
Garner	SL 2004-57
Gastonia	SL 2003-30
Godwin	SL 2001-37
Greenville	SL 2005-71
Grimesland	SL 2006-130
Hickory	1987 N.C. Sess. Laws ch. 179
Holly Ridge	SL 2004-57
Kenly	1987 N.C. Sess. Laws ch. 67
Kannapolis	SL 2005-173
Knightdale	SL 2004-57
Landis	SL 2005-173
Leland	SL 2004-57
Locust	SL 2003-30
Louisburg	SL 2001-37
Maggie Valley	SL 2005-79
Maiden	SL 2002-121
Marion	SL 2001-37
Mayodan	SL 2004-57
Midland	SL 2002-121
Mocksville	SL 2001-37
Mooresville	SL 1997-219
Morrisville	SL 2004-57
Mount Airy	SL 1999-232; SL 2003-281

Table 1.1 *(continued)*

Mount Holly	SL 2004-57
New Bern	1993(94) N.C. Sess. Laws ch. 605
Newton	SL 2002-121
Oxford	SL 2001-37
Pembroke	SL 2001-37
Pine Level	SL 2003-30
Princeton	SL 2006-62
Randleman	SL 2004-57
Ranlo	SL 2003-30
Rockingham	SL 2001-37
Rolesville	SL 2004-57
Rutherfordton	SL 2001-37
Salisbury	SL 2001-72
Sanford	SL 2002-121
Shallotte	SL 2005-173
Smithfield	SL 2006-62
Southport	SL 2002-121
Spencer	SL 2005-173
Statesville	1989(90) N.C. Sess. Laws ch. 882
Stem	SL 2006-130
Stovall	SL 2006-130
Surf City	SL 2005-71
Swansboro	SL 2002-121
Taylorsville	SL 2005-52
Troy	1993 N.C. Sess. Laws ch. 159
Wallace	SL 2004-57
Warsaw	SL 2002-121
Washington	SL 2004-57
Waynesville	SL 2001-37
Wendell	SL 2004-57
Windsor	SL 2005-71
Yadkinville	SL 2006-122
Zebulon	SL 2004-57

For the following cities, the 10-percent limit on the cumulative size of satellite annexation areas has been increased to the percentage noted:

Asheboro, 20 percent	SL 1998-203
Canton, 75 percent	1985(86) N.C. Sess. Laws ch. 979
Hope Mills, 20 percent	SL 1997-151
Marvin, 50 percent	SL 2002-140
Morehead City, 25 percent	SL 1998-42
Union County cities, 20 percent	SL 2003-321
Weaverville, 23 percent	SL 1997-151

Table 1.1 *(continued)*

For the following cities, the 10-percent limit does not apply to a specific area:

Apex	1993 N.C. Sess. Laws ch. 312
Brevard	1987 N.C. Sess. Laws ch. 254; SL 2001-105
Clayton	1993 N.C. Sess. Laws ch. 63; SL 1999-10
Holly Springs	1991 N.C. Sess. Laws ch. 243
Reidsville	SL 1997-343
Seagrove	SL 2000-32
Wake Forest	1989(90) N.C. Sess. Laws ch. 882

Modifications to Annexation Procedures

Durham	1993 N.C. Sess. Laws ch. 342	City may make annexation undertaken pursuant to G.S. 160A-58.1 effective up to three years after ordinance is adopted. City may change the effective date or repeal annexation ordinance adopted pursuant to G.S. 160A-58.2 at any time before it becomes effective.
Durham	SL 1997-452	Any action brought to challenge a voluntary satellite annexation must be brought within thirty days after the ordinance is adopted.
Tarboro	N.C. 1991 Sess. Laws ch. 305	City may make annexation undertaken pursuant to G.S. 160A-58.1 effective up to eighteen months after ordinance is adopted if a property owner so requests.

Other Modifications

Canton	1983 N.C. Sess. Laws ch. 301	City may exercise extraterritorial land-use jurisdiction from the satellite area.
Iredell County municipalities	1989 N.C. Sess. Laws ch. 598	Owner of satellite area may enter into a binding waiver of specific city services.
Mooresville	1991 N.C. Sess. Laws ch. 289	City may exercise extraterritorial land-use jurisdiction from satellite area.

Modifications to the Procedures for Involuntary Annexations

Modifications to Annexation Procedures

Durham	1993 N.C. Sess. Laws ch. 342	City may make annexation undertaken pursuant to G.S. 160A-46 effective up to three years after ordinance is adopted. City may change the effective date of or repeal annexation ordinance adopted

Table 1.1 *(continued)*

		pursuant to G.S. 160A-49 at any time before it becomes effective.
Raleigh	1977 N.C. Sess. Laws ch. 351	City may change the effective date of annexation ordinance adopted pursuant to G.S. 160A-49 at any time before it becomes effective.
Miscellaneous Modifications		
Asheville	SL 2005-139	City may not condition extension of utility service upon customer's submission of annexation petition.
Cabarrus County municipalities	1991 N.C. Sess. Laws ch. 685	County land-use regulations remain in effect for up to 120 days after an area is annexed by a city
Durham	SL 2003-26	City may annex street rights-of-way when both sides already within the city.

Table 1.2

Local Acts Modifying the Annexation Statutes, by City (through 2006)

Angier	SL 2004-99	There is no limit on the cumulative size of satellite annexation areas.
Apex	1993 N.C. Sess. Laws ch. 312	Annexations within a described area will not count against the 10 percent cumulative limit on the size of satellite areas.
Asheboro	SL 1998-203	Satellite areas may total up to 20 percent of area within primary corporate limits.
Asheville	SL 2005-139	City may not condition extension of utility service on customer's submission of petition for annexation.
Ayden	SL 2005-71	There is no limit on the cumulative size of satellite annexation areas.
Banner Elk	SL 1998-77	City may annex area closer to Sugar Mountain if area within Banner Elk's ETJ.
Beaufort	SL 2003-204	There is no limit on the cumulative size of satellite annexation areas. In addition, the satellite annexation requirements that the area be within three miles of the city and not closer to another city are deleted and replaced by a described line and authorization to satellite-annex any area east of that line.
Benson	SL 2006-122	There is no limit on the cumulative size of satellite annexation areas.
Bermuda Run	SL 1999(94)	City may not undertake any annexation without "vote or consent" of a majority of residents of the annexation area.
Bethania	1995 N.C. Sess. Laws ch. 74	City may annex only those areas within its sphere of influence under annexation agreement with Winston-Salem.
Bladenboro	SL 2003-30	There is no limit on the cumulative size of satellite annexation areas.
Brevard	1987 N.C. Sess. Laws ch. 254; SL 2001-105	Each act annexes described areas to the town and provides that these areas shall not be counted in determining the cumulative size of satellite areas.

Table 1.2 *(continued)*

Burgaw	SL 2006-122	There is no limit on the cumulative size of satellite annexation areas.
Cabarrus County municipalities	1991 N.C. Sess. Laws ch. 685	County land-use regulations remain in effect for up to 120 days after an area is annexed by a city.
Calabash	SL 2001-37	There is no limit on the cumulative size of satellite areas.
Canton	1983 N.C. Sess. Laws ch. 301	City may annex satellite areas that are up to five miles from city. City may exercise extraterritorial land-use jurisdiction from satellite area.
	1985(86) N.C. Sess. Laws ch. 979	Satellite areas may total up to 75 percent of area within primary corporate limits.
Catawba	SL 1997-2; SL 2001-37	There is no limit on the cumulative size of satellite areas.
Claremont	SL 2002-121	There is no limit on the cumulative size of satellite annexation areas.
Clayton	SL 2006-122	There is no limit on the cumulative size of satellite annexation areas.
Columbia	SL 2005-433	There is no limit on the cumulative size of satellite annexation areas.
Concord	SL 2002-121	There is no limit on the cumulative size of satellite annexation areas.
Conover	SL 2002-121	There is no limit on the cumulative size of satellite annexation areas.
Cornelius	SL 1999-103	Three-mile limit does not apply to any satellite area within city's sphere of influence under an intercity annexation agreement.
Craven County towns	1985 N.C. Sess. Laws ch. 92	Requires referendum before annexation by certain small towns in Craven County.
Creswell	SL 2004-57	There is no limit on the cumulative size of satellite annexation areas.
Currituck County	SL 2003-27	No city located outside Currituck County may annex territory within that county.
Dallas	SL 2001-37	There is no limit on the cumulative size of satellite annexation areas.
Davidson	SL 1999-85	Three-mile limit does not apply to any satellite area within city's sphere of influence under an intercity annexation agreement.

Table 1.2 *(continued)*

Dobbins Heights	1983 N.C. Sess. Laws ch. 658	City may not annex, except upon receipt of petition from owners of contiguous property pursuant to G.S. 160A-31.
Dobson	SL 2006-122	There is no limit on the cumulative size of satellite annexation areas.
Durham	1993 N.C. Sess. Laws ch. 342	City may make annexation undertaken pursuant to G.S. 160A-31 effective up to three years after ordinance is adopted. City may change the effective date or repeal annexation ordinance adopted pursuant to G.S. 160A-31 at any time before it becomes effective. In annexation undertaken pursuant to G.S. 160A-31, petition need not be signed by owners of tax-exempt property or by railroad companies, public utilities, or electric or telephone membership corporations. City may make annexation undertaken pursuant to G.S. 160A-58.1 effective up to three years after ordinance is adopted. City may change the effective date or repeal annexation ordinance adopted pursuant to G.S. 160A-58.2 at any time before it becomes effective. City may make annexation undertaken pursuant to G.S. 160A-46 effective up to three years after ordinance is adopted. City may change the effective date of or repeal annexation ordinance adopted pursuant to G.S. 160A-49 at any time before it becomes effective.
	SL 1997-452	Any action brought to challenge a voluntary contiguous annexation must be brought within thirty days after the ordinance is adopted. Any action brought to challenge a voluntary satellite annexation must be brought within thirty days after the ordinance is adopted.
	SL 2003-26	City may annex streets when properties abutting both sides of the street are already within the city.

Table 1.2 *(continued)*

Eden	SL 2002-74, SL 2003-316	City may contract not to involuntarily annex described industrial areas until 2013.
Elizabeth City	SL 2005-71	There is no limit on the cumulative size of satellite annexation areas.
Fletcher	1989 N.C. Sess. Laws ch. 44	City may not annex property in Buncombe County.
Fuquay-Varina	SL 2004-57	There is no limit on the cumulative size of satellite annexation areas.
Garner	SL 2004-57	There is no limit on the cumulative size of satellite annexation areas.
Gastonia	SL 2003-30	There is no limit on the cumulative size of satellite annexation areas.
Godwin	SL 2001-37	There is no limit on the cumulative size of satellite areas.
Greensboro	SL 1997-344	City may annex satellite area closer to Pleasant Garden.
	SL 1997-444	City may annex satellite area closer to Sedalia.
	SL 1998-113	City may annex satellite area closer to Oak Ridge.
Greenville	SL 2005-71	There is no limit on the cumulative size of satellite annexation areas.
Grimesland	SL 2006-130	There is no limit on the cumulative size of satellite annexation areas.
Henderson	1996 N.C. Sess. Laws (2d extra sess.) ch. 3	City may annex satellite areas that are up to five miles from city. City may annex satellite area closer to another city if the other city consents.
Hickory	1987 N.C. Sess. Laws ch. 179	There is no limit on the cumulative size of satellite areas.
Holden Beach	1991 N.C. Sess. Laws ch. 638	City may not complete any annexation without approval from city's voters if (a) town commissioners call referendum or (b) 40 percent of town's registered voters sign petition for referendum within twenty days after adoption of annexation ordinance.
Holly Ridge	SL 2004-57	There is no limit on the cumulative size of satellite annexation areas.
Holly Springs	1991 N.C. Sess. Laws ch. 243	The limit on cumulative size is inapplicable to a described area if it is annexed by a specific date.

Table 1.2 *(continued)*

Hope Mills	SL 1997-151	Satellite areas may total up to 20 percent of area within primary corporate limits.
Huntersville	SL 1999-19	If property annexed pursuant to G.S. 160A-31 is subject to use-value taxation, the effective date of the annexation is delayed in the same manner as in an involuntary annexation.
	SL 1999-24	Three-mile limit does not apply to any satellite area within city's sphere of influence under an intercity annexation agreement.
Iredell County municipalities	1989 N.C. Sess. Laws ch. 598	Owner of satellite area may enter into a binding waiver of specific city services.
Kannapolis	SL 2005-173	There is no limit on the cumulative size of satellite annexation areas.
Kenly	1987 N.C. Sess. Laws ch. 67	There is no limit on the cumulative size of satellite areas.
Kernersville	SL 1998-113	City may annex satellite area closer to Oak Ridge.
	SL 2004-37	City may annex satellite areas closer to Wallburg.
Knightdale	SL 2004-57	There is no limit on the cumulative size of satellite annexation areas.
Landis	SL 2005-173	There is no limit on the cumulative size of satellite annexation areas.
Leland	SL 2004-57	There is no limit on the cumulative size of satellite annexation areas.
Lewisville	1991 N.C. Sess. Laws ch. 116	City may not annex to the east except by agreement with Winston-Salem; city may not annex to the south except by agreement with Clemmons.
Lincoln County	SL 2006-22	No city located outside Lincoln County may annex territory within that county.
Locust	SL 2003-30	There is no limit on the cumulative size of satellite annexation areas.
Louisburg	SL 2001-37	There is no limit on the cumulative size of satellite areas.
Maggie Valley	SL 2005-79	There is no limit on the cumulative size of satellite annexation areas. Subdivision requirement does not apply to satellite annexations.
Maiden	SL 2002-121	There is no limit on the cumulative size of satellite annexation areas.

Table 1.2 *(continued)*

Marion	SL 2001-37	There is no limit on the cumulative size of satellite areas.
Marvin	SL 2002-140	The limit on the cumulative size of satellite annexation areas is raised to 50 percent.
Mayodan	SL 2004-57	There is no limit on the cumulative size of satellite annexation areas.
Midland	SL 2002-121	There is no limit on the cumulative size of satellite annexation areas.
Midway	SL 2006-37	City may not annex into Forsyth County and may not annex in Davidson County west and north of specified lines without agreement of Winston-Salem.
Mocksville	SL 2001-37	There is no limit on the cumulative size of satellite areas.
Mooresville	1991 N.C. Sess. Laws ch. 289	City may exercise extraterritorial land-use jurisdiction from satellite area.
	SL 1997-219	There is no limit on the cumulative size of satellite areas.
Morehead City	SL 1997-219	City may annex satellite area closer to Newport if within Morehead City's ETJ.
	SL 1998-42	Satellite areas may total up to 25 percent of area within primary corporate limits.
Morrisville	SL 2004-57	There is no limit on the cumulative size of satellite annexation areas.
Mount Airy	SL 2003-281	There is no limit on the cumulative size of satellite annexation areas.
Mount Holly	SL 2004-57	There is no limit on the cumulative size of satellite annexation areas.
New Bern	1989 N.C. Sess. Laws ch. 382	City may annex satellite area even if closer to Trent Woods.
	1993(94) N.C. Sess. Laws ch. 605	City may not undertake involuntary annexation across the Trent River. There is no limit on the cumulative size of satellite areas.
Newport	SL 1997-219	City may annex satellite area closer to Morehead City, if within Newport's ETJ.
Newton	SL 2002-121	There is no limit on the cumulative size of satellite annexation areas.
North Topsail Beach	1995 N.C. Sess. Laws ch. 489	City may not annex territory on the mainland.
Oak Ridge	SL 1998-113	City may not annex until after July 1, 2018.

Table 1.2 *(continued)*

Oxford	SL 2001-37	There is no limit on the cumulative size of satellite areas.
Pembroke	SL 2001-37	There is no limit on the cumulative size of satellite areas.
Pine Level	SL 2003-30	There is no limit on the cumulative size of satellite annexation areas.
Pleasant Garden	SL 1997-344	City may only annex toward the south, within a specifically described area, and may not undertake involuntary annexations at all.
Princeton	SL 2006-62	There is no limit on the cumulative size of satellite annexation areas.
Raleigh	1977 N.C. Sess. Laws ch. 351	City may change the effective date of annexation ordinance adopted pursuant to G.S. 160A-49 at any time before it becomes effective.
Randleman	SL 2004-57	There is no limit on the cumulative size of satellite annexation areas.
Ranlo	SL 2003-30	There is no limit on the cumulative size of satellite annexation areas.
Reidsville	SL 1997-343	An area annexed by a specific ordinance will not count in determining the cumulative size of satellite areas.
	SL 1997-360	City may not annex west of a described line.
River Bend	SL 1997-363	City may not undertake involuntary annexation without approval from voters in annexation area if 25 percent of registered voters who own real property in the annexation area sign petition for referendum by date of public hearing on annexation.
Rockingham	1995(96) N.C. Sess. Laws ch. 654	City need not annex entire subdivision if area developed for commercial or industrial use.
	SL 2001-37	There is no limit on the cumulative size of satellite areas.
Rolesville	SL 2004-57	There is no limit on the cumulative size of satellite annexation areas.
Rutherfordton	SL 2001-37	There is no limit on the cumulative size of satellite areas.

Table 1.2 *(continued)*

Salisbury	SL 2001-72	There is no limit on the cumulative size of satellite areas.
Sanford	SL 2002-121	There is no limit on the cumulative size of satellite annexation areas.
Seagrove	SL 2000-32	Annexes a described area to the Town of Seagrove and provides that this area shall not be counted in determining the cumulative size of satellite areas
Sedalia	SL 1997-444	City may not annex until after July 1, 2017.
Shallotte	SL 2005-173	There is no limit on the cumulative size of satellite annexation areas.
Smithfield	SL 2006-62	There is no limit on the cumulative size of satellite annexation areas.
Southport	SL 2002-121	There is no limit on the cumulative size of satellite annexation areas.
Spencer	SL 2005-173	There is no limit on the cumulative size of satellite annexation areas.
Statesville	1989(90) N.C. Sess. Laws ch. 882	There is no limit on the cumulative size of satellite areas.
Stem	SL 2006-130	There is no limit on the cumulative size of satellite annexation areas.
Stovall	SL 2006-130	There is no limit on the cumulative size of satellite annexation areas.
Sugar Mountain	1985 N.C. Sess. Laws ch. 395	City may not annex using involuntary procedure. Voluntary annexations are still permitted.
Surf City	SL 2005-71	There is no limit on the cumulative size of satellite annexation areas.
Swansboro	SL 2002-121	There is no limit on the cumulative size of satellite annexation areas.
Swepsonville	SL 1997-448	City may not annex northeast of State Highway 54 until after August 26, 2017.
Tarboro	1991 N.C. Sess. Laws ch. 305	City may make annexation undertaken pursuant to G.S. 160A-58.1 effective up to eighteen months after ordinance is adopted if owner of property so requests.
Taylorsville	SL 2005-52	There is no limit on the cumulative size of satellite annexation areas.
Trent Woods	1989 N.C. Sess. Laws ch. 382	City may annex satellite area even if closer to New Bern.

Table 1.2 *(continued)*

Troy	1993 N.C. Sess. Laws ch. 159	There is no limit on the cumulative size of satellite areas.
Union County cities	SL 2003-321	The satellite annexation standards are modified as follows: (1) the satellite area must be within two miles of the annexing city or be contiguous to an existing satellite area; (2) the satellite area may be closer to another city if it is contiguous to an existing satellite area; (3) the subdivision standard is deleted; and (4) the cumulative size of satellite areas may not exceed 20 percent of the primary city area.
Wake Forest	1989(90) N.C. Sess. Laws ch. 882	If an area meeting specific standards is annexed, the limit on cumulative size of satellite areas does not apply.
Wallace	SL 2004-57	There is no limit on the cumulative size of satellite annexation areas.
Wallburg	SL 2004-37	City may not annex into Forsyth County; and may not annex in Davidson County east of line set out in act.
Warsaw	SL 2002-121	There is no limit on the cumulative size of satellite annexation areas.
Washington	SL 2004-57	There is no limit on the cumulative size of satellite annexation areas.
Waynesville	SL 2001-37	There is no limit on the cumulative size of satellite areas.
Weaverville	SL 1997-151	Satellite areas may total up to 23 percent of primary corporate limits.
Wendell	SL 2004-57	There is no limit on the cumulative size of satellite annexation areas.
Wentworth	SL 1997-322	City may not annex east of a described line. City may not undertake involuntary annexation without approval from voters in annexation area.
Whitsett	1991 N.C. Sess. Laws ch. 684	City may not annex to south, east, or north except by annexation agreement with Gibsonville.
Windsor	SL 2005-71	There is no limit on the cumulative size of satellite annexation areas.

Table 1.2 *(continued)*

Winston-Salem	SL 2004-37	City may annex satellite areas closer to Wallburg.
Yadkinville	SL 2006-122	There is no limit on the cumulative size of satellite annexation areas.
Zebulon	SL 2004-57	There is no limit on the cumulative size of satellite annexation areas.

2

Annexation Boundaries: Existing Political Borders, Federal Facilities, and Islands

2

Annexation Boundaries: Existing Political Borders, Federal Facilities, and Islands

Section 2.01. Annexation of Territory Already within Another City

[a] In general

One city may never annex territory that is already within another city (although, as noted in Section 1.04, the General Assembly may remove territory from one city and place it in another). This prohibition is explicit in the two involuntary annexation statutes. One of the standards for any annexation area under those statutes states that "no part of the area shall be included within the boundary of another incorporated municipality."[1] Although there is no comparable language in either of the voluntary statutes, the North Carolina court of appeals has recognized that the prohibition on annexing territory that is already in a city is implicit in those statutes as well. In *Town of Valdese v. Burke, Inc.*,[2] Valdese attempted a voluntary annexation of property separated from the town by the Interstate 40 right-of-way. Under G.S. 160A-31(f), property separated from a town by a street or highway right-of-way is, in normal circumstances, considered contiguous to the town and so may be annexed. This particular right-of-way, however, was already within the neighboring town of Rutherford College, having been annexed to that town by the General Assembly the year before. The court of appeals therefore invalidated Valdese's annexation, noting that when a city annexes property on the other side of a right-of-way, "the annexing municipality, in effect, annexes the intervening . . . rights-of-way."[3]

1. N.C. GEN. STAT. § 160A-36(b)(3) and 160A-48(b)(3) (hereinafter G.S.).
2. 125 N.C. App. 688, 482 S.E.2d 24 (1997).
3. *Id.* at 691, 482 S.E.2d at 25.

Because the Interstate 40 right-of-way was already in another city, Valdese could not annex it and therefore could not annex the property that lay beyond it. Indeed, the court seemed to be applying the statutory prohibition on annexing territory in another city, found in the involuntary statutes, to annexations undertaken pursuant to the voluntary statutes. Because allowing Valdese's annexation would have the effect of placing the Interstate 40 right-of-way in Valdese, the result "would be at odds with the clear prohibition established in G.S. 160A-48(b)(3)" (the involuntary statute).[4]

[b] Inactive municipalities

Sometimes small towns die as a practical matter but not as a legal matter. People stop running for the town board, taxes are no longer levied, and town government ceases to operate. Unless the General Assembly repeals the town's charter, however, the town retains a shadowy existence. At one time, an important consequence of not repealing the charter of an inactive town was that another city or town could not annex territory within the inactive town. That territory was, after all, "within the boundary of another incorporated municipality." In 1986, however, the General Assembly ended this bar to annexation. It amended G.S. 160A-1(2) to provide that the term "incorporated municipality" does not include "a municipal corporation that, without regard to its date of incorporation, would be disqualified from receiving gasoline tax allocations by G.S. 136-41.2(a)." That statute prohibits the distribution of state street assistance (that is, Powell Bill funds) to a city that has not conducted the most recent city election required by its charter or by the general law. Therefore, if a city has stopped holding elections, its territory is no longer considered within a city for purposes of annexation, and the territory may be annexed by another city.

Section 2.02. Annexation of Territory within Another City's Extraterritorial Land-Use Jurisdiction

G.S. 160A-360 entitles most North Carolina cities to an extraterritorial land-use jurisdiction (or ETJ) of one mile. No statutory prohibition, though, prohibits one city from annexing territory that is within another city's ETJ. The ETJ is by definition *extraterritorial*; as it is not within the

4. *Id.*

city, the statutory and judicial prohibitions on annexing territory already within another city do not apply.

Section 2.03. Annexation of Territory within a Special District

[a] Cities may annex territory within special districts

The involuntary annexation statutes prohibit annexation of territory that lies within another "incorporated municipality." That term includes only cities, towns, and incorporated villages; it does not include special districts, such as sanitary districts, fire districts, or county water and sewer districts. This point has been made by the North Carolina supreme court and court of appeals and is implicitly recognized in a number of statutes.

In *State ex rel. East Lenoir Sanitary District v. City of Lenoir*,[5] the city undertook an annexation that included territory within the sanitary district. The annexation was undertaken under the 1947 annexation statute, which, like the current law, permitted annexation only of "land not embraced within the corporate limits of some other municipality." The sanitary district claimed that it was a "municipality" for purposes of the annexation statute, making the city's attempted annexation invalid. The supreme court disagreed:

> Does the word "municipality" as [used in the annexation statute] mean another city or town, or does it comprise sanitary districts and other quasi-municipal corporations? It is, we think, apparent that the word was intended to mean cities and towns and is limited to that meaning.[6]

The current annexation statutes use the term *incorporated municipality* rather than the single word *municipality*, but there is no reason to believe the General Assembly intended any difference in meaning when it enacted the current statutes. The latter also use the single term *municipality* throughout to describe the types of governments authorized to annex, and the session laws enacting the current statutes make it plain that they were intended as direct replacements of the 1947

5. 249 N.C. 96, 105 S.E.2d 411 (1958).
6. *Id.* at 100, 105 S.E.2d at 414.

statutory procedure.[7] The court of appeals recognized the continuing validity of the *Lenoir* decision in 1989 in *Thrash v. City of Asheville*.[8] In that case petitioners argued that the city could not annex territory within a county water and sewer district, which was characterized in G.S. Chapter 162A as a "municipal corporation." Despite that characterization, the court, relying squarely on the *Lenoir* decision, held that the district was not an "incorporated municipality" under the annexation laws.

The General Assembly has also recognized that cities may annex territory within certain special districts. Under G.S. 69-25.15, when territory within a rural fire protection district is annexed by a city, it ceases being part of the fire district; G.S. 153A-304.1 enacts a comparable rule applicable to county service districts established to provide fire protection.[9] Neither statute would make any sense if cities were not able to annex territory within fire protection districts or county service districts. Furthermore, G.S. 162A-93 protects the utility systems of county water and sewer districts from city competition and clearly recognizes that cities might annex territory within such a district.[10] Finally, one of the annexation statutes itself recognizes that cities may annex special districts: G.S. 160A-49(f) provides for reduced taxation by owners of property within a sanitary district that has been annexed by a city.[11]

[b] Effect of annexation on special district boundaries

Unless another statute makes a different provision, territory within a special district that has been annexed by a city remains in the special district as well. The supreme court recognized this situation in its *Lenoir* decision, remarking that it is "not unusual for one governmental agency to occupy the same territory as another governmental agency, and this is particularly true when the governmental objects are not coequal and coextensive."[12] The General Assembly has recognized it as well, as the

7. 1959 N.C. Sess. Laws ch. 1009, § 11 and ch. 1010, § 11.

8. 95 N.C. App. 457, 383 S.E.2d 657 (1989), *rev'd on other grounds*, 327 N.C. 251, 393 S.E.2d 842 (1990).

9. These statutes are discussed in section 9.02, Service Contracts with Rural Fire Departments, and section 14.02, City Reimbursement of Fire District Taxes.

10. The statute makes several references to annexations within a district by a city. This statute was enacted in the spring of 1989, several months before the *Thrash* decision was announced. The court of appeals, however, made no mention of the statute, perhaps because it was not brought to the court's attention. The statute is discussed in section 8.03[a].

11. This statute is discussed below in subsection [c], p. 7.

12. 249 N.C. at 100, 105 S.E.2d at 414. This is the law nationally as well. *See, e.g.*, City of Sacramento v. Southgate Recreation and Park Dist., 41 Cal. Rptr. 452 (1964).

above-noted statutory provisions affecting county water and sewer districts and sanitary districts make plain.

The General Assembly has made a different provision with respect to two kinds of special districts—rural fire protection districts and county service districts providing fire protection. G.S. 69-25.15(a) specifies that on the effective date of an annexation of some or all of the territory of a rural fire protection district, the annexed territory ceases to be part of the fire district. Similarly, G.S. 153A-304.1(a) specifies that on the effective date of an annexation of some or all of the territory in a county service district organized for fire protection, the annexed territory ceases to be part of the service district. It should be noted that this latter provision applies only to a service district organized for fire protection. When territory within a county service district organized for any other purpose is annexed by a city, it both remains in the service district and becomes part of the city.

[c] Effect of annexation on special district taxes

Constitutional concerns. Unless provided for in another statute, property that is within both a city and a special district is liable for taxes levied by both governments. This is made clear by the supreme court's 1969 decision in *State ex rel. Dyer v. City of Leaksville*.[13] In 1967 the General Assembly had enacted legislation that, subject to approval by the community's voters, consolidated three existing cities and an existing sanitary district into the new city of Eden. Part of the community was also served by a metropolitan sewerage district that was not included in the consolidation and continued to exist independently after the voters had approved the new city. Because the sewerage district did not encompass the entire area of the new city, not all the city's property owners paid district taxes. A number of property owners brought suit to challenge the consolidation; they argued, among other things, that it violated the state constitution's requirement of tax uniformity for some Eden taxpayers to pay taxes only to Eden while others paid taxes both to Eden and to the sewerage district. The supreme court rejected the argument:

> Unquestionably the Constitution requires that the rule of uniformity be observed. It is observed if the rate is uniform throughout each taxing authority's jurisdiction. When property is within more

13. 275 N.C. 41, 165 S.E.2d 201 (1969).

> than one taxing authority, each has the right to make its own levy. The constitutional requirement is that taxing powers shall be exercised "by uniform rule". The rule of uniformity is not violated by double taxation resulting from taxes levied by different authorities if each authority adheres to the uniformity rule in its levies. . . .
>
> The plaintiffs allege the failure to abolish [the sewerage district] and transfer its duties and obligations (including its heavy bonded debt) to the new municipality resulted in an unequal tax burden on the property within the [district's] taxing area. True, this burden is not shared by property which is within the city but is outside [the district]. Inequality in tax burdens follows the creation of municipal corporations with partially overlapping boundaries. The remedy, if one is due, must be supplied by the agency which created the taxing districts and fixed their boundaries. The General Assembly and not the court, has the requisite power.[14]

Statutory concerns. The argument in *Dyer* concerned whether subjecting property to both city and special district taxes violates the state constitution. It does not. Nonetheless, that fact does not settle related questions about the effect of such double taxation on a city's *statutory* ability to annex property within a special district—particularly under the involuntary annexation statutes.[15] The involuntary annexation statutes require that the annexing city provide major municipal services to annexed property on essentially the same basis as those services are provided to property already within the city. This requirement is explicit for four major municipal services—police, fire, solid waste collection, and street maintenance[16]—and implicit for the other two—water and sewer.[17] But if annexed property is

14. *Id.* at 49, 165 S.E.2d at 206. *See also* Town of Kenilworth v. Hyder, 197 N.C. 85, 147 S.E. 736 (1929) (uniformity requirement not violated when town is included in territory of new special district).

15. In a voluntary annexation, the property owner presumably understands the likelihood of double taxation and seeks annexation anyway.

16. G.S. 160A-35(3)a. and 160A-47(3)a. each provide that an annexing city must provide the four listed services to annexed property "on substantially the same basis and in the same manner as such services are provided within the rest of the municipality prior to annexation."

17. The two annexation statutes do not include comparable language for water or sewer services. They do, however, require that the city be prepared to extend water or sewer lines to annexed property "according to the policies in effect in such municipal-

subject to an additional tax not paid by the rest of the city because it is part of a special district, that property might not be receiving municipal services on essentially the same basis as other property in the city.[18]

This possibility underlies an argument between majority and dissent in the North Carolina court of appeals' 1989 decision in *Thrash v. City of Asheville*.[19] A portion of the area being annexed by Asheville in this case was within a county water and sewer district established a decade earlier pursuant to G.S. Chapter 162A, Article 6. The district had subsequently issued $1.5 million in general obligation debt for sewers, almost all of which was still outstanding at the time of annexation. To help retire the debt, the district levied a tax of eight cents, for which the property within the district being annexed by the city would remain liable. Although city and county officials had held discussions about arrangements for the district's operation and obligations, the county had refused to conclude an agreement. Thus the annexation report made no special provision for the district's obligations or for the tax burden that would fall on district property owners in the annexation area. In the court of appeals, one set of petitioners[20] argued that this continuing double taxation violated the involuntary annexation statute and persuaded one of the judges on the panel to agree with them. In his dissent, Judge Greene noted that the statute provides that annexed property is "entitled to the same privileges and benefits as other parts" of the city; he concluded that because annexed property that was within the district "was subject to additional ad valorem taxes, the 'benefits' [it receives] from the City are not the 'same' as the 'benefits' received by [property] in the 'other parts of the municipality.'"[21] The other two

ity." Once the lines are extended, the city is subject to a general obligation to provide water and sewer services according to a uniform rate structure.

18. The fact that property owners pay an additional tax does not automatically mean that they are not receiving services on the same basis as other property owners in the city. If the tax is for a water or sewer system and the special district is the provider of that service, how the district's utility rates compare with the city's utility rates would also affect whether the annexed property owners are receiving services within the statutory standards.

19. 95 N.C. App. 457, 383 S.E.2d 657 (1989), *rev'd on other grounds*, 327 N.C. 251, 393 S.E.2d 842 (1990).

20. The reported case joined three separate petitions challenging the annexation.

21. 95 N.C. App. at 478, 383 S.E.2d at 669. Judge Greene also argued that the annexed property would not be "subject to municipal taxes on the same basis as is the preexisting territory of the municipality," as G.S. 160A-58.10(c) requires. The reference to municipal taxes in the quoted language, though, is clearly to taxes levied by the municipality and not taxes levied by overlapping governments.

members of the panel disagreed, although their reasoning is not compelling. The majority opinion noted that the city had tried "to negotiate an equitable distribution of revenue with county staff prior to adoption of the annexation ordinance" and that the county ultimately had not responded.[22] The majority clearly thought the city's proposals would satisfy its statutory obligations and expressed confidence that "in light of the proposals made by the City to date, an equitable solution will be reached and this is not a bar to annexation of the area."[23]

There are two difficulties with the majority's response to this issue. First, the city was in a difficult position. It was trying to negotiate an arrangement with the county (which governs the district), and the county refused to negotiate. Therefore, the matter remained unresolved—but through no fault of the city. The majority's recognition of the city's dilemma probably explains how it handled this issue. Yet, if the city did need to make some special provision because of the special district tax, as the majority seems to accept, then the annexation statutes require that it do so *before* annexation, so that the solution can be included in the annexation report. This point was made by Judge Greene in his dissent, and he appears to be correct. Second, even if negotiations had been concluded before annexation on the basis of the city's proposals, it is not clear that those proposals would have dealt adequately with the problem created by the special district's tax levy. Although the court's majority and dissenting opinions do not detail the city's proposals, they are set out in the record. In essence, the proposals attempted to accommodate the interests of both the city and the district as follows: (1) the county would continue its scheduled construction of lines within the district, but the city would reimburse the county's costs of doing so; (2) the city would contract to operate sewer services within the entire district; and (3) the city would pay the county the amount necessary to meet that portion of the district's annual debt service obligations not satisfied by the eight-cents tax (which would continue to be collected).[24] The proposals might have satisfied the political and budgetary concerns of the county, but they did not deal directly with the concerns of property owners or the annexation statutes' requirement for equal treatment of annexed property. Instead, the city appears to have relied on a proviso in G.S. 160A-49(f) to protect property owners. That proviso directs that if a city annexes

22. 95 N.C. App. at 471, 383 S.E.2d at 665.
23. *Id.* at 471–72, 383 S.E.2d at 665.
24. Letter from City Manager to County Manager, Record at 407–08.

property in a sanitary district that has installed water and sewer lines paid for by residents of the district, that property is not liable for city taxes levied for debt service during the first five years after the effective date of annexation. In its brief, the city argued that the term *sanitary district* should be read broadly, to include county water and sewer districts, which would provide adequate relief to individual property owners. The majority opinion did not address this argument, but Judge Greene's dissenting opinion rejected it, pointing out that sanitary districts and county water and sewer districts are distinct, and different, governmental entities.[25]

In any event, the proviso itself is poorly conceived and probably unconstitutional. It is poorly conceived because the remedy provided does not fit the problem it addresses. Its authors obviously thought that it was unfair, and perhaps in violation of the annexation statute itself, for the city to tax sanitary district property owners for the same kind of facilities that the district had taxed them for and presumably would continue to tax them for. But instead of limiting the exemption from city taxes to taxes for debt service on water or sewer debt, the proviso creates an exemption for taxes levied for debt service on any debt. Why should property within a sanitary district be exempt from paying city taxes to retire city debt for streets, or parks, or any other city purpose except water and sewer? Moreover, the statutory direction appears to contravene the constitution's requirement of uniform taxes within a taxing jurisdiction. The court in *Dyer v. City of Leaksville* made clear that the constitution requires that the rate of tax be uniform throughout each taxing unit's jurisdiction. Exempting a portion of a city from city taxes violates that rule of uniformity. Even if it is claimed that the proviso establishes a tax classification, Article V, section 2(2) of the constitution requires that such classifications apply in *every* city, county, and other unit of local government, whereas this one applies only in cities of five thousand or more. There is no comparable proviso in the involuntary annexation statute for cities smaller than five thousand. The authors of the proviso recognized its vulnerability to constitutional attack. They added a sentence to G.S. 160A-49(f) specifying that if a

25. Judge Greene is clearly correct under current law. Of course, in 1959, when the proviso was inserted in the statute, sanitary districts were the only form of special districts then authorized by general law to provide water or sewer services. There were, however, a few special districts created by local act—usually also called sanitary districts—that provided water and sewer services. It is possible that in 1959 the General Assembly intended that the term *sanitary district* be given the broad meaning argued for by the city.

court found the proviso unconstitutional, it was to be severed from the remainder of the annexation law and not be the cause of the entire law's being held unconstitutional.

The General Assembly has made more effective provision for reduction or remission of special district taxes for two other kinds of special districts—rural fire protection districts and county service districts organized for fire protection. The statutes relating to each of these districts direct a city annexing territory within such a district to refund to district property owners a portion of the fire taxes paid for the fiscal year in which the annexation becomes effective.[26] (This requirement is discussed in detail in Chapter 14.) With other sorts of special districts, such as county water and sewer districts, a city probably could agree, as part of its annexation plans, to make comparable payments to owners of annexed property when that property continues to be subject to district taxes.

[d] Effect of annexation on property owned by a special district

When a city annexes territory within a special district, the annexation does not work any transfer of the special district's property to the city. As the supreme court held in the *Lenoir* case, "[w]ithout specific language to so indicate, we will not assume that the Legislature intended to permit a city to acquire property of a quasi-municipal corporation by a mere enlargement of the city's boundaries."[27]

Section 2.04. Annexation across a County Line

The annexation statutes present no bar to a city annexing territory on the other side of a county line. The statutes allow cities to expand along with patterns of urban development, and urban development is indifferent to county boundaries. At least two appellate cases have involved annexations across county lines, and neither the petitioners nor the court thought that fact worthy of mention.[28] That nothing in public

26. G.S. 69-25.15 (rural fire protection districts) and G.S. 153A-304.1 (county service districts).

27. 249 N.C. at 101, 105 S.E.2d at 415.

28. Wallace v. Town of Chapel Hill, 93 N.C. App. 422, 378 S.E.2d 225 (1989), and Chapel Hill Country Club v. Town of Chapel Hill, 97 N.C. App. 171, 388 S.E.2d 168 (1990). In both cases, the annexation area was bisected by the Durham–Orange County line.

policy opposes a city annexing across county lines is evidenced by the existence of at least thirty-four North Carolina cities that lie in at least two counties, most notably Rocky Mount, a city of almost sixty thousand that straddles the line between two counties. Indeed, portions of two North Carolina cities, Hickory and Sharpsburg, lie in three counties; and portions of one, High Point, in four.

Section 2.05. Annexation of Federal Facilities

In 1947 and 1950, the city of Louisville, Kentucky, annexed a naval ordnance plant operated by the federal government. When, in 1950, the city attempted to collect the city's payroll tax from employees of the plant, a number of employees brought suit, alleging that annexing federal facilities violated federal law. In *Howard v. Commissioners of Sinking Fund*,[29] the United States Supreme Court upheld the annexation. Even though the state had ceded exclusive jurisdiction over the area to the United States, the Court held that the state, through its cities, retained the power to adjust local political boundaries as long as the federal government did not object.

> A state may confirm its municipal structures [within the federal enclave] to its own plan, so long as the state does not interfere with the exercise of jurisdiction within the federal area by the United States. . . . A change of municipal boundaries did not interfere in the least with the jurisdiction of the United States within the area or with its use or disposition of the property.[30]

The North Carolina supreme court also recognized a city's ability to annex federal property, in *In re Annexation Ordinance No. 1977-4*, in which the court upheld Goldsboro's annexation of Seymour Johnson Air Force Base.[31]

It should be noted that it is not necessary for the federal government to consent to an annexation of federal facilities. Rather, the annexation may go ahead as long as the federal government does not object. As a practical matter, a city considering annexation of a significant federal facility is well advised to discuss the matter beforehand with the

29. 344 U.S. 624 (1953).
30. *Id.* at 626–27.
31. 296 N.C. 1, 249 S.E.2d 698 (1978).

appropriate federal officials, to ensure that there will be no federal objection.[32]

Section 2.06. Islands within—or Caused by—an Annexation

Sometimes an annexation area wraps around an area that does not, for one reason or another, qualify for annexation, resulting in an island of unincorporated territory within the boundaries of the annexing city. Indeed, sometimes the city annexing an area itself excludes one or more properties within its perimeters, bringing an unincorporated island into the city as part of the annexation. Although the existence of such islands may create administrative problems for the city in the provision of services, their creation does not appear to violate any public policy of the state.

In *Abbott v. Town of Highlands*,[33] the North Carolina court of appeals upheld a legislative annexation to the town, even though the annexation excluded and completely surrounded a 105-acre golf course. The court noted that neither the constitution nor the General Statutes required "contiguity and cohesiveness" in an annexation and held that a court would not substitute its judgment about boundaries for that of legislators. If the General Assembly may annex territory that includes an unincorporated island, it is hard to see why a city might not do so as well. After all, by creating a statutory procedure for satellite annexations, the General Assembly has shown that state policy does not forbid the inclusion of unincorporated land between the incorporated parts of a single city.[34]

32. *See* Chapter 1 note 12, for Novato Fire Protection Dist. v. United States, 181 F.3d 1135 (9th Cir. 1999), in which a federal court of appeals held that *deannexation* of a federal property violated the federal Constitution.

33. 52 N.C. App. 69, 277 S.E.2d 820 (1981).

34. In Kalb v. City of West Helena, 463 S.W.2d 368 (Ark. 1971), the court upheld an annexation that was attacked because it resulted in two island areas within the city. The annexed areas were still, the court held, contiguous to the city.

3

Competition between Cities to Annex the Same Area

3

Competition between Cities to Annex the Same Area

Section 3.01. Introduction

When two cities are neighbors, they might both become interested in annexing the same area. Should that happen, they may compete for the annexation area—driven by either their own ambitions or the preferences of the area's residents or property owners. If the two cities start annexation proceedings at about the same time, which proceeding prevails? The judicial response in North Carolina, which has been recognized by statute,[1] is to give preference to the proceeding with *prior jurisdiction*. The first part of this chapter explains the prior jurisdiction doctrine.

Rather than compete for the same territory, cities can resolve the potential conflict by mutual agreement *before* specific annexation proposals arise. During the 1980s, cities in a few counties chose this option and obtained local legislation from the General Assembly to allow them to enter into binding annexation agreements that designated areas in which only a single city could annex territory. As these agreements were successful, the General Assembly enacted statewide legislation allowing all cities to enter into them. The second part of this chapter discusses these annexation agreements.

Section 3.02. The Prior Jurisdiction Doctrine: The Basic Doctrine

If two cities each begin proceedings to annex the same land, the city that begins its proceeding first is entitled to complete the proceeding or abandon it while the other city stands by. The first city has *prior*

1. N.C. Gen Stat. § 160A-37(i) and 160A-49(i) each make reference to prior jurisdiction (hereinafter G.S.).

jurisdiction. If it completes the proceeding and annexes the contested land, the second city is foreclosed from annexing that land.[2]

The prior jurisdiction doctrine had a somewhat fitful beginning in North Carolina. In 1971 the state supreme court first recognized the doctrine in *Town of Hudson v. City of Lenoir*[3] but held that it did not apply when one city was undertaking a voluntary annexation and the other city an involuntary annexation. The prior jurisdiction doctrine, the court held, only applies to "equivalent" proceedings, and the two annexation procedures in question were not equivalent. Just a few years later, however, the court revisited the issue and repudiated its first holding. In *City of Burlington v. Town of Elon College,*[4] the court held that all statutory annexation procedures are equivalent; therefore, if one city begins a statutory annexation proceeding of any kind, it has prior jurisdiction to annex the area covered in that proceeding. No other city may simultaneously attempt to annex any part of that area under the same or any other statutory annexation procedure.

Section 3.03. The Prior Jurisdiction Doctrine: Gaining Prior Jurisdiction

For a city to acquire prior jurisdiction to annex an area, three conditions must be met. First, the city must take the first mandatory step of the annexation procedure it is using. Second, that first step must be valid. And third, the city must take that step before the competing city begins its own annexation procedure. This section reviews each of these three steps.

[a] The first mandatory step

Involuntary annexations. In the two involuntary annexation procedures, the first mandatory step is the city's adoption of a resolution of intent to annex the property. In *Town of Hazelwood v. City of Waynesville,*[5] Hazelwood argued that adoption of a resolution of consideration should be considered the first mandatory step in an involuntary

2. One potential side effect of having prior jurisdiction is illustrated in an Illinois case. In Village of Mundelin v. Village of Long Grove, 580 N.E.2d 599 (Ill. Ct. App. 1991), the court held that a city with prior jurisdiction had standing to bring an action to challenge the attempt by a second city to annex the same area. The issue of one city's standing to challenge an annexation by a second city is discussed in section 7.05.

3. 279 N.C. 156, 181 S.E.2d 443 (1971).

4. 310 N.C. 723, 314 S.E.2d 534 (1984).

5. 320 N.C. 89, 357 S.E.2d 686 (1987).

annexation, but the supreme court disagreed. The court pointed out that adoption of a resolution of consideration is not mandatory and that the annexation statutes set no standards for the territory that might be included in a resolution of consideration.[6] Furthermore, while the case was progressing through the appellate system, the General Assembly amended the two involuntary procedure statutes to specify that adopting a resolution of consideration did not confer prior jurisdiction to annex upon the city adopting the resolution.[7]

Voluntary annexations: private property. In the two voluntary procedures, the first mandatory step in annexing property owned by someone other than the city itself is presentation to the city of a petition signed by the relevant property owners. In *Town of Hazelwood v. Town of Waynesville*, the state supreme court stated that "[r]eceipt of the petition initiated the voluntary annexation procedure authorized by N.C.G.S. § 160A-31," the statute authorizing voluntary contiguous annexations.[8] In most cases, landowners present an annexation petition to the city council at a council meeting; the council then refers the petition to the city clerk, who must certify that the petition is legally sufficient. In some cities, however, a slightly different procedure is followed. In those cities, property owners submit their petitions directly to the city clerk, who conducts the necessary investigation before the petition is presented to the council. In that procedure, the council receives the clerk's certification at the same time as it receives the petition and can proceed directly to calling a public hearing on the petition. In this second procedure, however, what constitutes *receipt* of the petition by the city? Submission of the petition to the city clerk or presentation of the petition to the council?

In contiguous annexations, it seems clear that presentation to the governing board is the way a city receives a petition and thereby acquires prior jurisdiction to annex the property in question. G.S. 160A-31(a) authorizes the voluntary annexation of contiguous property "upon presentation *to the governing board* of a petition" signed by the property owners. Subsection (c) of the same section provides that "[u]pon receipt of the petition, the municipal governing board shall cause the clerk of the municipality to investigate the sufficiency thereof and to certify the result of his investigation." These statutory provisions indicate that the petition is to be presented to the governing board; this

6. The resolution of consideration is discussed in full in Volume 3 of this series.
7. G.S. 160A-37(i) and 160A-49(i).
8. 320 N.C. 89, 92, 357 S.E.2d 686, 688 (1987).

presentation is, therefore, the mandatory step that begins the annexation proceeding.

With noncontiguous annexations, the statute is not quite as clear, but it is likely that the answer is the same. G.S. 160A-58.1 authorizes the voluntary annexation of noncontiguous property upon *the city's* "receipt of a valid petition." There is no direct mention of presenting the petition to the governing board in this statute, in contrast to the contiguous annexation statute. The next section, however, states that upon receipt of a petition "*the city council* shall cause the city clerk to investigate the petition." This suggests that there must be a formal presentation to the governing board under this procedure as well; for that reason, such a presentation is probably the first mandatory step in a noncontiguous annexation.

There are at least two policy considerations that support this reading of the statutes. First, requiring a presentation to the board, rather than simply filing the petition with the clerk, mandates a public beginning of the annexation procedure—one comparable to the formal beginning of an involuntary annexation in which the governing board adopts a resolution of intent. Indeed, in discussing the prior jurisdiction doctrine, the authors of one of the leading treatises on local government law state that prior jurisdiction attaches when a city takes the "first mandatory *public* procedural step" in the annexation process.[9] Second, presentation of the petition to the board and its consequent mention in the board's minutes also provide stronger evidence of its receipt than the clerk's office date-and-time stamp.[10]

Voluntary annexations: city-owned property. When a city wishes to annex its own property voluntarily, either through the contiguous procedure or the satellite procedure, it begins by adopting a resolution of intent to annex.[11] In such a case, that resolution is clearly the first mandatory step in the annexation.[12]

[b] A valid first mandatory step

In order to result in prior jurisdiction, the city's first mandatory step must be in substantial compliance with the appropriate annexation

9. 2 Eugene McQuillin, The Law of Municipal Corporations § 7.22 (3d ed. 1996).

10. In McCune v. City of Phoenix, 317 P.2d 537 (Ariz. 1957), the court held that the first mandatory step of a petition annexation was presentation of the petitions to the city council, not filing them with the city clerk.

11. G.S. 160A-31(g), 160A-58.7.

12. City of Kannapolis v. City of Concord, 326 N.C. 512, 391 S.E.2d 493 (1990).

statute. If there is not substantial compliance, the city has not obtained jurisdiction to proceed with its annexation and, therefore, has not foreclosed a competing city from beginning its own proceeding. (That a city's first step is not in substantial compliance with the annexation statute does not necessarily render the annexation void; it simply denies the city prior jurisdiction. In many cases where there is no contest with a nearby city—and therefore prior jurisdiction is not in question—the city will be able to correct its error and complete the annexation.) The North Carolina supreme court has decided two cases that directly raised the issue of whether there had been substantial compliance and that illuminate the meaning of "substantial compliance."

City of Kannapolis v. City of Concord.[13] In this case, both cities had taken steps to annex Lake Concord, the water supply for Concord. Concord had first received petitions for voluntary annexation of the property between the current city limits and the lake. When the petitions were received, the city council adopted a resolution acknowledging their receipt and directing the city clerk to investigate their sufficiency. At the same meeting, the Concord council also adopted a resolution of intent to voluntarily annex the lake, which it owned. Both the city and the courts construed this second resolution as initiating an annexation proceeding separate from the one begun with the voluntary petitions. Kannapolis began its own annexation proceeding by adopting a resolution of intent under the involuntary annexation statute.

Each city's resolution of intent was flawed. Concord's difficulty was that it adopted its resolution under the voluntary contiguous annexation statute, but the lake would not, in fact, be contiguous to the city until the voluntary petition annexation, begun the same day, became effective. Kannapolis's difficulty was that its resolution did not state that the annexation ordinance would not become effective until at least one year after its adoption; this statement was required because the city had not previously adopted a resolution of consideration that included the annexation area.[14] The issue before the court was whether the flaw in either city's resolution was serious enough to constitute failure to be in substantial compliance with the relevant annexation statute. If so, the city that had adopted the faulty resolution would not secure prior jurisdiction.

The court first held that Concord's resolution was fatally flawed, because an area subject to voluntary contiguous annexation must be

13. *Id.*

14. This requirement is imposed by G.S. 160A-37(j) and 160A-49(j). It is discussed in Volume 3 of this series.

contiguous to the city at the time the city begins the proceeding; contiguity at the time of the resolution is an "essential requirement" of the statute. Therefore, Concord's resolution was not in substantial compliance with the statute; indeed it was void, and therefore could not secure prior jurisdiction for the city. Turning then to the Kannapolis resolution, the court held that omitting the information about the eventual effective date of the annexation was but a "slight irregularity" and not grounds for invalidating the resolution or the proceeding as a whole. The court noted that the statute itself mandated the delayed effective date and that the city did in fact comply with the statute by setting the effective date in the annexation ordinance more than a year after the ordinance's adoption. Therefore, the date's omission from the resolution of intent caused no material injury to the residents or property owners being annexed.

Town of Spencer v. Town of East Spencer. In this second case, both cities had adopted resolutions of intent to undertake involuntary annexations, with East Spencer's being earlier by almost three months. In its resolution, however, East Spencer inadvertently included in the proposed annexation area two acres already within the town of Spencer. Therefore, the question before the court was whether East Spencer's error was substantial enough to invalidate its resolution of intent and thereby deprive the city of prior jurisdiction to continue its annexation proceeding. The court noted that the annexation statute prohibits annexation of territory already within another city and held that a resolution of intent that includes such territory is fatally flawed. East Spencer thus lost its prior jurisdiction.

Reconciliation of the two cases. Do these three holdings (two in *Kannapolis* and one in *Spencer*) create a coherent set of principles regarding the meaning of "substantial compliance"? And if so, what are those principles?

The holding on Concord's resolution is straightforward and seemingly based on the language of the statute. The city adopted its resolution of intent to annex the city-owned property (the lake) pursuant to G.S. 160A-31(g). That subsection sets out the required content of the resolution, including a statement "that the property is contiguous to the municipal boundaries." The language certainly implies that the property must be contiguous to the boundary when the resolution is adopted, and Lake Concord was not. Such a requirement is consistent with petition annexations under the same section. G.S. 160A-31(b) directs that a petition for annexation submitted to the city include a statement that "the area to be annexed is contiguous" to the annexing city. It is quite clear that the statute intends that the property be contiguous at the time the annexation proceeding begins. The principle to be drawn from the Concord example, then, is that when the relevant annexation statute requires that important conditions be true at the time the annexation proceeding begins, those conditions must be met in order for the first mandatory step to be in substantial compliance with the annexation statute and for prior jurisdiction to attach.

The Concord principle, though, doesn't satisfactorily explain the other two holdings. The East Spencer holding was based on the requirement, in G.S. 160A-36(b)(3), that "no part of the [annexation] area shall be included within the boundary of another incorporated municipality." That requirement is one of three set out in that subsection, as follows:

- The annexation area must be adjacent or contiguous to the city's boundaries "at the time the annexation proceeding is begun."
- At least one-eighth of the aggregate external boundary of the annexation area must coincide with the city's boundary.
- No part of the annexation area may be within another city or town.

The first of the three requirements specifically states that it must be met at the time the city council adopts the resolution of intent; but that timing obligation is conspicuously absent from the other two requirements, including the one forbidding annexation of territory already within another city. The statute can readily be understood to require contiguity at the time the resolution of intent is adopted but to allow compliance with the other two requirements to be delayed to some later point. That is, a failure to meet the other two requirements initially could be cured by subsequent compliance with the annexation statute—for example, by adopting a proper annexation ordinance.

In that regard, East Spencer's error is very similar to that made by Kannapolis, which, it will be recalled, did not defeat that city's prior jurisdiction. The statute, G.S. 160A-49(j), required that the resolution of intent include a statement about the delayed effective date of the ordinance—and Kannapolis forgot to include the statement. The city did, however, include it in the annexation ordinance itself—thus the error was curable and so did not invalidate the first mandatory step. In any event, the court noted that the statute itself required that the effective date of the annexation be delayed. By the same token, East Spencer could have corrected the description of the annexation area in the ordinance itself or, for that matter, in the report, deleting the small area that was in Spencer and thereby curing the error. And, as the court pointed out in *Kannapolis*, the statute itself prohibits annexing territory within another city. Indeed, if the city's error, once cured, had been brought forward by a property owner seeking judicial review of the annexation, it is hard to imagine that a court would have found that the property owner had suffered a material injury sufficient to invalidate the annexation on this ground. The dissenting justice in the East Spencer case noted the comparability between the situations of East Spencer and Kannapolis, but he spoke alone.

The majority in the East Spencer case did try to bring that case within the principle established in the Concord decision—that is, as a statutory requirement that clearly applies at the time the proceeding is begun—but its attempt is not satisfactory. The court noted (1) that G.S. 160A-37 requires the annexation report to be adopted within 15 to 60 days after adoption of the resolution of intent, and (2) that G.S. 160A-35 requires that the annexation report include a statement showing that the annexation area meets the three requirements set out above. Therefore, because "these boundary requirements . . . are specifically required to be met *shortly after* the passage of the resolution of intent, it would at least seem incongruous not to apply these same standards to the . . . resolution of intent itself." That the city might be able to use the report to correct an error made in the resolution might not seem incongruous to others, but it apparently did to the court. The court went on to argue, somewhat heroically, that because the first requirement is specifically made to apply "at the time the annexation proceeding is begun," we should assume that the same timing requirement applies to the other two requirements. This argument really stands the statute on its head. The General Assembly could have included the quoted words at the beginning of the subsection, thereby clearly applying them to all three requirements—but it did not. It only included them in the first paragraph of the subsection; thus the more natural reading of the result is that the timing requirement *does not* apply to the latter two requirements. If we are to derive coherent principles from these cases, it cannot be on the basis of the majority's arguments in the East Spencer case.

We could perhaps derive such principles by distinguishing between *substantive* and *procedural* annexation requirements. Under such a distinction, a purely procedural error would not defeat prior jurisdiction unless the error were significant, could not be readily cured, and, perhaps, caused material injury to persons being annexed. Kannapolis's failure to include the delayed effective date in its resolution of intent does not meet these conditions: it was not significant, because the statute imposed the requirement in any case; it could be cured, and in fact was; and it caused no material injury to property owners in the annexation area. On the other hand, if a requirement is substantive—going to the definition of what property may be annexed—and if it is plain on the face of the relevant document that the requirement was not met at the beginning of the proceeding, then the failure is fatal to prior jurisdiction. This would hold even if the error can be cured, and even if there is no material injury to persons being annexed. In a voluntary contiguous annexation, the substantive requirements are that the property be contiguous and that property owners consent to the annexation. If either is not true when the proceeding is begun, there is no substantial compliance. In a voluntary noncontiguous annexation, the requirements are that the property meet the standards listed in the statute[15] and that property owners consent to the annexation. Again, if either is not true when the proceeding is begun, there is no substantial compliance. And in an involuntary annexation, the substantive requirements are that the annexation area be contiguous, that at least one-eighth of the perimeter of the annexation area coincide with the city's existing boundary, and that no property within the annexation area be within another city. If any of these substantive requirements are not met when the annexation begins, there is no substantial compliance.

Nonetheless, this substantive procedural distinction is not fully satisfactory. To begin with, there is always the question of which category a particular requirement falls under. If the resolution of intent includes an error in the description of the territory, but not one that inadvertently includes territory in another city, is that procedural or substantive? More seriously, in an involuntary annexation, why should failure attach only to the three requirements set out in G.S. 160A-36(b) and 48(b)—contiguity, the one-eighth requirement, and exclusion of property within another city? Why not also consider whether the area proposed in the resolution of intent is developed for urban purposes? To allow one city to challenge, for prior jurisdiction reasons, the resolution of intent of another city by challenging whether the area meets the urban development

15. These are set out in G.S. 160A-58.1(b).

standards of the involuntary annexation statute would transform a prior jurisdiction case into a full-fledged challenge to the annexation. So far, no case debating prior jurisdiction has raised those sorts of issues, perhaps because the standards of urban development are complicated and compliance or noncompliance is not readily apparent or even necessary when a proceeding is begun. After all, the resolution of intent simply asserts that the city is considering annexation of the described territory, which might imply that the city is still determining whether the area does meet the urban development standards. It is, in fact, clearly the province of the annexation report—which is due some weeks later—to demonstrate compliance with those standards.[16]

Examples. The above analysis of the court's treatment of the issue suggests the kinds of flaws that will invalidate a mandatory first step and the kinds that will not invalidate that step. The list of invalidating flaws would thus include the following:

- in a contiguous annexation, that the property is not contiguous at the time the proceeding begins;[17]
- in a noncontiguous annexation, that the property does not meet the mandatory standards for annexation at the time the proceeding begins;[18]
- that the city is prohibited by local act from undertaking this sort of annexation;[19]
- that the property being annexed is already in another city;[20]

16. The appellate courts have, however, been willing to allow cities to challenge completed involuntary annexations on the grounds that the annexation did not meet the statutory standards. *See* the discussion in section 7.05, especially at notes 58–62. It therefore appears that a city challenging the prior jurisdiction of another city whose annexation is involuntary and has been completed, may raise the issue of whether the annexation meets the standards—not as a challenge to prior jurisdiction but as a challenge to the annexation itself.

17. *See* City of Kannapolis v. City of Concord, 326 N.C. 512, 391 S.E.2d 493 (1990), for voluntary annexations. The two involuntary statutes specify that the annexation area must be contiguous to the city "at the time the annexation proceeding is begun." G.S. §§ 160A-36(b)(1) and 160A-48(b)(1).

18. These standards are set out in G.S. 160A-58.1(b).

19. See Table 1.1 at the end of chapter 1.

20. Town of Spencer v. Town of East Spencer, 351 N.C. 124, 522 S.E.2d 297 (1999). *See* People *ex rel.* First Nat'l Bank of Chicago v. City of North Chicago, 510 N.E.2d 577 (Ill. Ct. App. 1987) (annexation area already in another city at time proceeding begun and therefore city does not gain prior jurisdiction). *See also* the discussion in section 2.01 concerning the inability of one city to annex territory already in another city.

- in an involuntary annexation, that at least one-eighth of the aggregate external boundaries of the annexation area are not contiguous to the city at the time the council adopts the resolution of intent;[21]
- in a voluntary annexation, that the petitions do not include all the owners of the property being annexed;[22]
- in an involuntary annexation, that the resolution of intent does not describe the annexation area.[23]

The court's discussion of the Kannapolis resolution drew on the case law developed for reviewing attacks on annexations after adoption of annexation ordinances.[24] Unless a challenger has suffered material injury because of a city's error under the statute, the courts uphold annexations that are otherwise in substantial compliance with the annexation statute. Such an approach is consistent with the above suggestion that procedural errors might not be fatal to a city's prior jurisdiction. Although such a list must be speculative, the following sorts of errors might be held to be "slight irregularities" that do not destroy a city's prior jurisdiction (at least if they are promptly cured):

21. "[W]e hold . . . that at least one eighth of the aggregate external boundaries of the [annexation] area coincide with the municipal boundary . . . 'at the time the annexation proceeding is begun'" and that this is an essential element "with regard to a 'prior jurisdiction' determination." Town of Spencer v. Town of East Spencer, 351 N.C. 124, 132, 135, 522 S.E.2d 297, 303, 305 (1999).

22. Both G.S. 160A-31(a), for contiguous annexations, and 160A-58.1(a), for noncontiguous annexations, specify that annexation proceedings begin when the city receives a petition signed by *all* the owners of land within the proposed annexation area. *See also* Petition of Village of Long Grove, 509 N.E.2d 1041 (Ill. Ct. App. 1987) (petition does not contain signatures from sufficient number of owners and therefore city does not gain prior jurisdiction).

23. This might be thought of as a procedural error, but failing to define the area under consideration at all is so fundamental an omission that a court would be unlikely to accept such a resolution of intent. Of course, because a description is so fundamental, it is hard to imagine a city making this particular error.

24. The court quoted from and relied on *In re* Annexation Ordinance, 278 N.C. 641, 180 S.E.2d 851 (1971), in which the court held that petitioners did not suffer material injury when the annexation report was not explained orally at the public hearing, inasmuch as it had been carefully reviewed by their attorney. Other cases in which the courts have found errors to be immaterial include Humphries v. City of Jacksonville, 300 N.C. 186, 265 S.E.2d 189 (1980) (petitioners suffered no material disadvantage from the city's not including the entire city in a map in the annexation report); and Scovill Manufacturing Co. v. Town of Wake Forest, 58 N.C. App. 15, 293 S.E.2d 240 (1982) (city's failure to include in the annexation ordinance a statement that the subdivision test had been met is an immaterial error, given that everything else was done correctly).

- minor errors in the description of the proposed annexation area, such as a description that does not close;[25]
- in a voluntary annexation, failure to include with the petition the addresses of the signers;[26]
- in an involuntary annexation, a resolution of intent that does not set the dates for the public informational meeting or the public hearing;[27]
- in a noncontiguous annexation, failure to include in the petition a metes and bounds description of the annexation area and a map showing its location relative to the city annexing it.[28]

[c] First steps on the same day

Normally, it will be clear whether one city has taken its first mandatory step before the other city. One city will act on one day and the other city will act on some subsequent day. Occasionally, however, the two cities will act on the same day. In *Town of Hudson v. City of Lenoir*,[29] the supreme court held that in such a circumstance, neither city gains prior jurisdiction. Presumably that means that both cities may proceed and the first to accomplish its annexation prevails.

25. *See* Conover v. Newton, 297 N.C. 506, 256 S.E.2d 216 (1979) (no material injury from fact that metes and bounds description in resolution of intent omitted one small parcel, because resolution referred to map and map showed parcel as included).

26. Both G.S. 160A-31, for contiguous annexations, and 160A-58.1, for noncontiguous annexations, require that the petition include the addresses of the signing property owners. It is hard to see any material injury to the annexees from a failure to include the addresses; the requirement is probably intended to assist the city in determining whether all owners have signed.

27. It is possible that a court might see failure to set the date for the public informational meeting or the public hearing as analogous to the failure of Kannapolis to mention the required delayed effective date of its annexation in its resolution of intent. Even when a city does not include the dates in that resolution, it must still publish a notice of the meeting and hearing and mail a copy of the notice to each property owner in the annexation area. Therefore, a court might hold that no one is materially injured by the failure to set the date in the resolution. Still, these seem more serious flaws than the one in the Kannapolis resolution, and a court might well reject the analogy.

28. As these are procedural requirements imposed by G.S. 160A-58.1(c), a court might forgive them if promptly cured.

29. 279 N.C. 156, 181 S.E.2d 443 (1971).

Section 3.04. Abandoning or Ending a Proceeding That Has Prior Jurisdiction

Once one city gains prior jurisdiction to annex property, it retains that priority until the annexation proceeding ends or is abandoned. What does it mean to end or to abandon an annexation proceeding?

One obvious way to end an annexation proceeding is to annex the property. Once the annexation is effective and the time for further appeals has run, the proceeding is over. At that point, it is presumably over for the competing city as well. Another way that a proceeding can end is for the courts to hold that the city's attempted annexation is invalid because of some failure to meet statutory standards or procedures. That a trial court has invalidated an annexation, however, does not end the city's proceeding or cause the city to lose its prior jurisdiction. The proceeding ends only if the city fails to appeal or loses its appeal in a higher court.[30] Furthermore, the court must hold that the annexation is invalid and cannot be corrected. If a trial or appellate court remands a city's attempted involuntary annexation, the city may correct the errors that led to the remand, retain its prior jurisdiction, and complete the annexation.[31]

Abandoning an annexation proceeding is a more slippery concept and arises when a city simply fails to move the procedure along in a deliberate way. The city that does so runs the risk that a court might hold that its failure to actively continue the proceeding constitutes abandonment of the proceeding. It should be noted that this is only at issue in voluntary annexations. The involuntary annexation statutes set out a detailed procedure that requires each step to be taken within a specific number of days from the preceding step; if those time limits are not met, the annexation will fail because it no longer complies with the statute. As there are no such deadlines for voluntary annexations, a city that has received a petition for voluntary annexation but has not acted on it might be susceptible to an allegation that it has abandoned the proceeding. There are no North Carolina cases that deal with the issue of abandonment, but a number of cases from other states illustrate the fairly consistent way in which courts around the country have dealt with

30. Town of Delavan v. City of Delavan, 484 N.W.2d 343 (Wis. Ct. App. 1992) (first city retains prior jurisdiction during appeal of trial court decision).

31. *See* Food Town Stores v. City of Salisbury, 303 N.C. 539, 279 S.E.2d 557 (1981), in which it is clear that the city's actions on remand are part of the original and continuing annexation proceeding.

claims of abandonment. Basically, if a city does nothing to move the process along and continues to do nothing for several months, a court is likely to find abandonment. In two Illinois cases, for example, the city took no action whatsoever on petitions for annexation for periods of eight and ten months. The courts held in each case that the city had abandoned the annexation proceeding.[32] If a city is actively working on the annexation, however, the passage of several months or possibly even years will not be taken as abandonment of the proceeding. Two other Illinois cases illustrate this point. In one, four months passed between receipt of the petition and passage of the annexation ordinance; the city's staff was actively studying the annexation during that time, and the court held there was no abandonment.[33] In the other case, receipt of the petition led the city to undertake extended and difficult negotiations with the landowners and neighboring cities, negotiations that continued for more than four years. Again, the court held that, despite the passage of several years, the proceeding had not been abandoned.[34]

Section 3.05. The Effect of Prior Jurisdiction on the Second Proceeding

The apparent law. If a city loses the race to claim prior jurisdiction, what is the effect on its own proceeding? Is that proceeding void, or is the city merely foreclosed from using the proceeding to annex the area covered by the first city's proceeding? This issue becomes important if the first city is held not to have gained prior jurisdiction or if its annexation effort is abandoned or held invalid.

32. People *ex rel.* Village of Worth v. Ihde, 177 N.E.2d 313 (Ill. 1961) (petition received in November, discussed by council in December, and then no action taken until succeeding September); City of Countryside v. Village of LaGrange, 180 N.E.2d 488 (Ill. 1962) (petition received in June, and no action taken by the succeeding February). *See also* People *ex rel.* Village of Long Grove v. Village of Buffalo Grove, 515 N.E.2d 438 (Ill. Ct. App. 1987) (no action on petition for six years), and City of Milwaukee v. Town of Oak Creek, 98 N.W.2d 469 (Wis. 1959) (no action for two years). *Contra*, City of Terrell Wells v. City of San Antonio, 216 S.W.2d 657 (Tex. Ct. Civ. App. 1948) (city took no action for nineteen months, but court finds no abandonment).

33. People *ex rel.* Village of Buffalo Grove v. Village of Long Grove, 557 N.E.2d 643 (Ill. Ct. App. 1990).

34. *In re* Annexation to City of Joliet, 668 N.E.2d 1073 (Ill. Ct. App. 1996). *See also* City of Muscatine v. Waters, 251 N.W.2d 544 (Iowa 1977) (annexation proceeding continued over thirteen months, but court found no unreasonable delay and that the city moved promptly to rectify problems as they arose).

None of the North Carolina cases discuss this point, but the facts of one case suggest that the second proceeding is not void but rather in abeyance during the time the first proceeding has real or apparent prior jurisdiction. In *Kannapolis v. Concord*,[35] Concord acted first; while that proceeding was pending, Kannapolis took its own first step. When Concord's first step was held invalid, and so did not give Concord prior jurisdiction, the Kannapolis proceeding automatically gained prior jurisdiction. The city did not have to start anew once the Concord action had been held invalid. This outcome accords with the case law from other states.

In *Town of Clive v. Colby*,[36] the second city received an annexation petition while the first city's annexation was before the courts. When the first proceeding was held invalid, the second city claimed that its proceeding, begun with receipt of the petition, now had priority. The first city, however, responded that its "jurisdiction [had been] exclusive until the final decree and that all action taken [by the other city] between the first step and the final decree is void and of no effect."[37] The court sided with the second city, holding that the first city's proceedings were void *ab initio* (that is, from the beginning) and therefore could not affect later actions by the second city. "A winner [in the initial race to start annexation proceedings] who has been disqualified by a decision of this court is not entitled to a fresh start. The race goes to the party which instituted the first valid proceeding and complied with the statute."[38]

In *In re City of Wood Dale*,[39] an Illinois appellate court made the same point in more general terms.

> [A]s to the same territory or a part thereof, an annexation petition or proceeding may not *legally* be initiated or effectuated *so long as* a prior petition or proceeding remains pending and undefeated or unresolved. In other words, a later petition, filed during the pendency of an earlier initiated petition, does not lawfully come into being and enjoy jurisdictional priority so long as the earlier petition remains pending and unresolved. This does not mean that a petition may not be filed during the pendency of a prior petition.

35. 326 N.C. 512, 391 S.E.2d 493 (1990).
36. 123 N.W.2d 331 (Iowa 1963).
37. *Id.* at 332.
38. *Id.* at 333.
39. 611 N.E.2d 606 (Ill. Ct. App. 1993).

As a practical matter, successive petitions or proceedings are routinely "initiated" (but not legally) during the pendency of others prior in time. However, a later-filed petition, even though initiated during the pendency of another petition, may become "legally" initiated if the prior petition is abandoned, defeated or otherwise deemed invalid; that is, a later petition may acquire "jurisdictional priority."[40]

Examples. If we apply these principles to a series of possible scenarios, we get these outcomes.

1. While City A has prior jurisdiction to undertake an annexation, City B receives an annexation petition covering some or all of the same territory. City B proceeds through the voluntary procedure, investigating the petition, holding a public hearing, and adopting an annexation ordinance. If City A abandons its proceeding, or if its attempt to annex is held invalid, City B succeeds to prior jurisdiction and its annexation ordinance becomes effective.[41]
2. While City A has prior jurisdiction to undertake an annexation, City B receives an annexation petition covering some or all of the same territory. City B may accept the petition and then do nothing more until City A's proceeding is resolved. If City A abandons the annexation, or if its attempt to annex is held invalid, City B now has prior jurisdiction and may continue the appropriate statutory procedure for voluntary annexation.
3. While City A has prior jurisdiction to undertake an annexation, City B begins an involuntary annexation proceeding that includes some or all of the same territory as City A's proceeding. City B follows its proceeding through to completion, and property owners in the annexation area petition the superior court to review the annexation. If City A's proceeding is still pending, or if has ended with a successful annexation, the superior court can either invalidate City B's annexation or, if

40. *Id.* at 613. *See also*, Loyd v. City of Russellville, 696 S.W.2d 741 (Ark. 1985), in which City A obtained an injunction halting City B's annexation proceeding, because City A had priority. When City A's annexation was held invalid, the court set aside the earlier injunction, which indicates that City B's proceeding was not void simply because City A had priority at the time City B began it.

41. This is, in fact, the sequence of events in Town of Hudson v. City of Lenoir, 279 N.C. 156, 181 S.E.2d 443 (1971), although the court held that the two proceedings were not equivalent.

B's annexation would still be valid with A's territory removed, remand the annexation to the city to amend the report and ordinance to remove the areas annexed by City A. If City A, however, has abandoned its annexation or if its attempt to annex has been held invalid, then City B would succeed to prior jurisdiction and City A's annexation would be irrelevant to the validity of B's annexation.[42]

4. While City A has prior jurisdiction to undertake an annexation, City B begins an involuntary annexation proceeding that includes some or all of the same territory as City A's proceeding. After adopting the resolution of intent, City B decides to place its proceeding on hold until City A's annexation is resolved. If doing so, however, causes City B to miss the deadlines for various actions under the involuntary procedure, its own annexation will be invalid should it ever gain prior jurisdiction. Therefore, attempting to begin an involuntary proceeding but then not carrying it through to completion will probably not be successful.

Section 3.06. When the Prior Jurisdiction Doctrine Is Inapplicable

The prior jurisdiction doctrine only applies when two cities are engaged in equivalent proceedings. It does not bar the General Assembly from annexing an area to a city or from incorporating a new city, even if the area involved is the subject of a pre-existing annexation proceeding. Although the proceedings might be equivalent, the parties are not, and the General Assembly is not bound by the fact that a city has acted first.[43] Furthermore, the North Carolina court of appeals has held that an annexation proceeding and an eminent domain proceeding are not equivalent. Therefore, the earlier commencement of an annexation proceeding by a town did not stop a county from beginning an action to condemn the property subject to the annexation.[44]

42. This is the sequence of events in City of Kannapolis v. City of Concord, 326 N.C. 512, 391 S.E.2d 493 (1990).

43. See the discussion in sections 1.02 and 1.03 on the power of the General Assembly over annexations and deannexations.

44. Yandle v. Mecklenburg County, 85 N.C. App. 382, 355 S.E.2d 216 (1987).

Sections 3.07 through 3.10. Reserved.

Section 3.11. Annexation Agreements: Introduction and Summary

In 1984 the General Assembly enacted a local act that permitted cities in Mecklenburg County to enter into agreements delineating areas in which one or more of the cities could not annex.[45] The purpose was to allow the cities in that county to agree upon their respective annexation "spheres of influence" in order to avoid annexation fights and races to obtain prior jurisdiction. The cities in Mecklenburg County immediately implemented the local act by entering into the authorized agreements, and cities in other counties took note. During the next four years, the General Assembly enacted comparable authority for the cities in at least three other counties.[46] The League of Municipalities asked that the authority be made statewide rather than piecemeal, and in 1989 the General Assembly complied. The result is Article 4A, Part 6, of G.S. Chapter 160A, beginning at G.S. 160A-58.21.

Summary of the statute. G.S. 160A-58.21 identifies the purpose of the statute as authorizing two or more cities to enter into binding agreements concerning their future annexations. Under such an agreement, the cities delineate one or more areas in which one or more of the cities *may not* annex.[47] The agreements apply to annexations under all the statutory procedures, both involuntary and voluntary. An annexation agreement may be set for any period up to twenty years; and, unless all participating cities agree, a city may prematurely terminate the agreement only after giving five years' notice to the other city or cities. While an annexation agreement is in effect, no participating city may adopt an annexation ordinance in violation of the agreement. If a city attempts to do so, the statute authorizes any other party or parties to the agreement to petition superior court for an order invalidating the attempted annexation. If the court finds that the

45. 1983 (1984) N.C. Sess. Laws ch. 953.

46. 1987 N.C. Sess. Laws ch. 204 (cities in Gaston County), ch. 233 (cities in Orange County); 1987 (1988) N.C. Sess. Laws ch. 1009 (cities in Guilford County).

47. In Anderson v. City Development Board of State of Iowa, 631 N.W.2d 671 (Iowa 2001), the Iowa supreme court held that such an agreement did not violate any constitutional rights of property owners who might prefer to be annexed by a city other than the one whose sphere of influence they found themselves in.

annexation violates the agreement, it either invalidates the annexation ordinance or, if the annexation can be saved by deleting the disputed territory, remands the ordinance to the annexing city for amendment.

Section 3.12. The Content of an Annexation Agreement

G.S. 160A-28.24 sets out the provisions that must or may be included in an annexation agreement.

[a] Duration

As noted above, G.S. 160A-58.23 permits participating cities to fix the term of an annexation agreement for any period up to twenty years.

[b] Description of the areas subject to the agreement

The agreement must "describe clearly the area or areas subject to the agreement"—that is, the areas into which one or more of the participating cities may not annex. In the usual case, the annexation agreement provides each participating city with an area—that city's sphere of influence—in which it alone can annex property. The statute does not set out any preferred method for delineating the various spheres of influence as long as the method selected clearly describes each such area. While it is possible to use courses and distances or some other form of metes and bounds, the cities need not use those methods. A boundary may be described by reference to roadways or tax maps, or even by reference to a map incorporated into the agreement. The key requirement is to identify the boundaries of each sphere of influence so that they can be located on the ground.

The statute does require that the agreement designate *areas* into which one or more cities may not annex. Therefore, an agreement cannot simply designate a *line* between two cities and state that neither city will annex across the line. Some agreements do, however, draw a line between two cities and then extend it to meet other lines, such as county boundaries, so that areas are delineated as required by the statute.

Once an agreement has delineated annexation spheres of influence, G.S. 160A-58.24(a)(2) provides that a participating city's subsequent annexations may follow the boundaries of its sphere of influence, "whether or not such boundaries follow roads or natural topographical features." The quoted language reflects the boundary requirements applicable to involuntary annexations in 1989, when the annexation agreement statute was enacted. At that time, a city undertaking an involuntary annexation was required to, "wherever practical, use natural topographic features . . . and may use streets as boundaries." Thus, the clear policy of the annexation agreement statute was to allow a city participating in an annexation agreement to annex up to the edge of its sphere of influence under the agreement, even if doing so used boundaries that did not comply with the usual statutory directive. A number of annexation agreements, for example, prohibit a particular city from annexing across a county line; such a city would want to use the county line as the edge of its annexation area, even if that line did not otherwise qualify under the statute. In 1998 the General Assembly amended the involuntary annexation statutes to require that henceforth cities were to use as boundaries "recorded property lines and streets." Although the annexation agreement statute was not amended at the same time, there is no reason to think that the policy underlying G.S. 160A-58.24(a)(2) has changed. Therefore, even though that latter statute does not refer to recorded property lines, a city probably can still annex up to the edge of its sphere of influence, even if doing so requires that it follow something other than streets or recorded property lines in setting the boundaries of the annexation area.

[c] Identification of which cities cannot annex into which areas

Although this is not the principal intention of the statute, it is possible for participating cities to specify that *none* of them will annex land in a specific area during the duration of the agreement, thus rendering one or more parcels completely off-limits to annexation while the agreement is in force. At least one pair of cities has included such a provision to protect a nearby rural buffer area; other cities could use such an agreement to protect an industrial project against annexation.

[d] Effective date of the agreement

As the statute provides no direction about how soon or late after adoption the agreement may become effective, that date is entirely up to the participating cities.

[e] Notice of annexations

The statute directs that the agreement require each participating city proposing to undertake an annexation to give each of the other cities notice of that annexation. This notice, which must be given at least 60 days before the annexing city adopts its annexation ordinance, remains in effect, under G.S. 160A-58.24(b), for 180 days. Apparently, if the city does not adopt the annexation ordinance within that 180 days, it must give a new 60-days' notice. Subsection (b) further amplifies the notice requirement by directing that the notice include a map identifying the proposed annexation area by reference to the relevant sphere or spheres of influence under the agreement and also by reference to roads, waterways, and other prominent geographical features. It should be noted that the annexation agreement statute requires a city undertaking an annexation to notify each participating city, regardless of whether the annexation is near or far from that city

The statute states that the agreement may permit "a waiver of this *time period* by the notified city" (emphasis added). On its face, this seems to allow the notified city to waive the 60-day requirement but still requires the annexing city to provide notice, though not as soon as otherwise required. In practice, however, many cities have understood the statute to mean that a city may waive the requirement of notice altogether. Thus, some agreements provide that as long as a city annexes only within its own sphere of influence, it need not give notice of annexation to the other participating city or cities. The cities that are party to such agreements apparently see no need to be notified of annexations undertaken within the terms of the agreements; and it is unlikely that their interpretation of the statute's requirement would be cause for invalidating their agreements or any annexations undertaken pursuant to them.

If the agreement permits a waiver of the notice period but does not actually waive the notice itself, the agreement should set out how each city's waiver will be made and communicated. The agreement might require each city's governing board to issue the waiver; it might authorize each governing board to delegate the issuance of waivers to the mayor or an administrative official; or it might designate a particular official, such as the mayor or city manager, to waive the notice. Typically, the agreement requires that a waiver be in writing and specifies how it is to be delivered to the annexing city.

[f] Other provisions

The statute permits an agreement to include any other provisions the parties think necessary or proper. Some agreements have included provisions about whether participating cities may extend utility lines into each other's spheres of influence, and about the operation of those lines should the areas they serve be annexed by another city. Others have established time periods during which the city with jurisdiction over an area agrees not to undertake involuntary annexations in that area, such as for five years after the agreement is executed. In one agreement that was the subject of an unpublished decision of the North Carolina court of appeals, two cities agreed that during the term of the agreement neither city would annex property that was subject to agricultural use-value taxation.[48]

Section 3.13. The Procedure for Approving and Executing an Annexation Agreement

Public hearing. Before a city may enter into an annexation agreement, the city council must hold a public hearing on the proposed agreement.[49] (Alternatively, all the participating cities may, if they wish, hold a joint public hearing.) The statute requires that the city give public notice of the hearing pursuant to the rules for voluntary contiguous annexations set out in G.S. 160A-31(c). Those rules require that notice of the hearing be published at least ten days before the hearing in a newspaper with general circulation within the city.[50] At the hearing, the city must receive any public comment related to the proposed agreement.

48. Bowers v. City of Thomasville, No. COA97-1391, filed in the North Carolina court of appeals, 1 December 1998.

49. G.S. 160A-58.24(c).

50. If there is no such newspaper, G.S. 160A-31 requires that the city post the notice of the voluntary contiguous annexation in three or more public places within the annexation area and in three or more public places within the city. Applying this requirement to a public hearing on an annexation agreement suggests that any such notices be posted in at least three places within the city and at least three places within the city's sphere of influence as proposed under the agreement.

A form for the required notice is included in the North Carolina League of Municipalities (NCLM) handbooks, MECHANICS OF ANNEXATION (UNDER 5,000 POPULATION and 5,000 OR MORE POPULATION), available from NCLM, PO Box 3069, Raleigh, NC 27602 or through its Web site: http://www.nclm.org/Pubs/pub-link.html (last visited May 16, 2002).

County commissioner approval. If the sphere of influence assigned to a city by an annexation agreement extends more than three miles from the primary corporate limits of that city, the agreement is not binding in any area more than three miles from the city unless the board of county commissioners with jurisdiction over the area has approved the agreement.[51] (If the commissioners do not approve the agreement and the city's primary limits subsequently grow, bringing some or all of the area within three miles of the limits, the agreement automatically comes into force in the areas of the city's sphere of influence that are now within three miles of the new corporate limits.) Before the county commissioners may approve an agreement, they must hold a public hearing and comply with all the notice requirements that apply to the cities' public hearings on the agreement. The commissioners indicate their approval by resolution.

Approval by ordinance. G.S. 160A-58.24(c) directs that each participating city approve the annexation agreement by adopting an ordinance to that effect. [52]

Amending an agreement. G.S. 160A-58.24(d) permits cities that are party to an annexation agreement to amend or terminate it by mutual agreement. Before doing so, however, the cities must each hold a public hearing, using the same forms of notice as those for the public hearing on the original agreement.

Section 3.14. Enforcing an Agreement

[a] Enforcement by the participating cities

Introduction. Once an agreement becomes effective, G.S. 160A-58.25 prohibits a city from adopting an annexation ordinance that violates the agreement. If one of the cities adopts an ordinance another participating city believes violates the agreement, G.S. 160A-58.27 permits the second city to file a petition seeking review of the ordinance in superior court within thirty days of its adoption. If such a petition is filed before the ordinance becomes effective, and if the petition proceeding or any appeal from the proceeding is pending when the ordinance is to become effective, the statute automatically defers the effective date until the litigation is concluded. If the ordinance has

51. G.S. 160A-58.24(e).

52. Mechanics of Annexation includes a sample form for the required ordinance.

already become effective when the petition is filed, the petitioning city may seek to stay the annexation until the litigation is concluded.

If a city files a petition pursuant to G.S. 160A-58.25, the issue before the court is whether the annexation ordinance and the annexing city's annexation proceeding violate either the annexation agreement statute or a particular annexation agreement. In hearing the case, the court sits without a jury. Should the judge find that there has been no violation of the statute or any agreement, the court may enter an order affirming the annexation ordinance. If, however, the judge finds that the annexing city violated either the statute or the agreement, he or she chooses one of the remedial choices set out in G.S. 160A-58.27.

Involuntary annexation. If the annexation was attempted incorrectly under the involuntary annexation laws, the court must remand the annexation ordinance to the annexing city for revision. The city may amend the annexation area boundaries or take any other action necessary to make the ordinance or the annexation proceeding conform to the statute or to the applicable annexation agreement. If the city cannot do so and still qualify the area for annexation under the statute, the annexation fails. In any event, the annexing city must take whatever action it intends to take within three months after the remand; if it does not, the attempted annexation is void.

Voluntary annexation. If the annexation was attempted under either of the voluntary annexation laws, the statute directs the trial court to declare the ordinance void. The city will simply have to begin again with a new petition, avoiding the errors that led to the court's invalidation the first time.

[b] Third-party enforcement

The annexation agreement statute says nothing about enforcement of an agreement by third parties. Assume, for example, that a city undertakes an involuntary annexation that in some fashion violates an annexation agreement. May petitioners challenging the annexation raise violation of the agreement as one reason to invalidate the annexation—assuming that the other city or cities participating in the agreement have not raised the issue in a separate action pursuant to G.S. 160A-58.27? It is a little difficult to see how petitioners might do so. G.S. 160A-38 and 160A-50, the statutes that govern petitions appealing the validity of an involuntary annexation, set out three kinds of arguments on which petitioners may challenge an annexation: (1) that the statutory procedure was not followed; (2) that the annexation report does not show that the city will provide the services required by the statute; and (3) that the annexation area does not meet the standards of urban development necessary for annexation.[53] Of these three bases for a challenge, only the first offers any room for arguing that the annexation violates an annexation agreement with another city or cities—and even that basis may be interpreted as referring only to the procedures specifically included in the involuntary annexation statutes. Indeed, the fact that the annexation agreement statute only mentions enforcement by the participating cities might be an indication that the legislature did not intend third parties to play a role in enforcing these agreements. After all, persons normally do not have the power to enforce contracts to which they are not party. Nevertheless, in one unreported decision, the court of appeals did allow petitioners to raise a challenge to an involuntary annexation by alleging violation of an annexation agreement; and the court did remand the annexation on that ground.[54] Although as an unreported decision the case creates no precedent, it does indicate a willingness on the part of the court to allow third-party enforcement of an annexation agreement.

Section 3.15. Court Approval of Annexations That Violate an Agreement

G.S. 160A-58.27(i) permits a city that is party to an annexation agreement to petition the superior court for permission to undertake an annexation that violates the agreement. (A city may also seek this permission in response to a petition by another city challenging a completed annexation as violative of the agreement.) If the court finds that "there is an imminent threat to public health or safety that can be remedied only by the city seeking annexation," it may authorize the annexation to proceed despite the annexation agreement.

53. G.S. 160A-38(f), 160A-50(f).

54. Bowers v. City of Thomasville, No. COA97-1391, filed in the North Carolina court of appeals, 1 December 1998. The agreement had included a provision that neither city party to it could annex property that held agricultural use valuation; despite that provision, Thomasville's annexation did include such property, and the court remanded the annexation on that ground.

Section 3.16. Compliance with Other Annexation Statutes

Even though a city has a sphere of influence under an annexation agreement, any annexation it undertakes must still conform to the appropriate annexation statute.[55] There are two exceptions to this statement. First, the boundaries of an involuntary annexation area can follow the boundary of the sphere of influence, rather than streets or recorded property lines. (This point is discussed above in section 3.12[b].) Second, if a proposed satellite annexation area is within one city's exclusive sphere of influence, that city may annex the area even if it is closer to another city, as long as the other city is party to the annexation agreement and is prohibited by the agreement from annexing the satellite area.[56]

Section 3.17. Terminating an Agreement

If all the cities that are party to an annexation agreement concur, the agreement may be terminated at any time. As noted above, mutual termination of an agreement requires the cities to follow the same procedures they followed in originally adopting it.[57] If all the cities do not agree, however, a city that wishes to withdraw from the agreement must repeal the ordinance by which it approved the agreement and give the other city or cities five years' written notice of withdrawal.[58] If only one other city is party to the agreement, the agreement terminates once the five-year period has ended. If more than one other city is party to the agreement, the agreement terminates once the five-year period has ended unless each of the remaining cities adopts an ordinance reaffirming it. Apparently this ordinance may be adopted at any time during the five-year notice period and does not require any hearings, notices, or other proceedings before it is adopted.

55. G.S. 160A-58.26.
56. G.S. 160A-58.1(b1).
57. G.S. 160A-58.24(d).
58. G.S. 160A-58.24(f).

4

Contracts with Private Parties Regarding Annexation

4

Contracts with Private Parties Regarding Annexation

Section 4.01. Introduction

This chapter examines legal issues associated with three kinds of contracts concerning annexation that a city might enter into with private parties: (1) contracts under which the city agrees not to annex specific property for some period of time; (2) contracts that tie city utility services to immediate or eventual annexation of the utility customer's property; and (3) contracts regarding city services, or comparable matters, with landowners seeking voluntary annexation.

Section 4.02. Contracts Not to Annex

[a] In general

Cities are sometimes asked, as part of an economic development project, to agree not to annex a facility being purchased or constructed by a private company. A city might, for example, be asked to agree not to annex a new manufacturing facility that will be served by city water and sewer lines. The General Statutes do not address such contracts, but decisions in the state's appellate courts indicate that a contract in which the city agrees not to annex a property would not be enforceable against the city.

One of the basic doctrines regulating the contracting authority of local governments is that, absent specific legislative authority, they may not enter into certain sorts of contracts that bind the discretion of the local government's governing board.[1] The leading case establishing and illustrating this doctrine in North Carolina is *Plant Food Company v.*

1. This doctrine is described at length in David M. Lawrence, *Contracts That Bind the Discretion of Governing Boards*, Popular Government, Summer 1990, 38–42. The discussion in this chapter is drawn from that article.

City of Charlotte.[2] Plant Food had contracted with the city to remove sewage sludge from city drying beds, paying the city according to a schedule set out in the contract. The contract was for ten years, with an option for either party to extend it for another ten years. Within a year or two of the contract's execution, however, a new governing board took over in the city and sought to terminate the contract. When Plant Food sued the city for breach of contract, the city argued that the previous board had no power to enter into a contract that bound the current one.

The national rule, as developed by the courts of many states, was (and is) that a city may enter into a contract that binds future boards if the subject of the contract is a *proprietary* activity of local government. If, however, the subject is a *governmental* activity, such a contract is beyond the power of the local government and therefore void. The city pointed out that sewer services had been held to be a governmental activity in the context of local government immunity from tort liability; therefore, it argued, the Plant Food contract involved a governmental activity and could not bind a later board. The trial court agreed. On appeal, the North Carolina supreme court accepted the dichotomy between proprietary and governmental activities but refused to transfer automatically the distinction made in tort law to this different context. The court reasoned that as the public policies behind the distinction were very different in the two contexts, they called for drawing the line between proprietary and governmental activities in a different place. "The true test," according to the court, "is whether the contract itself deprives a governing body, or its successor, of a discretion which public policy demands should be left unimpaired."[3] If that sort of discretion is not involved, the contract is not invalid simply because it extends beyond the contracting board's term of office. If that discretion is involved, however, the contract cannot be enforced, even against the board that entered into it. In *Plant Food*, the court found that this sort of discretion was not involved and ordered the city to pay damages to the company.

The court in *Plant Food* did not attempt to define the category of discretionary powers concerning which binding contracts may not be made. Rather, it set out a number of examples to "roughly indicate the quality of the power involved." This list included the powers

2. 214 N.C. 518, 199 S.E. 712 (1938).
3. *Id.* at 520, 199 S.E. at 714.

- to adopt ordinances,
- to lay out and maintain streets,
- to preserve order,
- to regulate rates,
- to levy taxes,
- to levy special assessments.[4]

The list does not specifically include the power to annex, perhaps because cities did not enjoy statutory authority to annex at the time the case was decided; nonetheless, there is little doubt that the power to annex is one of the powers that may not be impaired by contract. The list does include the power to adopt ordinances, and cities annex property by adopting ordinances. Furthermore, the power to adopt ordinances is part of a city's legislative power, and the courts have made it clear that annexation is also the exercise of legislative power. It is hard to imagine a situation in which a governing body has a greater need to retain its discretion unimpaired by contract than when it is legislating.[5]

The North Carolina court of appeals agreed with this analysis in *Thrash v. City of Asheville*.[6] In this case, several petitioners were challenging an annexation by Asheville; one of them sought to enforce an alleged agreement under which the city would not annex some of the property included in the annexation area. In 1928—sixty years before the annexation—the city was attempting to attract a textile plant to a location in Buncombe County at some distance from the city. In a letter to the company, the city wrote

> [t]hat owing to the distance of the proposed plant location from the City Limits of the City of Asheville, and the vast amount of vacant land lying between said location and said City Limits, that the incorporation of said plant and land adjoining the same into the City of Asheville is impractical, and said City of Asheville would oppose such a proposition.[7]

4. *Id.* at 520, 199 S.E. at 713.

5. The prohibition of contract zoning is another means by which the courts prevent cities from contracting away their legislative power. Chrismon v. Guilford County, 322 N.C. 611, 370 S.E.2d 579 (1988); see section 4.06[c] below.

6. 95 N.C. App. 457, 383 S.E.2d 657 (1989), *rev'd on other grounds,* 327 N.C. 251, 393 S.E.2d 842 (1990).

7. 95 N.C. App. at 472, 383 S.E.2d at 666.

The city later repeated this statement in a formal resolution adopted by the city council and indicated that the resolution was to apply to the company's successors in interest. In the court of appeals, the current owner of the textile facility argued that the city's 1928 representations barred it from annexing the facility some sixty years later. The court rejected the argument. Quoting at length from *Plant Food*, the court wrote:

> We conclude that the power to annex is such a discretionary power[,] which must remain unfettered for the public good. The annexation power, like a municipality's power to lay out and maintain streets, to build bridges and to levy taxes, is an exercise of a City's governmental discretion. . . . Any attempt by the City to abridge this governmental power in 1928 was *ultra vires* and gives [the plant's owner] no right of action for noncompliance.[8]

The judicial prohibition against entering into annexation contracts with property owners is not constitutionally based; therefore, the General Assembly can authorize all cities, or particular cities, to enter into such contracts—and in fact has done so. In 1993 the General Assembly authorized Eden to enter into a contract[9] that delayed annexation for ten years; the Attorney General's office subsequently issued an advisory opinion supporting the constitutionality of the legislation.[10]

[b] Lawsuit settlements

During the four decades since the involuntary annexation statutes were enacted, there have been a number of instances in which a city has wished to settle a legal challenge to an annexation by agreeing to delay the annexation for some number of years; in return, the petitioning

8. *Id.* at 473–74, 383 S.E.2d at 666–67. In City of Leeds v. Town of Moody, 319 So.2d 242, 246 (Ala. 1975), the Alabama supreme court too held that cities may not enter into binding contracts not to annex ("The powers [of annexation] which the City of Leeds was purporting to give up [by contract] are legislative powers delegated to the municipality by the legislature. Neither the mayor nor the council had authority to relinquish these legislative powers. Since a municipality cannot by any provision or terms of a contract delegate or barter away a governmental power, the agreement which purported to do so in the present case was null and void.").

9. 1993 N.C. Sess. Laws ch. 418. Comparable authorizations have been given to Huntersville, SL 1997-266; and Mount Holly, SL 2000-24.

10. Letter to Charles L. Nooe, Op. Att'y Gen. No. 79 (November 24, 1993), on the Web site of the North Carolina Department of Justice: www.jus.state.nc.us/lrframe.htm (last visited May 16, 2002).

property owner was willing to accept annexation at the end of the agreed-upon period. The widespread recognition that cities are prohibited from contracting not to annex property made cities hesitant about entering into settlements or consent judgments that included such agreements. The concern was that if a city could not directly contract not to annex specific property, it might not be able to do so as a feature of a consent judgment or other settlement of a lawsuit. After all, settlements and consent judgments are contractual in nature, and it seemed unlikely that a court could approve a judgment including contractual provisions that could not otherwise bind a city.[11] As a result, cities in this position usually sought specific legislative authority to enter into such consent judgments or settlements.[12]

In 1998, however, the General Assembly amended the involuntary annexation statutes and specifically permitted cities to reach settlements in annexation lawsuits. If the court approves a settlement, therefore, General Assembly authorization or approval is unnecessary.[13] Although cities are still unable to enter into direct contracts in which they promise not to annex specific parcels of property for some stated period of years, they now may settle a legal challenge to an involuntary annexation ordinance by making such a promise as part of the settlement, and the promise will be enforceable against the city.

Section 4.03. Contracts Tying Annexation to Extension of Utility Lines: In General

Cities throughout the United States, including in North Carolina, frequently use their utility systems as carrots for annexation. These cities refuse to provide utilities to a property located outside the city unless the owner petitions, or agrees to petition, for annexation. If a city

11. A number of courts in other states have also reached this conclusion: Ad-Ex, Inc. v. City of Chicago, 565 N.E.2d 669 (Ill. Ct. App. 1990) (settlement that purported to change city sign ordinance invalid because city did not follow proper procedures for changing ordinance); PMC Realty Trust v. Town of Derry, 480 A.2d 51 (N.H. 1984) (city may not bargain away discretion regarding zoning through consent judgment); Midtown Properties, Inc. v. Township of Madison, 172 A.2d 40 (N.J. Super. Ct., Law Div. 1961) (city may not contract away zoning power through consent judgment). *See also* Cleveland County Ass'n for Gov't by the People v. Cleveland County Bd. of Comm'rs, 142 F3d. 468 (D.C. Cir. 1991), in which the court held that a North Carolina county could not enter into a settlement that expanded its authority under state law.

12. *E.g.*, 1987 N.C. Sess. Laws ch. 201 (Charlotte); 1991(92) N.C. Sess. Laws ch. 897 (Elizabethtown).

13. N.C. Gen. Stat. § 160A-38(l), 160A-50(m) (hereinafter G.S.).

follows such a policy impartially, it is clearly acting in accord with North Carolina law and is not violating federal law.

State law. When a city offers water or sewer services to its own residents, it is considered a public utility; that is, it is obligated to extend service to all properties within the city that are within a reasonable distance of existing utility lines and to offer service to customers on a nondiscriminatory basis.[14] A city can refuse to extend service to a potential customer inside the city only for reasons directly related to the utility itself, such as lack of adequate water supply or sewage treatment capacity or the property's unusual distance from existing utility lines.[15] Outside its borders, however, a city has no such obligation to extend service. That is, outside its borders, it is not a public utility[16] and can condition extension of utility service on matters not directly related to the utility, such as the customer's agreement to be annexed.[17]

Federal law. The federal courts have made it clear that utility policies requiring annexation as a condition of service do not violate federal law.[18] The most serious potential challenge under federal law involves the application of the antitrust statutes to these utility policies. In certain circumstances, antitrust laws prohibit tying one product to

14. *E.g.,* Dale v. City of Morganton, 270 N.C. 567, 155 S.E.2d 136 (1967); Fulghum v. Town of Selma, 238 N.C. 100, 76 S.E.2d 368 (1953).

15. *Cf.* Dale v. City of Morganton, 270 N.C. 567, 155 S.E.2d 136 (1967) (city may terminate electrical service because wiring in house is unsafe but may not as a means of enforcing the housing code); State *ex rel.* Utilities Commission v. National Merchandising Corp., 288 N.C. 715, 220 S.E.2d 304 (1975) (telephone utility may not terminate service to subscribers who place another company's cover over the cover of the utility-provided telephone book).

16. Fulghum v. Town of Selma, 238 N.C. 100, 76 S.E.2d 368 (1953).

17. *See* City of Fort Collins v. Park View Pipe Line, 336 P.2d 716 (Colo. 1959) (city may terminate service to existing extraterritorial customers unless they agree to be annexed by city); State *ex rel.* Indian Hill Acres, Inc. v. Kellogg, 79 N.E.2d 319 (Ohio 1948) (city requirement that extraterritorial water service be conditional upon annexation not against public policy); Andres v. City of Perrysburg, 546 N.E.2d 1377 (Ohio Ct. App. 1988) (city policy of requiring annexation as a condition of utility connection does not deprive potential customers of equal protection; nor is it a taking of their property).

18. Such a policy might, however, violate the terms of a city's loan contract with a federal agency. In Wayne v. Village of Sebring, 36 F.3d 517 (6th Cir. 1994), the village had received a water system loan from the Farmers' Home Administration (FmHA). One of the terms of the loan required the village to provide service to all persons within its service area. Because the village had earlier extended service to extraterritorial customers without requiring annexation, the extraterritorial area was considered part of the village's service area. The federal appeals court held that when the village changed its extension policy and began to require annexation as a condition of receiving water service, it violated its contract with FmHA.

another, and requiring annexation as a condition of receiving water or sewer service does tie one "product"—annexation—to another—utility service. In *Town of Hallie v. City of Eau Claire,*[19] the United States Supreme Court established the framework for considering whether a policy requiring extraterritorial customers to agree to annexation as a condition of receiving utility services violates the federal antitrust statutes. The city of Eau Claire, Wisconsin, owned the only sewage treatment plant serving a particular area; it would extend service to an extraterritorial area only if the area's residents voted to be annexed by the city. A group of nearby towns brought suit in federal court, arguing that the city's policy constituted an illegal tying arrangement under federal antitrust statutes. The Supreme Court had earlier held that local governments acting in apparent violation of the antitrust statutes were insulated from antitrust liability if their anticompetitive actions were undertaken pursuant to a clear state policy replacing competition with regulation.[20] In *Hallie,* the Court found evidence of such a policy in two Wisconsin statutory provisions that, first, authorized cities to provide utility services and, second, expressly excused cities from any duty to extend those services to properties outside their borders. The Court held that this statutory combination "clearly contemplate[s] that a city may engage in anticompetitive conduct. Such conduct is a foreseeable result of empowering the City to refuse to serve unannexed areas."[21] Therefore the city was insulated from federal antitrust liability.[22] Four years later, a federal district court applied this framework to a North Carolina city and found that North Carolina's statutes also created a clear policy that permits cities to engage in similar anticompetitive conduct. Indeed, the court found that "the North Carolina scheme more explicitly contemplates anticompetitive activity than the Wisconsin statutes cited in *Hallie* because [in addition to including the same statutory authorizations as Wisconsin's, North Carolina law] *expressly* authorizes cities to require those within its limits to use its sewer facilities."[23]

19. 471 U.S. 34 (1985).

20. Lafayette v. Louisiana Power & Light Co., 435 U.S. 389 (1978).

21. 471 U.S. at 42.

22. In Amalgamated Trust and Savings Bank v. Village of Glenview, 423 N.E.2d 1230 (Ill. Ct. App. 1981), the court held that a city policy of tying utility service to annexation did not violate the *state's* antitrust statute.

23. Pinehurst Enterprises, Inc. v. Town of Southern Pines, 690 F. Supp. 444, 449 (M.D.N.C. 1988).

Furthermore, it does not seem to violate Equal Protection to refuse to serve an extraterritorial customer who has not agreed to annexation, even though the city may have in the past extended service to other extraterritorial customers without requiring it. A city may change its extension policies.[24]

Possible assumption of utility responsibilities extraterritorially. There is a possible exception to the general rule that cities may, under state law, condition extension of water or sewer lines on acceptance of annexation. In a number of states (although not as yet in North Carolina), the courts have imposed public utility responsibilities on cities that provide utility services beyond their borders. As stated by the Florida supreme court, "through its conduct a municipality may assume the legal duty to provide reasonably adequate [utility] services for reasonable compensation to all of the public in an unincorporated area."[25] The cases from these states suggest perhaps three ways in which a city might assume a public utility's duty to provide utility service to an extraterritorial area. First, it might agree to do so as a matter of contract, perhaps in an interlocal agreement with the county.[26] Second, it might provide service to a specific area and by doing so become bound by public utility principles.[27] Third, it might purchase a private utility system that has been subject to public utility duties and assume

24. *E.g.,* Shipman v. Lorain County Board of Health, 414 N.E.2d 430 (Ohio Ct. App. 1979); Melton v. City of Wichita Falls, 799 S.W.2d 778 (Tex. Ct. App. 1990). *See also,* Jeld-Wen, Inc. v. Environmental Quality Comm'n, 986 P.2d 582 (Or. Ct. App. 1999).

25. Allen's Creek Properties, Inc. v. City of Clearwater, 679 So.2d 1172, 1176 (Fla. 1996).

26. Delmarva Enterprises, Inc. v. Mayor and Council of City of Dover, 282 A.2d 601 (Del. 1971) (under contract with county, city had exclusive authority to provide water or sewer in buffer area surrounding city); City of Clearwater v. Metco Development Corporation, 519 So.2d 23 (Fla. Ct. App. 1987) (under contract with county, city agreed to undertake public utility responsibilities in a designated unincorporated area). *See* State *ex rel.* Indian Hill Acres, Inc. v. Kellogg, 79 N.E.2d 319 (Ohio 1948) (during term of 20-year contract with county under which city agreed to provide water service within county utility districts, city assumed county's public utility responsibilities); Vine Street Commercial Partnership v. City of Marysville, 989 P.2d 1238 (Wash. Ct. App. 1999) (city contract to provide service to improvement district formed to finance sewer-line installation foreclosed ability of city to require annexation of property within district as condition of receiving city sewer service).

27. Robinson v. City of Boulder, 547 P.2d 228 (Colo. 1976) (city assumes public utility responsibilities because of these actions: city extended service to area; city entered into agreement with other public providers of utility services, thereby preventing those other entities from providing service in the area; city held itself out as only provider of utility service in area); Schroeder v. City of Grayville, 520 N.E.2d 1032 (Ill. Ct. App. 1988) (once a city has begun serving extraterritorial customers, it may not discriminate among such customers unreasonably); Bair v. Mayor and City Council of Westminster, 221 A.2d

those duties with the purchase.[28] When a city assumes public utility responsibilities for extraterritorial areas, it cannot condition further extensions of the utility within that area on property owners' agreement to be annexed. If the North Carolina courts were to adopt the reasoning of this line of cases from other states,[29] a North Carolina city that already has a widespread system of extraterritorial utility customers might find that state law bars it from conditioning utility services on annexation.

Section 4.04. Contracts Tying Annexation to Extension of Utility Lines: Annexation at a Future Time

[a] Introduction

Assume that a city has not assumed public utility responsibilities for an extraterritorial area, or that the North Carolina courts have refused to impose those responsibilities on cities operating outside their borders in any circumstances. In either case, the city may properly condition extension of utility services to an area on agreement to be annexed. Sometimes the city will not want to annex the property at the time it extends utility service—because it is not ready, perhaps, to extend all city services to the property; or perhaps the city cannot annex the property at this time—because it is not contiguous to the city and does

643 (Md. 1966) (if a city has undertaken to supply water to an area outside its borders, it must do so impartially to all those within a reasonable distance of its lines).

28. North Little Rock Water Co. v. Waterworks Comm'n of City of Little Rock, 136 S.W.2d 194 (Ark. 1940); Fellows v. City of Los Angeles, 90 P. 137 (Cal. 1907). *See* Amalgamated Trust and Savings Bank v. Village of Glenview, 423 N.E.2d 1230 (Ill. Ct. App. 1981).

29. The cases cited are inconsistent with the rhetoric of the North Carolina decisions. *See, e.g.,* Fulghum v. Town of Selma, 238 N.C. 100, 104–05, 76 S.E.2d 368, 371 (1953) in which the court wrote that "when a municipality exercises this discretionary power [to extend water lines to extraterritorial customers], it does not assume the obligations of a public service corporation toward non-resident customers." *But see* Hall v. City of Morganton, 268 N.C. 599, 151 S.E.2d 201 (1966), in which the court affirmed a preliminary injunction prohibiting the city from cutting off service to an extraterritorial water customer who refused to switch to the city's electrical system.

Not all courts in other states have accepted the idea that a city can become saddled with public utility responsibilities toward nonresident customers. *See, e.g.,* County of Del Norte v. City of Crescent City, 84 Cal. Rptr. 2d 179 (Cal. Ct. App. 1999) (although a majority of its customers were outside the city, the city could refuse to make any further connections for extraterritorial customers); Dateline Builders, Inc. v. City of Santa Rosa, 194 Cal. Rptr. 258 (Cal. Ct. App. 1983) (court refuses to follow the Delaware and Colorado cases cited in notes 25 and 26).

not currently qualify for satellite annexation. In these circumstances, a number of cities have asked the property owner to sign a contract agreeing to submit an annexation petition at a later time (upon the city's request) or to abstain from participation in any legal challenge to an involuntary annexation that includes his or her property. Can such a contract be enforced against the property owner? And, a more difficult question, can such a contract be enforced against someone who has purchased the property from the owner who signed the contract—against, that is, successors in interest?

[b] Enforcement against the contract signer

A contract of this sort can certainly be enforced against the property owner who signed it. This issue was before the Washington state supreme court in the case of *Yakima County (West Valley) Fire Protection District No. 12 v. City of Yakima*.[30] For more than twenty years, the city of Yakima had had a policy requiring annexation of any area to which it extended water or sewer service. When extraterritorial property owners wanted city utility services, they had to sign an agreement saying they would sign any petition presented to them that would lead to annexation of their property. In 1981 one couple signed such an agreement; when the city presented them with an annexation petition ten years later, they sought to avoid their contractual obligation. The Washington supreme court held that the agreement was enforceable. It noted that the city had had no statutory obligation to provide utility services to extraterritorial customers and that the agreements were therefore supported by consideration. In addition, and for the same reason, the court rejected the plaintiffs' argument that the contracts were unconscionable.[31]

[c] Enforcement against successors in interest

As noted, a more difficult issue arises when the property owner who signed the contract has conveyed the property to someone else. Can the contract be enforced under those circumstances? The following

30. 858 P.2d 245 (Wash. 1993).

31. The contracts in the case required the property owners to sign petitions that initiated the annexation process under Washington law. The court noted that the contract did not require the property owners to waive their right to challenge in court any final annexation, and that seemed an important distinction to the court. For that reason, the case does not support a contractual provision under which the property owner agrees not to join in any legal challenge to an involuntary annexation.

discussion examines three ways in which a city might attempt to ensure enforcement of the contract.

Signing a new contract with each successor in interest. When a property owner conveys property, he or she normally ceases being a customer of the city's utility system. As a condition of continuing utility service, the city can require the new property owner (and each subsequent new property owner) to sign a new contract with the city agreeing to petition for annexation when requested to do so. If a city follows that procedure, the current property owner will always be subject to a current, and enforceable, contract. In *Yakima County*, the city followed this procedure, and the local banks cooperated by requiring a new contract to be signed at the property closing. The court upheld the enforceability of the contract when it was challenged by new owners.

Terminating the service of customers who refuse to be annexed. Because the city is under no statutory obligation to extend service to an extraterritorial customer, it might be able to terminate service if a subsequent property owner refuses to sign an annexation petition. Courts in a number of states have permitted cities to terminate existing extraterritorial service under these circumstances, except where the city is contractually barred from doing so. For example, in *Flex-O-Glass, Inc. v. City of Dixon*,[32] the city had provided utility services to an extraterritorial property owner for almost thirty years; it then implemented a policy requiring such owners to agree to annexation in order to continue receiving services. The Illinois Court of Appeals upheld the city's actions, even though the property owner had been using the city's service for decades and, indeed, had made expensive plant improvements based on the expectation that the service would continue. If the property owner would not agree to annexation, the city could terminate service.[33] A city intending to use this route to ensure that later owners will petition for annexation when asked to do so would be wise to adopt a formal policy; this policy would become part of the city's contract with

32. 718 N.E.2d 730 (Ill. Ct. App. 1999).

33. Other courts reaching a similar conclusion are City of Fort Collins v. Park View Pipe Line, 336 P.2d 716 (Colo. 1959) (unless contract with extraterritorial customer limits reasons for which city may terminate service, city has complete discretion to terminate); Rehm v. City of Batavia, 125 N.E.2d 831 (Ill. Ct. App. 1955) (city may terminate service to existing extraterritorial customer in absence of contract to contrary); Exchange Nat'l Bank of Chicago v. Behrel, 292 N.E.2d 164 (Ill. Ct. App. 1972) (city may terminate service to existing extraterritorial customer in absence of contract to contrary); Adkisson v. Ozment, 370 N.E.2d 594 (Ill. Ct. App. 1977) (once contract with extraterritorial customer has expired, city may unilaterally terminate service); Davisworth v. City of Lexington, 224 S.W.2d 649 (Ky. 1949) ("Non-residents have no lawful claim upon any city service. Any use of city facilities by nonresidents is

extraterritorial utility customers and state that the city may terminate the service at any time if the customer refuses the city's request to petition for annexation.

Recording contracts: equitable servitudes. Some cities have recorded their contracts with property owners in the office of the register of deeds in hopes that the obligation to sign an annexation petition will run with the land and so be enforceable against later owners with record notice of the contract (i.e., by giving them notice of the contract). Although the law on this point is not fully developed, it is likely that recording such a contract would cause the contract to be enforceable against later owners of the property. North Carolina law distinguishes between two types of interests that run with the land: real covenants at law and equitable servitudes. In the 1992 case of *Runyon v. Paley*,[34] the North Carolina supreme court discussed these two kinds of interests at length; the court's discussion suggests that a city's recorded agreement with a property owner tying annexation to utility service does successfully create an equitable servitude. To understand the matter fully, it is useful to begin with a discussion of real covenants at law, then move on to equitable servitudes.

For an agreement to create a real *covenant at law* that runs with the land, it must meet three tests. First, the agreement must indicate the parties' intention to have the promise run with the land. This is a simple matter for an annexation agreement; language specifically saying that it runs with the land can be included in the contract. Second, there must be a close connection between the covenant and the land, so that the promise can be said to "touch and concern" the land of both the party making the promise and the party to whom the promise is made. "It is essential, however, that the covenant in some way affect the legal rights of the covenanting parties as landowners. Where the burdens and benefits created by the covenant are of such a nature that they may exist independently from the parties' ownership interests in land, the covenant does not touch and concern the land and will not run with the

---

wholly permissive (in the absence of contract or estoppel) and not based upon legal right. . . . It follows that the City's consent [to use of its utility facilities] could be withdrawn at will.").

34. 331 N.C. 293, 416 S.E.2d 293 (1992). In maintaining a separate analysis of real covenants and equitable servitudes, the court was resisting recent attempts to merge these two areas of law into a single law of servitudes. *See* RESTATEMENT OF THE LAW (THIRD), RESTATEMENT OF THE LAW: PROPERTY: SERVITUDES (2000). If the North Carolina courts were to adopt the recommendations of this restatement, it would be easier for a city to enforce an annexation agreement against subsequent owners.

land."[35] An annexation agreement cannot meet this test. While the property owner's promise to petition for annexation certainly affects the owner's interest in the property—because it creates future liability for city property taxes[36] —the promise has no connection to property *owned* by the city to which the promise is made. Instead, the promise is made to the city "personally" (or "in gross"). Third, there must be *privity* between the party seeking to enforce the covenant and the party against whom the promise is being enforced. This test requires both horizontal privity—between the two original parties—and vertical privity—between the parties to the original promise and the parties seeking or defending against enforcement of the promise. As a practical matter, to achieve horizontal privity, the original promise must be made in the context of a conveyance of the subject property from one of the parties to the other.[37] Here again, an annexation agreement cannot meet the test: it will not have been entered into as part of a conveyance of land. Rather it is simply a contract for the extension of utility services. Therefore, because an agreement tying a promise to petition for annexation to the receipt of utility service does not meet either the "touch and concern" test or the privity test, it does not create a real covenant at law.

On the other hand, based upon the court's discussion in *Runyon*, it seems probable that an annexation agreement does create an *equitable servitude*. The primary difference between a real covenant at law and an equitable servitude is that the latter does not have to meet the third test noted above, that of privity. Even though the promise to petition for annexation is not made as part of a transaction conveying the property, it can still qualify as an equitable servitude.[38] In addition, although an equitable servitude must also touch and concern the land, the court in

35. *Runyon v. Paley*, 331 N.C. 293, 300, 416 S.E.2d 177, 183.

36. Generally, if the promise decreases the value of the promisor's land—which a promise to seek annexation might seem to do, because of the burden of additional taxation on the land—it is held to touch and concern the promisor's land. 9 RICHARD R. POWELL, ON THE LAW OF REAL PROPERTY § 60.04[2] (Michael Allan Wolf, ed., 2000). *See also,* William B. Stoebuck, *Running Covenants: An Analytical Primer*, 52 WASH. L. REV. 861, 874 (1977).

37. *Runyon v. Paley*, 331 N.C. 293, 303, 416 S.E.2d 177, 184–85 ("In order to show horizontal privity, it is only necessary that a party seeking to enforce the covenant show that there was some 'connection of interest' between the original covenanting parties, such as, here, the conveyance of an estate in land.").

38. Stoebuck, *supra* note 36 at 897 ("A major difference between real covenants and equitable [servitudes] is that the latter may run even if they are not created in connection with the transfer of an interest in land. In other words, horizontal privity . . . is not an element of equitable [servitudes].").

Runyon made a crucial modification in the requirement of "touch and concern" as it applies to equitable servitudes: "[I]t is not always necessary to show that both the burden and the benefit touch and concern land. . . . Where, for example, a covenantee or a named beneficiary seeks to enforce the restriction against the covenantor's successor in interest, the party seeking enforcement need not show that the benefit touches and concerns his land but need show only that the burden touches and concerns the land of the party against whom he seeks to enforce the restriction."[39] That is, the party to whom the promise was originally made may enforce the promise against a successor owner of the property, even if the promise does not touch and concern property owned by the enforcing party—even if it is merely "personal" to that party. This describes exactly the situation of a city enforcing a promise to petition for annexation against a subsequent owner of the property to which utilities have been extended.

In order for such an agreement to be enforceable against subsequent owners as an equitable servitude, it is essential that subsequent owners have notice of the covenant through the chain of title to the property.[40] Although the opinion in *Runyon* contains language that might be read to require that the notice be contained in a deed within the chain of title,[41] that is clearly not the case. If the covenant were required to be in a deed to the property, there would always be horizontal privity, and therefore no need to resort to the doctrine of equitable servitudes (as opposed to real covenants at law). Furthermore, it is clear that the notion of the "chain of title" includes documents other than deeds, including contracts, as long as those other

39. *Runyon v. Paley*, 331 N.C. at 310, 416 S.E.2d at 189. In footnote 3 of the opinion, the court elaborated upon this point: "We recognize that at least one scholar has suggested that our courts will not permit the covenantee to enforce a restrictive covenant, at law or in equity, against the covenantor's successor in interest unless the covenantee is able to demonstrate that the benefit of the covenant touches and concerns land owned by him and is not personal to him. We do not agree. . . . Equity will intervene to enforce a covenant the benefit of which is in gross [that is, personal to the covenantee] just as it will intervene to enforce a covenant appurtenant to the covenantee's land." *Id.* at 310–11, 416 S.E.2d at 189.

40. *Id.* at 313–15, 416 S.E.2d at 191–92.

41. "A purchaser is chargeable with notice of the existence of the restriction only if a proper search of the public records would have revealed it. . . . If the restrictive covenant is contained in a separate instrument or rests in parol and *not in a deed* in the chain of title and is not referred to in such a deed[,] a purchaser, under our registration law, has no constructive notice of it." *Id.* at 313, 416 S.E.2d at 191 (emphasis added).

documents present evidence of burdens on the title and are properly indexed in the office of the register of deeds.[42]

In summary, if the city's agreement with the property owner is reduced to writing and signed by both parties, and if the written agreement specifies that it is to run with the land, the court's discussion in *Runyon* supports enforcement of the agreement as an equitable servitude. Of course, some crucial parts of the discussion in *Runyon* are not simply dicta but also dicta found only in footnotes to the opinion. Therefore, a city hoping to enforce such agreements against later owners is well-advised to include in its utility-extension policies—which would become part of the utility contract with all customers—a statement that extraterritorial service is conditioned upon the property owner's agreement to petition for annexation whenever requested to do so by the city. That the policy has been formally stated by the city, and included in the basic contract with all customers, would offer a second basis—in addition to the individual, recorded contract—for enforcing it against a recalcitrant customer.

Section 4.05. Requiring Annexation from Existing Extraterritorial Customers

Suppose a city has extended utility services to properties outside the city without any reference to eventual annexation and later changes policy to require agreement to submit to annexation as a condition of utility service. Can such a policy change be enforced retroactively against existing extraterritorial customers?

It probably can, unless the city is somehow contractually barred from terminating service for this reason. The same set of cases that support a city's capacity to terminate service when a subsequent owner refuses to comply with a promise to petition for annexation made by the original recipient of the utility service supports a city's ability to modify its policies and require annexation from existing extraterritorial customers.[43] Those cases, in fact, involved situations in which a city did

42. *Webster's* notes that party-wall agreements, which "are nothing more than contractual agreements" respecting the property, are part of the chain of title. 2 Webster's Real Estate Law in North Carolina: Possessory Estates and Present Interests in Real Property § 24.21 (Patrick K. Hetrick and James B. McLauglin Jr., eds., 5th ed., 1999).

43. Those cases are set out in notes 32 and 33 and the accompanying text.

change its policy and begin to require annexation as a condition of *continued* utility service, and so are directly on point. There is one cryptic North Carolina case, however, that suggests some limitations on a city's ability to terminate a customer who was connected before the city established a policy tying annexation to receipt of utility services. In *Hall v. Morganton*,[44] the plaintiff, an extraterritorial customer, alleged that the city had provided water service until he had contracted with a private power company to provide electrical service to the house. The city had then notified the owner that if the property was not connected to the city's electric system (rather than the private utility's), the city would terminate water service. On receipt of these allegations, the trial court granted a preliminary injunction against the city barring it from disconnecting the property's water service. The city immediately appealed. The North Carolina supreme court affirmed the injunction.

> More is involved in this case than the right to require the City to serve a customer outside the City limits. On the present showing the question is whether the City may force the home owner to switch from Duke Power to City power by a threat to sever the owner's connection with the City water system for which he paid $300.00. The court has power to restrain a municipal corporation's threatened wrongful acts.
>
> The complaint and affidavit filed by the plaintiff furnish sufficient factual basis for Judge Froneberger's order continuing the restraint to the hearing.[45]

There may well be a difference between requiring existing water or sewer customers to petition for annexation, thereby becoming part of the city providing the service, and requiring such customers to take an unrelated city service they do not want or need. Nonetheless, any attempt to enforce an annexation requirement will have to deal with the language in *Hall*.

44. 268 N.C. 599, 151 S.E.2d 201 (1966).
45. *Id.* at 601, 151 S.E.2d at 202.

Section 4.06. Contracts Regarding City Services with Persons Being Annexed

[a] Introduction

Cities that are undertaking voluntary annexations sometimes ask, or are asked, to enter into contracts—side agreements, really—with the persons petitioning for annexation. If these contracts attempt to add conditions to a voluntary annexation that are not expressly supported by the annexation statute, they are probably not enforceable. There is, however, very little case law about such contracts anywhere in the United States, and none in North Carolina. The discussion that follows focuses on two specific categories of such side agreements between a city and a property owner, but the general points made probably apply more broadly.

[b] Lower levels of city services

Sometimes a property owner petitions for annexation to obtain a particular service or benefit available only if the property is within the city. In such a situation, the owner often doesn't care about other city services and will tell the city it need not supply those after annexation. For example, in counties where the sale of beer or wine is not permitted in unincorporated areas but is permitted inside a city, a convenience store or a restaurant owner might petition for annexation solely to be able to sell beer or wine. If the city expresses concern about the cost of extending city services to the property (which is especially likely in a satellite annexation), the property owner might offer to sign an agreement declining city services and agreeing not to seek them in the future. Such an agreement is probably not enforceable against the property owner who signs it and is certainly not enforceable against subsequent owners of the property.

As noted earlier in section 4.02, annexation is a legislative act. Despite the consensual elements of a voluntary annexation, it remains a legislative, not a contractual, act. As local governments may not ordinarily condition legislative actions upon agreements with private citizens, conditioning this legislative act—annexation—upon such an agreement would seem to require statutory authority that the city does not possess. Moreover, both voluntary annexation statutes specifically state that annexed properties are entitled to the same privileges and benefits as other parts of the city. A city has no authority to force (or even allow) a petitioner to forgo a statutory entitlement in order to be annexed. If the city is unwilling to provide services to a property, the appropriate course is simply not to annex the property.

A number of cities have entered into contracts that, in effect, delay the city's obligation to provide the full range of city services to voluntarily annexed property. Under these contracts, the property owners waive their entitlement to city services, most often water or sewer, for a specified number of years. They retain the right, however, to request those services before the expiration of the agreement upon complying with the city's usual policies for extending utility lines. Because a property owner can, in effect, renounce the contracts at any time and immediately assume his or her entitlement to city services, such a contract is not subject to the concerns voiced above. The contract merely offers documentation of the property owner's temporary consent to the nonextension of services. As long as that consent continues, the contract is unexceptionable.

[c] Specific zoning of annexed property or other exercises of the police power

Sometimes a property owner agrees to petition for annexation in return for the city's agreement to zone the annexed property in a particular manner. Such an agreement is a clear instance of *contract zoning*, which is prohibited under North Carolina law. The North Carolina supreme court has stated and explained the ban on contract zoning in this way:

> Illegal contract zoning properly connotes a transaction wherein both the landowner who is seeking a certain zoning action and the zoning authority itself undertake reciprocal obligations in the context of a *bilateral* contract. . . . [C]ontract zoning of this type is objectionable primarily because it represents an abandonment on the part of the zoning authority of its duty to exercise independent judgment in making zoning decisions.[46]

46. Chrismon v. Guilford County, 322 N.C. 611, 635, 370 S.E.2d 579, 593 (1988) (emphasis in original).

The court's explanation of the ban on contract zoning suggests that any attempt to connect annexation to a contract limiting the necessary legislative discretion of a city in other ways will also be invalid.[47]

47. The author has seen a contract proposed by a railroad company in response to a city's request that the railroad petition for annexation of a stretch of its right-of-way. The proposal includes a provision in which the city agrees not to seek or support any further grade crossings of the railroad's properties anywhere in the city. Because decisions about the need for and the location of grade crossings involve judgments of public safety and the efficient use of city streets (*see* G.S. 160A-298), it is unlikely that such an agreement could be enforced against the city.

5

Council Votes on Annexation Ordinances

5

Council Votes on Annexation Ordinances

Section 5.01. The General Rule

To adopt an ordinance, G.S. 160A-75 requires an "affirmative vote equal to a majority of all the members of the council not excused from voting on the question in issue." As cities accomplish annexations through adoption of an annexation ordinance, this requirement applies when a council votes on that measure. Adoption of an annexation ordinance, therefore, requires that a council with the following number of members cast the number of affirmative votes shown (assuming that no one is excused from voting on the measure):

No. of council members	No. of affirmative votes needed
3	2
4	3
5	3
6	4
7	4
8	5
9	5
10	6
11	6
12	7

Section 5.02. Is a Two-Third's Vote Necessary?

G.S. 160A-75 also states that "no ordinance . . . may be finally adopted on the date on which it is introduced except by an affirmative vote equal to or greater than two thirds of all the actual membership of the council, excluding vacant seats. . . . [A]n ordinance shall be deemed to have been introduced on the date the subject matter is first voted on by the council." Considerable uncertainty surrounds the application of this two-thirds vote requirement to annexation ordinances.

The purpose of the two-thirds requirement seems to be to prevent a council from quickly bringing up and adopting an ordinance before the entire council or the public has a chance to react to it, unless the ordinance has the support of at least two-thirds of the council's members. If this is the correct understanding of the requirement's purpose, that purpose is satisfied by the notice to the public and council members provided by any council action or vote that involves the ordinance or its subject matter and indicates that the council is considering adopting the ordinance. If this broad interpretation of the requirement is accepted, the first vote on an annexation ordinance's subject matter would be adoption of a resolution of intent (for an involuntary annexation), directing the city clerk to investigate an annexation petition, or, perhaps, calling the public hearing (for a voluntary annexation). This interpretation conforms to the statutory language, inasmuch as the votes on the resolution of intent, giving direction to the clerk, and calling the hearing all involve the subject matter of the ultimate annexation ordinance. Furthermore, given the elaborate steps that must be taken before any vote on an annexation ordinance is held, it is difficult to characterize the day of that first vote on adoption as "the date on which [the ordinance] is introduced." Certainly holding a public hearing before any annexation and carrying out the additional procedures associated with involuntary annexations more than adequately provide for the public notice the two-thirds vote requirement seems intended to ensure. Under this broad interpretation, a city council could adopt an annexation ordinance that receives a majority of affirmative votes on its first attempt, because the first vote on the subject matter has already taken place.

There is a narrower interpretation of the two-thirds vote requirement, however, born of some city attorneys' concern that their councils' votes be immune from attack on the ground that the two-thirds vote requirement has not been met. This narrower interpretation insists that the first vote on the subject matter of the ordinance must be a vote on adopting the ordinance. The statutory reference to the subject matter of the ordinance, in this interpretation, is intended to allow amendments after the first vote. If this narrower interpretation is accepted, a city council would need the affirmative votes of at least two-thirds of its members to adopt an annexation ordinance on its first attempt. If the ordinance received a simple majority but not two-thirds, the council would need to vote on it again, and on that second vote a majority vote would pass the ordinance.

There has been no reported appellate decision interpreting the two-thirds vote requirement. The requirement has, however, been the subject of at least one unpublished decision of the North Carolina court of appeals, and that panel accepted the narrower interpretation. In *Bowers v. City of Thomasville*,[1] the city council voted 4–3 to adopt an annexation ordinance in July 1996. Three weeks later it again voted 4–3 to adopt the ordinance, but in the interim the effective date of the ordinance had been changed. The court of appeals and all the parties appear to have agreed that the two-thirds vote requirement applied to the annexation ordinance; the issue before the court was whether the change in the effective date caused the second majority vote to be on a new ordinance and was therefore inadequate to meet the two-thirds requirement. The court held that a change in the effective date was a minor change that did not create a new ordinance and so the second vote was adequate to adopt the annexation ordinance. As an unpublished opinion, of course, this case carries no precedential value. Furthermore, the author is aware of at least one superior court decision that accepted the broader interpretation of the two-thirds vote requirement and held that it did not apply to annexation ordinances. Conclusive resolution of this issue must await either legislative clarification or a reported appellate decision.

If a city and its attorney decide to follow the narrower interpretation of the two-thirds requirement for adoption of an annexation ordinance on its initial vote, a council with the following number of members would have to cast the number of affirmative votes shown (assuming no vacant seats):

No. of council members	No. of affirmative votes needed
3	2
4	3
5	4
6	4
7	5
8	6
9	6
10	7
11	8
12	8

1. No. COA97-1391 (N.C. Ct. App. Dec. 1, 1998).

6

Metes and Bounds Boundary Descriptions and Annexation Maps

6

Metes and Bounds Boundary Descriptions and Annexation Maps

Section 6.01. Metes and Bounds Descriptions

[a] Introduction

Several sections of the various annexation statutes require that the proposed or actual annexation area be described by metes and bounds. The satellite annexation statute requires that the petition describe the area proposed for annexation in terms of metes and bounds,[1] while the two involuntary annexation statutes require that the annexation ordinance itself describe the annexation area by metes and bounds.[2] (The voluntary contiguous annexation statute does not explicitly require a metes and bounds description in either the petition or the annexation ordinance.) This section defines a metes and bounds description and describes the kinds of boundary statements that meet the statutory requirement.

[b] Basic meaning

There is some confusion among attorneys, planners, and others about the exact components of a metes and bounds description. One authority describes a metes and bounds boundary description as follows:

> The term *metes* means "measure," and the term *bounds* means the limits or boundaries of a tract of land. Although common usage places a number of types of description in this category, strictly speaking a *metes and bounds* description is one that has

1. N.C. GEN. .STAT. §160A-58.1(c) (hereinafter G.S.).
2. G.S. 160A-37(e)(1) and 160A-49(e)(1).

a defined point of beginning and travels around the parcel in a clockwise or counterclockwise direction, recites courses, distances, monuments and abutting parcels as they are encountered, and returns to the point of beginning. Generally, the description recites the area of the parcel so traversed. The theoretical parcel description should contain all of the above elements; however, the typical description includes some combination of the foregoing elements, with some information often lacking.[3]

One type of metes and bounds description results from an actual field survey by a registered land surveyor and might include calls (that is, compass bearings) and distances something like those in the excerpt below.

> [T]hence, S 39° - 54' E, 1,682.87 feet to a point; thence, N 51° - 38' W, 583.42 feet to a point; thence, S 39° - 50' W, 550.1 feet to a point; thence N 64° - 25' W, 522.75 feet to a point; thence, N 51° - 29' W, 456.7 feet to a point; thence, N 62° - 09' W, 35.83 feet to a point; . . .[4]

This is clearly a metes and bounds description (assuming that the complete description includes a determinable point of beginning), but it is not the only kind of metes and bounds description. The descriptions below are from two much older documents.[5]

> Beginning at the corner of Floyd's and Tanner's tracts and thence along a line North fifteen degrees West one hundred and sixty two poles crossing a cold branch to pointers in Joseph Motley's old line and thence along the same South eighty two and a half degrees West one hundred and four poles crossing the said branch several times to pointers. . . .

> Beginning at a corner sweet gum in William Carter's line, thence along the said Carter's line to a Red Oak corner, thence along

3. Donald A. Wilson, "Reading, Interpreting, and Writing Land Descriptions," in, Land Surveys: A Guide for Lawyers and Other Professionals 41 (Mitchell G. Williams, ed., A.B. A. Sec. Real Prop. Prob. & Tr. L. 2d ed. 2000).

4. This excerpt is from a 1960 annexation report prepared by the city of Raleigh.

5. Both excerpts are from late-eighteenth-century deeds recorded in Pittsylvania County, Virginia.

William Welcom Allen's line to a white oak on Elijah Adams' line, thence down the Little Rockey branch on the said Adams' line to the Big Rockey branch, thence up the Big Rockey branch to the mouth of the Pig Pen branch thence up the Pig Pen branch to the Beginning.

The compass readings and specific distances in the first of these two old descriptions suggest that the land was formally surveyed, while the tract in the second description apparently was not. Nonetheless, both use *monuments* (natural or artificial markers) and *courses*[6] to describe the perimeter of a tract of land, and both are metes and bounds descriptions. Obviously, these old style descriptions would not be used for a current annexation, but they do demonstrate the range of descriptions that fall within the meaning of metes and bounds.

The first metes and bounds description above measures directions to the nearest minute and distances to the nearest one one-hundredth of a foot; modern surveying equipment can measure directions to the nearest second.[7] Such precise measurements are not, however, necessary to meet the annexation statutes' requirement of a metes and bounds description. The North Carolina appellate courts have upheld descriptions that do not describe compass bearings and distances as precisely as is technically possible and that do not include corners marked by natural or artificial monuments.

Bearings. In *Blackwell v. City of Reidsville,*[8] for example, the petitioners argued that the city's boundary description was insufficient, in part, because it did not use precise bearings calculated from compass readings—that is, readings such as N 64° - 25' W. Rather than providing precise compass bearings, the description indicated directions in general terms like "easterly" and "southwesterly." Although the *Blackwell* court did invalidate the city's boundary descriptions (see below), it did so on a different ground. Indeed, several court of appeals decisions have specifically upheld descriptions that give directions in similar general terms. In *In re Annexation Ordinance (Asheville)*,[9] for

6. "Each course is composed of a bearing and a distance," according to CURTIS M. BROWN ET AL, BROWN'S BOUNDARY CONTROL AND LEGAL PRINCIPLES 99 (John Wiley & Sons, 4th ed. 1995).

7. *See* Knud E. Hermansen, "When is a Rod Not 16.5 Feet? (More Times Than Not)," in Williams, *supra* note 3, at 56.

8. 129 N.C. App. 759, 502 S.E.2d 371 (1998).

9. 62 N.C. App. 588, 303 S.E.2d 380 (1983).

example, the trial court invalidated a boundary description characterized by the following excerpt:

> [T]hence in a *southeasterly* direction following said City Limit boundary a distance of approximately 3,960 feet to a point, said point being 10 feet east of the eastern right-of-way margin of Sand Hill Road (SR 3412); thence in a *southwesterly* direction following a line 10 feet east of the eastern right-of-way margin of Sand Hill Road . . . .[10]

The court of appeals, however, reversed the decision, holding that this was a metes and bounds description that "could be established on the ground in substantial compliance with the applicable statutes."[11]

Distances. In another Asheville case, *Garland v. City of Asheville*,[12] the trial court invalidated the city's boundary description, in part, because it "contains only approximations as to distances."[13] Again, the court of appeals reversed, holding that the description "could be ascertained on the ground" and therefore was valid.[14]

Unmonumented points. The trial court in *Garland* also invalidated the city's description because it did not "refer to monuments for approximate distances, the only reference to approximate distances being that they are to run from 'point' to 'point,' which said points are not ascertainable in and of themselves."[15] As noted just above, the court of appeals reversed the decision, in effect holding that monumented corners are not a necessary component of a metes and bounds description.[16]

10. *Id.* at 594, 303 S.E.2d at 383 (emphasis added).
11. *Id.*
12. 63 N.C. App. 490, 305 S.E.2d 66 (1983).
13. The description is fairly characterized by this excerpt:

> [T]hence in a northerly direction following a line 10 feet west of the western right-of-way margin of Chunns Cove Road and running parallel to said right-of-way margin, a distance of *approximately* 1,400 feet to a point; thence crossing Chunns Cove Road in a northeasterly direction following a straight line a distance of *approximately* 60 feet to a point. . . .
>
> *Id.* at 491, 305 S.E.2d at 67 (emphasis added).

14. *Id.* at 493, 305 S.E.2d at 68. Note that the boundary description from *In re* Annexation Ordinance (Asheville), in the text accompanying note 10, also gives approximate distances.
15. *Id.* at 492, 305 S.E.2d at 67.
16. The court also specifically upheld descriptions with unmonumented corners in *In re* Annexation Ordinance (Asheville), 62 N.C. App. 588, 303 S.E.2d 380 (1983) and McKenzie v. City of High Point, 61 N.C. App. 393, 301 S.E.2d 129 (1983).

[c] Use of tax maps

Field surveys are not commonly used in North Carolina to prepare the metes and bounds description for an annexation ordinance. Much more often, the boundaries of an annexation area use monuments and courses that reference county tax maps or, less frequently, recorded plats. Using tax maps or recorded plats allows a city to avoid a field survey, thereby saving considerable costs. Case law has established that such a description is a sufficient metes and bounds description as long as references are clear. Several court of appeals decisions involving involuntary annexations have included challenges to ordinance descriptions of annexation areas that relied on tax maps. In all but one case, the court upheld the descriptions. The court found, for example, that the two descriptions containing the following excerpts met the statutory requirement.

> Beginning at an iron pipe at the northeast corner of the bridge crossing Richland Creek on the North Carolina highway 98, as so described in the Town of Wake Forest charter and dated 1909, and proceeding along the north side of highway 98 S84°30'E 474.50' to an iron stake; then across North Carolina highway 98 S15°00'E along the present corporation limits and through the lands of Thomas J. Byrne to the southern boundary of the aforementioned lands and the northern boundary of the lands of Mary Sue Byrne as according to the *Wake County tax maps, sheet number 103 and 106, parcel numbers 103-31 and 106-45*, a distance of approximately 325' . . .[17]
>
> Thence in a northerly direction along the Forsyth/Guilford County line to a point on the northern property line of *Parcel 27E of Block 5613 of Forsyth County Tax Map 5-2*, thence in an easterly direction along the northern property line of *Parcel 27E of Block 5613 County Tax Map 5-2* to a point on the center line of Tanglebrook Road (S. R. 1824); thence in a northeasterly direction along the northern property lines of *Parcels 20, 25, 26 and 8 of Block 1 of Guilford County Tax Map 320* for a distance of 836 feet more or less to the northeast corner of *Parcel 8 of Block 1 of Guilford County Tax Map 320*; . . .[18]

17. Record at 62, Scoville Manufacturing Co., Inc. v. Town of Wake Forest, 58 N.C. App. 15, 293 S.E.2d 240 (1982) (emphasis added). Both the court and the parties agreed that this was a metes and bounds description; the petitioners argued, unsuccessfully, that it was an inaccurate metes and bounds description. *Id.* at 21, 293 S.E.2d at 245.

18. Record at 63, McKenzie v. City of High Point, 61 N.C. App. 393, 301 S.E.2d 129 (1983) (emphasis added). "We have examined the descriptions used in the ordinance

The one boundary description not upheld demonstrates the need, when using tax maps or recorded plats, to designate clearly the specific maps being used and where they might be found. In *Blackwell v. City of Reidsville*, the city was attempting to annex several areas, in most areas using boundary descriptions similar to the following excerpt:

> Beginning at a point in the present City limits, said point being westerly about 108 feet from the southwest corner of lot 1, thence from the beginning point easterly about 138 feet to a point, said point being in the southern line of lot 1, thence from said point easterly about 890.97 feet to a point, said point being the southeast corner of lot 11 and a corner for lot 13, . . .[19]

The city's boundary description referred repeatedly to various numbered lots but included no indication of where the lots were located; and it contained no references to tax maps (as in the above descriptions) or to recorded plats. Because of that absence, the court of appeals held that Reidsville's "use of the tax maps, without incorporation by reference, was not a sufficient metes and bounds description."[20]

[d] Description by plat reference

Many annexations involve platted subdivisions for which plats have been recorded; properties within such subdivisions are commonly conveyed by lot number with reference to the recorded plat. For example, a deed might describe the property conveyed as "all of Lots 73, 74, 75, 76, Block B, of Rock Barn Extension, Section 10, as per plat and survey thereof now on file in Plat Book 6, page 18," in the office of the appropriate register of deeds. Such a description is entirely adequate to convey property, and probably to describe it, but it is not a metes and bounds description.[21] Therefore, a description that simply names an

---

and hold that they are in substantial compliance with the statutory requirement." *Id.* at 401–02, 301 S.E.2d at 132.

19. Record at 118, Blackwell v. City of Reidsville, 129 N.C. App. 759, 502 S.E.2d 371 (1998).

20. 129 N.C. App. at 763, 502 S.E.2d at 374.

21. "Some descriptions merely refer to a plan (commonly termed a *plat* when referring to a subdivision of land), which by rule of law makes the plan part of the property description. In such cases, one must consult the plan in order to determine the location of the parcel as well as the definition of its lines and corners." Wilson, *supra*, note 3, at 43 (emphasis in original). The author is distinguishing this form of boundary description from a metes and bounds description.

entire subdivision, or lots in a subdivision, and then refers to a recorded plat does not meet the statutory requirement that the boundaries of an annexation area be described by metes and bounds.

Section 6.02. Annexation Maps

A variety of statutes require that a map showing each annexation be prepared, filed, and recorded. This chapter reviews those requirements.

[a] The city clerk

G.S. 160A-22 requires that the city clerk maintain a map, or a written description, of the city's current boundaries. Because the statute requires that the map or description be current, the clerk or other official charged with updating the map should make the necessary changes after the effective date of each annexation approved by the city council or the General Assembly.

[b] The Secretary of State and the register of deeds

G.S. 160A-29 directs the mayor, after any statutory annexation by the city, to "cause an accurate map of such annexed territory, together with a copy of the ordinance duly certified," to be recorded in the office or offices of the appropriate register or registers of deeds and in the office of the Secretary of State. This statute applies explicitly to annexations undertaken pursuant to any of the four statutory annexation procedures;[22] but it is also good practice to record in those offices an appropriate map of any annexation to the city accomplished by local act of the General Assembly, together with a copy of the legislation. It is equally good practice to record a map and a copy of the legislation in those rare occasions when the General Assembly deannexes territory from a city.

The statute directs that the map and annexation ordinance be filed with the Secretary of State no later than thirty days after the effective date of the ordinance, but it goes on to state that failure to do so does not invalidate the annexation ordinance.[23] And, while there is no time

22. N.C. Gen Stat. § 160A-39, for involuntary annexations by cities under 5,000, and § 160A-51, for involuntary annexations by cities of 5,000 or more, contain identical (and redundant) recording requirements.

23. In so stating, the statute codifies the supreme court's holding in Dale v. Morganton, 270 N.C. 567, 155 S.E.2d 136 (1967). In that case the city did not record

requirement for filing the map and ordinance with the local register of deeds, it is, again, good practice to do so as soon as practicable. Indeed, if there is no challenge to an annexation ordinance, there is no reason not to file the map and ordinance promptly after the ordinance's adoption, even before the effective date.

The statute directs that any maps filed with the office of the Secretary of State comply with regulations adopted by the Secretary as to map size, material, and the like. In fact, however, the Secretary has never promulgated any such regulations and so, as a practical matter, will accept any map a city submits. The best approach is to file with the Secretary a copy of the map it files with the local register or registers of deeds. The Secretary's office prefers a certified copy of the annexation ordinance but will currently accept an uncertified version. As the Secretary has assigned responsibility for these maps to the Land Records Management Program, cities may send the maps and ordinances to that office.

G.S. 47-30 sets out the requirements that must be met for all land plats presented for recording to registers of deeds. Subsection (j) of the section explicitly provides that it does not apply to annexation maps. Nevertheless, a city that complies with, at least, the plat-size requirements imposed by the local register of deeds pursuant to G.S. 47-30(a) will substantially facilitate the register's storage of the city's annexation maps.

[c] The board of elections

G.S. 163-288.1 requires any city that has annexed territory, whether by one of the statutory procedures or through local legislation from the General Assembly, to prepare a map of the annexed territory and deliver it to the board of elections that conducts elections for the city. It makes sense to meet this requirement by using copies of the map filed with the Secretary of State and the register or registers of deeds. The board of elections uses this map to *activate*, or register for city elections, voters living within the annexed territory. (Section 13.03[a] describes the process by which the local board of elections activates voters residing within an annexation area.)

---

the map and ordinance until more than thirty months after adoption of the annexation ordinance.

7

Standing to Challenge an Annexation in Court

7

Standing to Challenge an Annexation in Court

Section 7.01. Introduction and Summary

Who has standing to bring a court challenge to an annexation, in what circumstances, at what time, and through what form of action? These are the questions investigated in this chapter. The law concerning these issues is not fully articulated in North Carolina, and for that reason some of what follows is inevitably speculative. It is clear, though, that bringing a legal challenge to an annexation is a difficult matter and that many potential plaintiffs do not have standing to prosecute a challenge. The chapter begins by reviewing the leading North Carolina cases and then addresses, in turn, the standing of several types of plaintiffs: the State of North Carolina, owners of property in the annexation area, nearby cities, residents of the annexing city, the county, and others.

In summary, these are the conclusions reached in the ensuing discussion.

1. The State may challenge a completed annexation through an action in the nature of quo warranto brought by the Attorney General.
2. An owner of property involuntarily annexed by a city may challenge an annexation pursuant to the involuntary annexation statute.
3. An owner of property voluntarily annexed by a city who denies that she or he gave consent to the annexation may challenge the annexation, pursuant to the Declaratory Judgment Act.
4. Another city may, in certain circumstances, challenge an annexation pursuant to the Declaratory Judgment Act. The most likely such circumstance arises when a city seeking to annex the same area as the defendant city brings a declaratory judgment action to determine which city has successfully obtained prior jurisdiction to undertake the annexation.

5. Occasionally some other person or entity might have standing to challenge an annexation, but it is also possible that no one else, in any other circumstances, may do so.

Section 7.02. The North Carolina Cases: The *Gaskill–Taylor* Rule

[a] Supreme court decisions

Seven North Carolina appellate decisions—two by the supreme court, five by the court of appeals—directly raise the question of standing to challenge an annexation in court. The first is *Gaskill v. Costlow*,[1] decided in 1967. The 1963 General Assembly enacted a local act exempting the town of Beaufort from the normal requirements for extending sewer services to involuntarily annexed property. Relying on the act, Beaufort proceeded with an annexation, referencing the local act in its annexation report. About a year after the annexation became effective, a number of persons owning property in the annexation area brought suit, arguing that the local act was unconstitutional and that, therefore, the annexation ordinance was invalid. The trial court agreed that the act was unconstitutional and invalidated the annexation ordinance. On appeal, the supreme court also agreed that the local act was unconstitutional but denied the plaintiffs the fruit of their argument. The court began by noting that

> [I]n many jurisdictions, unless such ordinance be absolutely void, e.g., on the ground of lack of legislative authority for its enactment, private individuals may not attack, collaterally or directly, the validity of proceedings extending the corporate limits of a municipality, this being an action to be prosecuted only by the state through its proper officers.[2]

The court then noted that the involuntary annexation statute allowed persons owning property within the annexation area to challenge the

1. 270 N.C. 686, 155 S.E.2d 148 (1967).

2. *Id.* at 689, 155 S.E.2d at 150. The court cited an *American Law Reports* annotation: "Capacity to attack the fixing or extension of municipal limits or boundary," 13 A.L.R.2d 1279 (1950).

validity of the annexation by filing a petition in superior court; it held that this statutory provision was the sole remedy for attacking an involuntary annexation. Because the statute (at the time) required the petition to be filed within thirty days after the annexation ordinance was adopted, and because the plaintiffs had missed that short statute of limitations, their attempt to have the annexation declared invalid failed.

The second case is *Taylor v. City of Raleigh*,[3] decided in 1976. In 1972 the city had annexed about forty acres through a voluntary satellite annexation and had begun preparations for extending utility lines to the annexed area. When it became clear that the city would have to condemn easements over certain property near the annexation area, the owners of that property brought suit challenging the validity of the annexation. Their strategy was to invalidate the annexation and thus remove the need for extending utilities and for condemning their properties. The plaintiffs, who brought suit about six months after the annexation became effective, owned property between the principal city limits and the annexed area; they did not own property in either the city or the annexed area. The trial court refused the motions of the various defendants to dismiss the suit for lack of standing but then upheld the annexation ordinance. The court of appeals affirmed, but on the ground that the plaintiffs did not have standing to challenge the annexation.[4] The supreme court affirmed on the same ground.

The court began by citing *Gaskill* and repeating that decision's statement of the general rule limiting court challenges to annexations. The court then conditioned the *Gaskill* statement, adding that "if the annexation is neither authorized by law nor made under color of law[,] it is void and is subject to attack by anyone having a sufficient personal interest in the litigation."[5] The court also admitted that the General Assembly may permit challenges to an annexation, as it had done in the involuntary annexation statute, but noted that the legislation permitting Raleigh's satellite annexation included no provision for private challenges to such an annexation. "It is clear, therefore, that the plaintiffs in this action lack standing to contest the annexation ordinance."[6]

3. 290 N.C. 608, 227 S.E.2d 576 (1976).
4. 22 N.C. App. 259, 206 S.E.2d 401 (1974).
5. 290 N.C. at 618, 227 S.E.2d at 582.
6. *Id.* at 227, S.E.2d at 582.

[b] Court of appeals cases

Taylor was followed by four court of appeals decisions that interpreted it as barring challenges to voluntary annexations by (1) neighbors of the annexed property, (2) residents and taxpayers of the annexing city, and (3) a city located near the annexing city. A fifth court of appeals decision also involved standing and is consistent with the others, although it does not cite the other standing cases.

The first of these five cases is *McKenzie v. City of High Point*,[7] decided in 1983. The petitioners challenging an involuntary annexation by High Point were property owners in the annexation area. One of their arguments was that the area was not in fact contiguous to the city because, they claimed, an earlier voluntary annexation was illegal. Thus, their case depended on their ability to challenge this earlier annexation of an area in which they were not property owners. The court refused to allow them to make the argument, because, among other reasons, they did not have standing to do so—not being residents of the area of that earlier annexation. The court's handling of the issue suggests that a property owner might be able to challenge such an annexation, but its decision does not reference either *Gaskill* or *Taylor*.

The second case is *Davis v. City of Archdale*,[8] decided in 1986. The city had voluntarily annexed two tracts of land contiguous to the city; within the next month, the city rezoned those tracts, apparently triggering opposition from persons owning property near the tracts but outside the city. These property owners brought a declaratory judgment action seeking to invalidate the annexation on the ground that not all owners of the annexed property had signed the petitions; the owners of the annexed property were also joined as defendants. Although the city readily admitted that the plaintiffs were correct—that not all owners had signed the petitions—the trial court still granted the motions from the defendant property owners to dismiss the action for lack of standing, and the court of appeals affirmed. The appellate court began by quoting from *Taylor* and then noted that the various annexation statutes permit a challenge to an annexation only by owners of property within the annexation area.[9] As these plaintiffs did not own property within the annexation area, they were not permitted to challenge the annexation.

7. 61 N.C. App. 393, 301 S.E.2d 129 (1983).
8. 81 N.C. App. 505, 344 S.E.2d 369 (1986).
9. The court's citations were only to the involuntary annexation statutes, inasmuch as the voluntary annexation statute, under which the annexation was accomplished, contains no provision whatsoever for making challenges.

In *Taylor*, after holding that the plaintiffs did not have standing because the applicable annexation statute included no provision for private challenge to a satellite annexation, the supreme court confused the matter somewhat by noting that the plaintiffs in *Taylor* "own no property in the annexed noncontiguous area . . . [nor] do they own property within the primary corporate limits" of the city.[10] This implicit suggestion—that persons owning property within a city's primary corporate limits might have standing to challenge a voluntary annexation—was tested in the next case in this series, *Joyner v. Town of Weaverville*.[11] After Weaverville annexed a satellite tract of almost ninety acres, citizens of the town brought suit, alleging that the annexation area did not meet the standards of the satellite annexation statute.[12] Noting that the satellite statute permitted town citizens to speak at the public hearing on annexation, the trial court held that the plaintiffs had standing but ruled against them on the merits. The court of appeals affirmed, but on the ground that even residents of the annexing city were without standing to challenge a voluntary annexation. Because the satellite annexation statute contains no provision for judicial review, the plaintiffs had to go without their day in court.

The fourth case is *Town of Seven Devils v. Village of Sugar Mountain*.[13] This case was triggered by a combination of two voluntary annexations by Sugar Mountain. The first was a long shoestring annexation running from the village's existing corporate limits down the highway and then along a property line for a total of some 3,430 feet. The shoestring was only 10 feet wide for its entire length. Once this annexation was complete, the village accepted an annexation petition from a commercial development at the other end of the shoestring. This second annexation area was literally across the highway from the corporate limits of Seven Devils. A satellite annexation of this second area by Sugar Mountain would not have met the statutory requirements in the satellite statute, because the area, minus the shoestring, was closer to Seven Devils than to Sugar Mountain. But the shoestring annexation made the second annexation a contiguous one for Sugar

10. 290 N.C. at 618, 227 S.E.2d at 582.

11. 94 N.C. App. 588, 380 S.E.2d 536 (1989).

12. N.C. GEN. STAT. § 160A-58.1 (hereinafter G.S.) can be read as prohibiting the satellite annexation of part (rather than all) of a platted subdivision. [This substantive issue is discussed in Volume 2 of this series.] The plaintiffs alleged that the ninety acres were part of a subdivision and therefore within the prohibition.

13. 125 N.C. App. 692, 482 S.E.2d 39 (1997).

Mountain, rendering its proximity to Seven Devils irrelevant. Seven Devils brought suit under the Declaratory Judgment Act, arguing that the shoestring annexation was invalid and that, therefore, the second annexation was invalid as well. The pair of annexations was nothing more, Seven Devils argued, than a disguised satellite annexation. The town argued that because the satellite statute prohibited annexing an area closer to a second city, it, as the second city, should have standing to enforce this requirement in the satellite law. The court of appeals would have none of it. The court, citing *Taylor*, stated that unless an annexation ordinance is void or unless a statute specifically grants standing, one city may not challenge the annexation of a second city. Because "there is no contention that the annexation is void,"[14] and because no statute granted standing to the plaintiff town, Seven Devils was without standing.

The final case of this set is *Town of Ayden v. Town of Winterville*,[15] decided in 2001. In 1997 Winterville undertook a voluntary annexation of territory that brought its borders nearer to those of Ayden; as a result of the annexation, the potential extraterritorial land-use jurisdictions (ETJs) of the two towns overlapped. In 1999, citing possible loss of its ETJ, Ayden brought suit, alleging that not all the owners of property had signed the petition and that the property was not in fact contiguous to Winterville. The trial court granted summary judgment to Winterville on the ground that Ayden did not have standing to challenge the annexation. Citing each of the six cases summarized above, the court of appeals affirmed the trial court's decision. Because G.S. 160A-31, the relevant annexation statute, does not authorize suit by neighboring municipalities, Ayden was without standing to challenge the annexation.[16]

[c] The *Gaskill–Taylor* rule

The foregoing seven cases are the only appellate cases directly addressing the issue of standing to challenge an annexation, and the rule they create (which, for convenience, we'll call the *Gaskill–Taylor* rule)

14. *Id.* at 694, 482 S.E.2d at 40.

15. 143 N.C. App. 136, 544 S.E.2d 821 (2001).

16. The court wrote that the "annexation statute upon which Winterville based its annexation . . . G.S. § 160A-31, does not identify categories of plaintiffs other than owners of land in the subject area, who are authorized to challenge an annexation pursuant to the statute." *Id.* at 140, 544 S.E.2d at 824. Of course, the voluntary annexation statute does not explicitly identify any category of plaintiff who may challenge an annexation, even the property owner.

provides but a narrow opportunity for challenging an annexation: First, an annexation may be challenged if the annexation statute itself provides a remedy; second, an annexation that is void may be challenged in some manner; and third, the state may challenge an annexation. With this background in mind, let's look at the chances of success for a range of possible plaintiffs.

Section 7.03. Standing: The State of North Carolina

[a] By the Attorney General, in an action in the nature of quo warranto

In *Taylor*, as noted above, the court stated that an action attacking the validity of an annexation may be brought "by the State through its proper officers."[17] Although the court does not clearly say so, the basic rule, in fact, is that *only* the state may challenge an annexation. All other opportunities for challenge are exceptions to this basic rule. Who, then, are the State's "proper officers" and what kind of action may they bring?

The answer almost certainly is that such an action may be brought by the Attorney General and that the proper form is an action in the nature of quo warranto, brought pursuant to G.S. 1-515. Although the *Taylor* court did not mention quo warranto, it supported its statement about a state challenge by citing an *American Law Reports* annotation, "Proper remedy or procedure for attacking legality of proceedings annexing territory to municipal corporations."[18] The annotation asserts that most state courts have acknowledged quo warranto as the appropriate remedy for a state challenge to annexations, an assertion that certainly accords with the scattered case law on the subject. This case law emerges from an even more basic rule: only the state can challenge the validity of a municipality's de facto corporate existence, doing so in a quo warranto action. This rule is asserted in various treatises on quo warranto and other extraordinary remedies[19] and has been repeated by

17. 290 N.C. at 617–18, 227 S.E.2d at 582.

18. 18 A.L.R.2d 1255 (1951).

19. *E.g.*, "The creation of municipal franchises being an attribute of sovereignty to be exercised only by the supreme power in the state, all who presume to exercise such franchises without due authority are liable to proceedings by information in the nature of a quo warranto. And when it is sought to exercise the privileges and powers of a municipal corporation without authority of law, an information is the proper remedy, and the court will give judgment that the pretended corporation be dissolved." JAMES L. HIGH, EXTRAORDINARY LEGAL REMEDIES § 684 (3d ed. 1896). *See also*, Charles W. Tooke, *De Facto Municipal Corporations under Unconstitutional Statutes,* 37 YALE L.J. 935

a number of courts as well.[20] Reasoning that challenges to annexations are comparable to challenges to the existence of the municipality itself, courts have extended the more basic rule to include annexation challenges as well.[21] The Oregon supreme court has made perhaps the fullest expression of this line of reasoning:

> It is important to note that an action brought to declare invalid the annexation of territory to a municipality is markedly different than the ordinary action in which the plaintiff seeks only the vindication of his individual rights. The validity of the annexation is a matter of importance not only to the plaintiff who brings an action questioning it but also to all persons who own property in the annexed territory. Of greater significance is the fact that the city itself may be vitally affected by the judgment in such a case. These factors, touching so directly upon the public interest, have prompted the courts to treat actions attacking the validity of annexations as constituting a special type of proceeding, governed by rules different from those applied in purely private actions. Thus it has been held that the corporate existence of a municipality as originally organized or as reorganized by the extension of its boundaries through annexation proceedings cannot be questioned in an action by private parties and that the question can be raised only in a direct proceeding prosecuted at the instance of the Attorney General or the District Attorney.
>
> A more refined statement of the rule is that once the municipality exercises dominion over the annexed territory in a de facto

---

(1928) ("The resulting incidents [of being a *de facto* corporation] are that the organization itself and those dealing with it as a corporation cannot attack its existence, that its acts are as valid as those of a *de jure* corporation, and that the legality of its existence cannot be inquired into collaterally, but may be challenged only by the state itself in quo warranto proceedings.").

20. *E.g.,* Enos v. District Court, 238 P.2d 861 (Colo. 1951); Farrington v. Flood, 40 So.2d 462 (Fla. 1949); State *ex rel.* Gibbs v. Mayor, 10 A. 377 (N.J. 1887).

21. *E.g.,* Port Valdez Co., Inc. v. City of Valdese, 522 P.2d 1147 (Alas. 1974) (quo warranto sole method for challenging annexation); City of Tallahassee v. Kovach, 733 So.2d 576 (Fla. Ct. App. 1999) (quo warranto sole method for challenging annexation); Edgewood Park No. 2 Homeowners Ass'n v. Countryside San. Dist., 246 N.E.2d 294 (Ill. 1969) (quo warranto sole method for challenging annexation); State *ex rel.* Condon v. City of Columbia, 528 S.E.2d 408 (S.C. 2000) (state may bring quo warranto to challenge annexation even when state does not own property in annexation area). Some additional cases in which quo warranto was in fact used to challenge an annexation are State *ex rel.* Martin v. City of Kansas City, 317 P.2d 806 (Kan. 1957), and State *ex rel.* Village of Fridley v. City of Columbia Heights, 53 N.W.2d 831 (Minn. 1952).

capacity, the validity of the annexation cannot be attacked by a party other than the state. Generally, it is said that quo warranto is the proper remedy and that quo warranto can be brought only at the instance of the state.[22]

The North Carolina quo warranto statute is not particularly plain in its authorization of a state challenge to an annexation, but it contains language that has been found adequate in other states to support challenges to municipal existence and municipal annexation. G.S. 1-515 permits the Attorney General to bring an action "when a person *usurps, intrudes into, or unlawfully holds or exercises* any public office, civil or military, or *any franchise within this State*, or any office in a corporation created by the authority of this State" (emphasis added). As courts in other states have held that the exercise of municipal power is a *franchise* within the meaning of the quo warranto statute, the statute gives the state the right to challenge the unlawful exercise of such power.[23]

The North Carolina case law, though sparse and not directly on point, supports these general propositions. First, the supreme court has expressly recognized the exclusive right of the state to challenge the validity of a de facto private corporation. In a 1914 case, *Claremont College v. Riddle,* the court held that once an entity achieved de facto corporate existence, "[i]ts powers to act could only be drawn in question by the State, on suit regularly entered."[24] Second, in *State ex*

22. Griffin v. City of Roseburg, 464 P.2d 691, 693–94 (Or. 1970).

23. *E.g.*, People *ex rel.* Adams v. City of Oakland, 28 P. 807 (Cal. 1891) ("The right and power [to govern and tax the inhabitants of a specified territory] is a franchise in addition to and distinct from that of being a corporation, and the exercise of such power by a municipal corporation over the inhabitants of territory outside of its charter limits is usurpation of a franchise, for which the attorney general is authorized to bring an action in the name of the people." *Id.* at 808); People *ex rel.* Rice v. McKinnie, 115 N.E. 526 (Ill. 1917) (In maintaining streets and installing sewer in an annexed area, the "city was exercising its franchise as a city over the lands" so annexed, and therefore the validity of the annexation may only be raised in an action in quo warranto. *Id.* at 526). *But see*, Red River Valley Brick Co. v. Grand Forks, 145 N.W. 725 (N.D. 1914) (statute allowing quo warranto to challenge usurpation of a franchise does not permit challenge to a municipal annexation).

24. 165 N.C. 211, 216, 81 S.E. 283, 285 (1914). *See also* Wood v. Staton, 174 N.C. 245, 93 S.E. 790 (1917), in which the court distinguished between de jure and de facto corporations in this way: "So far as the State is concerned, the final distinction [between the two types of corporations] is that the one can successfully resist a suit by the State or sovereign which created it, brought directly to test the rightfulness of its existence, and the other cannot; but as to individuals who have dealt with it as a corporation . . . there is no essential difference." *Id.* at 252–53, 93 S.E. at 794.

rel. Tillett v. Mustian,[25] the court acknowledged in 1956 that quo warranto is an appropriate form for bringing an action challenging the corporate existence of a municipality. That case was brought by a private relator in the name of the State, pursuant to G.S. 1-516, and was an attack on the continued corporate existence of the newly incorporated town of Kill Devil Hills. In its opinion, the court considered without deciding the question of whether such a suit could be brought by a private relator or could only be brought directly by the Attorney General.[26] Nonetheless, it was clear that a direct action by the Attorney General pursuant to G.S. 1-515 would have been appropriate. Third, in 1960, in *Starbuck v. Havelock*,[27] the court again acknowledged that quo warranto was the appropriate remedy for challenging the corporate existence of a de facto municipality. When the plaintiffs sought to enjoin the exercise of municipal powers by the officers of the newly incorporated town of Havelock, the defendants argued that quo warranto, rather than an action for an injunction, was the correct remedy. Although the court disagreed with the defendants about whether quo warranto was the sole remedy in the peculiar set of facts in that case, it did imply that had the town already achieved de facto status, quo warranto would be the correct remedy.[28]

Finally, the supreme court has at least once considered a challenge to an annexation brought pursuant to the quo warranto statute, although it did so without comment and without argument from the parties. In the 1958 case of *State ex rel. East Lenoir Sanitary District v. City of Lenoir*, the record discloses that the sanitary district petitioned the Attorney General for permission to file the lawsuit, which was granted upon payment of bond in the amount of $200.[29] Although the record does not disclose the statute under which the petition was made, the quo warranto statute is the only one that contains such a procedure, and the amount of bond required by the Attorney General pursuant to G.S. 1-516 remains $200 to this day.

25. 243 N.C. 564, 91 S.E.2d 696 (1956).

26. "Can an action to declare a municipal corporation nonexistent be brought except by the State, through the Attorney-General, acting *ex officio* as the representative of the public?" *Id.* at 568, 91 S.E.2d at 699.

27. 252 N.C. 176, 113 S.E.2d 278 (1960).

28. "The wrongs which may be corrected by quo warranto are specified by statute. G.S. 1-515 and 516. . . . None of these statutes apply to this action. This is not an action to determine a right to a public office nor to prevent the exercise of a franchise by a *de facto* corporation. This is an action to determine whether a *de jure* municipal corporation has been established." *Id.* at 178, 113 S.E.2d at 278.

29. 249 N.C. 96, 105 S.E.2d 411 (1958). The petition to the Attorney General and his response is found in Record, pages 10–11.

[b] By a private relator

Assuming that an action in quo warranto brought by the Attorney General is the appropriate method by which the State challenges the validity of an annexation, two of the cases discussed in the preceding paragraphs raise the question of whether a private individual (a *relator*) may bring such an action in the name of the State. Under G.S. 1-516, the Attorney General is permitted to allow a private individual to do so; but in *Tillett* the court posed the question of whether that statutory authorization applied to a challenge to the corporate existence of a de facto municipality or was only available to a relator challenging the right of someone to hold public office. Having posed the question, the court decided not to pursue it. Two years later, in *East Lenoir,* the court heard a quo warranto challenge to an annexation but did not acknowledge the issue raised in *Tillett* in any way. Let's begin with *Tillett.*

The town of Kill Devil Hills had been incorporated by act of the General Assembly in 1953; the initial town board was appointed in the legislation, and the first town election was scheduled for 1955. At that time, the general law included a procedure under which a town's citizens could, by petition, force a referendum on repeal of the town's charter; a number of citizens of Kill Devil Hills did present such a petition to the town board shortly before the 1955 election. The board placed the proposition on the ballot, where it narrowly carried; nonetheless, the town board elected at the same election refused to recognize the validity of the charter vote. Therefore, a private relator brought suit in quo warranto to declare the town's charter repealed and the town offices vacant. The North Carolina supreme court held that the referendum statute was inapplicable to Kill Devil Hills at the time the petition was presented and that the vote on repealing the charter was therefore without legislative authority and consequently invalid. Before reaching that decision, however, the court questioned the propriety of a private relator bringing the suit before it.

> This action was brought in the name of the State, *pro forma*, by a private relator. The Attorney-General has not participated in the action beyond requiring the bond and granting leave as prescribed by G.S. 1-515.
>
> Can an action to declare a municipal corporation nonexistent be brought except by the State, through the Attorney-General, acting *ex officio* as the representative of the public? Where the sole subject of controversy is the existence or nonexistence of the municipal corporation, can such action be brought against

> individuals rather than against the municipal corporation itself? Decision in other jurisdictions, based in part on statutory provisions, would seem to point toward conflicting answers. In this connection, it is noted that this action involved a municipal corporation alleged to have been created and organized as a *de jure* municipal corporation. Does this distinguish this action from cases where the corporate existence is challenged on the ground that, for failure to meet statutory requirements prescribed by general law for its valid organization, the purported municipal corporation did not come into existence either as a *de jure* or as a *de facto* municipal corporation?
>
> Since our decision is put on other grounds, we refrain from discussing the serious questions raised as to whether the relator could maintain the action as presently constituted if his legal position were otherwise correct.[30]

Despite the court's comment that decisions in other states seem to point toward conflicting answers to the court's questions, the overwhelming weight of the law in those jurisdictions that have addressed the issue (as well as all the cases on the question cited by the court) is that a private relator *may not* bring an action in quo warranto challenging the legal existence of a municipal corporation; only the state through its proper officers—in North Carolina, the Attorney General—may do so. The rationale for this limitation was stated more than a century ago by the New Jersey supreme court.

> [I]t was highly inexpedient that these municipalities, being the depositories of a part of the governmental power of the state, should have their very being put at hazard whenever any member of the community saw fit to make the assault. Being public institutions, it was determined that their existence was not to be challenged, except by the state, through its attorney general, he acting *ex officio*, as the representative of the public, and that in such a procedure his name could not be used *pro forma* by a private narrator.[31]

30. State *ex rel.* Tillett v. Mustian, 243 N.C. 564, 568, 91 S.E.2d 696, 699 (1956) (citations omitted).

31. State *ex rel.* Steelman v. Vickers, 17 A. 153, 154 (N.J. 1889). Other cases to the same effect include Enos v. District Court, 238 P.2d 861 (Colo. 1951); State *ex rel.* Wetzel v. Tracy, 51 N.W. 613 (Minn. 1892); and State *ex rel.* Mick v. Burke, 166 N.E. 354 (Ohio 1929). *See also* Thos. C. Spelling, II A Treatise on Injunctions and Other Extraordinary Remedies § 1840 (2d ed. 1901).

That is, because an attack on the existence of a municipal corporation is so serious, it may only be brought by the state, and not by individuals seeking to act through the state.

That being the case, does this prohibition on private relators challenging a muncipality's corporate existence apply as well to private relators attempting to challenge an annexation? On the one hand, because the state's exclusive power to challenge an annexation grows out of its exclusive power to challenge a municipality's corporate existence, it would be logical for the same limitations to apply to both actions. On the other side, however, the public cost of an invalidated annexation is clearly less heavy than the public cost of invalidating the very existence of the municipality itself; therefore a court could draw a principled line between the two sorts of cases.[32]

Section 7.04. Standing: An Owner of Annexed Property

The supreme court, in *Taylor*, identified two exceptions to the basic rule that only the state may challenge an annexation. First, the General Assembly may by statute permit others to bring a challenge. And second, if the annexation is void, any person with a sufficient interest may bring a challenge. Both exceptions come into play with respect to challenges by owners of property in an annexation area.

[a] Involuntary annexations

Both of the involuntary annexation statutes set out a procedure that allows an owner of property located within the annexation area to challenge the annexation. Within sixty days after an annexation ordinance is adopted, any person owning property within the annexation area may petition superior court to review the legality of the annexation. Such challenges are a common part of the involuntary annexation process. In such an action, a petitioner may question whether the annexation area in fact meets the statutory standards, whether the city

32. The Illinois courts have permitted private relators with a sufficient interest to bring quo warranto challenges to annexations. *E.g.*, People *ex rel.* Kirby v. City of Effingham, 356 N.E.2d 1315 (Ill. Ct. App. 1976) (city resident may bring quo warranto because of allegation that annexation will necessitate additional expenditure of city funds); Island Lake Water Co., Inc. v. LaSalle Development Corp., 493 N.E.2d 44 (Ill. Ct. App. 1986) (displaced private service provider may bring quo warranto); Village of Kildeer v. Village of Lake Zurich, 521 N.E.2d 1252 (Ill. Ct. App. 1988) (city undertaking competing annexation may bring quo warranto).

has followed the statutory procedures, and whether the city's annexation report sets out an adequate plan for providing services to the annexation area. A petitioner may also raise related legal issues, such as the constitutionality of any local legislation relied upon by the city in undertaking the annexation.[33] If a property owner does not act within the time set out in the statute, this remedy is lost, and there is no other statutory procedure for challenging an annexation on any of the above grounds.[34]

[b] Voluntary annexations

Neither of the voluntary annexation statutes includes a procedure for challenging the annexation.[35] Therefore, as summarized above, courts have denied standing to challenge such annexations to neighbors of the annexed property, residents of the annexing city, and a nearby city. Because a voluntary annexation begins with a petition from the affected property owners, one would not expect a challenge from a property owner. Occasionally, though, a property owner asserts that she or he has not assented to the annexation; the appellate courts have heard at least two challenges to attempted annexations by such property owners. In *Allman v. City of Newton*[36] (a case included in the official reports under the heading of a companion case, *Newton v. Conover*), several property owners who had signed a petition for voluntary annexation requested, at the public hearing, that their names and properties be removed from the petition. When the city refused and adopted an annexation ordinance that included their properties, they brought suit under the Declaratory Judgment Act to have the annexation declared void. In *County of Brunswick v. Town of Bolivia*, [37] the county had relocated its courthouse facilities to a site near Bolivia. Subsequently, the town was presented with a petition to annex the facilities. The county brought suit under the Declaratory Judgment Act to stop the

33. Gaskill v. Costlow, 270 N.C. 686, 155 S.E.2d 148 (1967). In Biltmore Square Assoc. v. City of Asheville, 113 N.C. App. 459, 439 S.E.2d 211 (1994), the court held that property owners in the annexation area did not have standing to challenge the annexation under the federal Voting Rights Act. The court noted that the petitioners were not members of minority groups nor were they voters of the city.

34. Gaskill v. Costlow, 270 N.C. 686, 155 S.E.2d 148 (1967).

35. Joyner v. Town of Weaverville, 94 N.C. App. 588, 380 S.E.2d 536 (1989) (satellite annexations); Town of Seven Devils v. Village of Sugar Mountain, 125 N.C. App. 692, 482 S.E.2d 39 (1997) (contiguous annexations).

36. 297 N.C. 506, 256 S.E.2d 216 (1979).

37. 56 N.C. App. 732, 289 S.E.2d 569 (1982).

annexation, because it had not signed the petition. Although the appellate courts heard both cases, and invalidated both annexations, in neither case did the parties or the court raise or discuss the property owners' standing to bring the action. How do these challenges fit, if at all, within the confines of the *Gaskill–Taylor* rule?

Because the Declaratory Judgment Act is not "specific statutory authority" to challenge an annexation,[38] these two cases, in order to fit within the rule, must involve void annexations. To determine whether that is true requires, first, that we ascertain what the courts mean by a *void annexation ordinance*. One fairly narrow possibility, suggested by the court in both *Gaskill* and *Taylor*, is that the annexing city is completely without legislative authority to undertake this kind of annexation or annexations of any kind. As summarized by Table 1.1 in Chapter 1, some towns are barred by local act of the General Assembly from undertaking involuntary annexations or from undertaking annexations of any kind until a specific date. Certainly a town subject to such a local act would be without authority to attempt an annexation included within the prohibition applicable to that town; thus any prohibited annexation would clearly be void within the meaning of *Gaskill*, *Taylor*, and their progeny.

From one point of view, it would appear that the court of appeals panels that decided *Davis* and *Joyner* had adopted this narrow sort of understanding of a void annexation. In *Davis*, plaintiffs alleged (and the city admitted) that not all property owners had signed the petitions; in *Joyner* the plaintiffs alleged (although the city denied) that the petition did not meet all the standards of G.S. 160-58.1(b). Despite these allegations, in each case the court held that the plaintiffs were without standing. If these cases depend on such a very narrow meaning of void annexations, however, they do not explain why the courts did not deny standing to the property owners in *Allman* or in *Brunswick County*. The defendant cities in *Allman* and *Brunswick County* enjoyed full statutory authority to undertake voluntary annexations; they simply did not comply with the statute.

Is there a way to reconcile these four cases? Yes, by first accepting a broader understanding of what constitutes a void annexation and then

38. In Town of Seven Devils v. Village of Sugar Mountain, 125 N.C. App. 692, 482 S.E.2d 39 (1997), the plaintiff town brought suit under the Declaratory Judgment Act. The court of appeals, however, thought some sort of statute "that expressly authorizes one municipality to challenge the annexation ordinance of another municipality" was what was required under the *Gaskill–Taylor* rule, *id.* at 694, 482 S.E.2d at 40. Because there was no such statute, the court held that the complaint was properly dismissed.

recalling the supreme court's additional point from *Taylor*: that a void annexation may be challenged by someone with a "sufficient personal interest in the litigation." That is, not only must the annexation be void, but the plaintiff must also have some adequate personal interest in order to prosecute the challenge.

To begin with, to fit *Allman* and *Brunswick County* within the framework of the *Gaskill–Taylor* rule, we need an understanding of what constitutes a void annexation broader than simply one carried out by a city totally lacking the legislative authority to annex. One possibility is to apply the substantive-procedural distinction suggested as an explanation for the North Carolina supreme court's decisions on prior jurisdiction.[39] Thus, if an annexation fails to comply with a basic substantive requirement, it is void. In a voluntary contiguous annexation, the substantive requirements are that the property be contiguous and that the property owners consent to the annexation. In a voluntary noncontiguous annexation, the requirements are that the property meet the standards listed in the statute[40] and that the property owners consent to the annexation. And in an involuntary annexation, the substantive requirements are that the annexation area be contiguous, that at least one-eighth of the perimeter of the annexation area coincide with the city's existing boundary, that no property within the annexation area be within another city, and that the annexation area meet the statutory standards of urban development. If the city makes only procedural errors, however, such as an inadequate property description in a published notice or a slightly shorter notice period than required by statute, the annexation would not be void for purposes of this rule of standing. Courts in other states considering the question of standing to challenge annexations have made this distinction between substantive and procedural requirements.[41]

It is possible, however, that the North Carolina courts might even accept challenges based on procedural grounds, given the approach the supreme court took in the above-noted *Starbuck v. Town of Havelock* (section 7.03[a]).[42] In that challenge to the corporate existence of the town of Havelock, the plaintiffs, residents of the new town, sought to enjoin town officials from exercising municipal powers. The defendants

39. See the discussion in section 3.03[b].

40. These are set out in G.S. 160A-58.1(b).

41. *E.g.*, City of Wilmer v. Laidlaw Waste Systems (Dallas), Inc., 890 S.W.2d 459 (Tex. Ct. App. 1994).

42. 252 N.C. 176, 113 S.E.2d 278 (1960).

argued that because the plaintiffs were challenging the corporate existence of the new town, their sole remedy was through an action pursuant to the quo warranto statute; therefore their injunction action should be dismissed. The court, however, held that, on the facts alleged and at that particular point in the history of the incorporation effort, the plaintiffs were not restricted to quo warranto but could proceed with their action for injunctive relief.

The case is relevant to this discussion because, as discussed above, the exclusive standing of the state to challenge municipal annexations derives from its exclusive standing to challenge the corporate existence of municipalities themselves. Because the court permitted a challenge to a city's corporate existence in an action by citizens for injunction, it would presumably permit a challenge to an annexation through a comparable action based on comparable grounds. What, then, were the grounds of attack in *Starbuck*? The plaintiffs argued that the incorporation act was void, first, because it unconstitutionally limited the qualifications necessary to run for city office, and, second, because the incorporation referendum had not complied with the requirements of the incorporation legislation. The second ground is essentially procedural. By hearing the case, the court seems to have signaled that it was willing to consider any argument that would show the incorporation effort had not complied with the constitution or with other applicable legislation. *Starbuck*, therefore, suggests quite a broad understanding of a void annexation as, basically, one that fails to meet the essential substantive or procedural requirements of the annexation statute. We need not choose between these two possible meanings of a void annexation at this point.[43] Both the very broad understanding and the narrower one based on a substantive–procedural distinction are consistent with the facts of the two property-owner cases that opened this discussion. In both *Allman* and *Brunswick*, plaintiffs alleged that all owners of the annexed property had not signed the annexation petition as required by the appropriate annexation statute.[44]

43. It should be noted, however, that if the notion of a void annexation includes annexations that suffer only from procedural errors, then the notion itself becomes meaningless as no kind of faulty annexation is left outside that notion. The court's firm assertion that standing exists only if the annexation is void–as if the term does mean something—suggests that only annexations that suffer from substantive errors are void.

44. Both understandings are also not inconsistent with the facts of *Gaskill*, which was also an action brought by owners of property being annexed. In *Gaskill*, the plaintiffs had a statutory remedy that they had failed to use; in addition, their delay in bringing the action distinguishes the case from *Allman, Brunswick County*, and *Starbuck*.

In this understanding of the *Gaskill–Taylor* rule, the problem for the plaintiffs in the four court of appeals decisions that explicitly implemented the rule is not that the plaintiffs failed to allege that the annexations in question were void but that they did not have a sufficient personal interest in the matter to support their own standing to make their arguments. That is, it is not the understanding of what is a void annexation that is narrow, but rather the understanding of what constitutes a sufficient personal interest in the litigation. An owner of property being annexed has a sufficient interest, but a neighbor (*Davis*), a city resident (*Joyner*), and a neighboring city (*Seven Devils* and *Ayden*) do not. In *Starbuck*, in holding that the plaintiffs in that case—owners of property in the challenged town—had a sufficient interest, the court wrote:

> A delay in challenging compliance with the statutory requirements might permit a *de facto* corporation to arise, thereby subjecting plaintiffs and their property to obligations and liabilities of municipal government. This gave plaintiffs a right to have the validity of the election determined without seeking authority from the Attorney General.[45]

The potential liability for town taxes, and perhaps the potential subjection to town regulations, was what gave standing. Property owners in an annexation area have just such an interest, but neighbors, current city residents, and a neighboring town do not.

Buyers of property in the annexation area. Perhaps persons who are in the process of acquiring property in the annexation area have standing as well. At least such a rule offers the best explanation of a court of appeals decision that allowed a county to seek injunctive relief against a voluntary annexation. In *Yandle v. Mecklenburg County*,[46] property owners had sought voluntary annexation by the town of Matthews at about the same time as the county was bringing an action to condemn their property for a sanitary landfill. Because annexation would have prohibited the county from constructing the landfill,[47] the property owners brought suit against the county, arguing that the pending annexation justified enjoining the condemnation action. The

45. 252 N.C. 176 at 180, 113 S.E.2d at 281.

46. 85 N.C. App. 382, 355 S.E.2d 216 (1987).

47. G.S. 153A-292 permits a county to "establish and operate solid waste collection and disposal facilities *in areas outside the corporate limits of a city*" (italics added).

county then brought suit against the town and the property owners to enjoin the annexation. The trial court initially enjoined both proceedings—the annexation and the condemnation—then concluded by allowing the annexation to go forward. The court of appeals reversed, holding that the annexation would "constitute irreparable harm to the County" and therefore enjoining the town from proceeding. Even though the decision makes no mention of the county's standing to bring the action, we can perhaps best understand it in terms of an extension of a property owner's right to challenge an annexation. Because the county had brought the condemnation action, and therefore had an expectation of owning the property, the court treated it as if it were a property owner who had not consented to a voluntary annexation.

When an action must be brought. One final point. If the owners of property annexed through a voluntary procedure in fact do not consent to the annexation, they need to bring their action challenging the annexation immediately—before the annexation becomes effective or very shortly thereafter. Once again, the court's discussion in *Starbuck* is revealing. The court acknowledged that quo warranto is the appropriate remedy for challenging the existence of a de facto corporation, just as, presumably, it would be the appropriate remedy for challenging a de facto annexation. But the plaintiffs in *Starbuck* were not challenging the existence of a corporation that had reached de facto status. As the court pointed out,

> [t]his is an action to determine whether a *de jure* municipal corporation has been established.
>
> . . .
>
> The [incorporation] election either created or failed to create a corporation. It could not produce a *de facto* corporation, but it could present an opportunity for a *de facto* corporation to arise. *De facto* corporate existence requires not only colorable compliance with a law authorizing its creation but the exercise of corporate power.[48]

That is, if the plaintiffs had waited for a time and allowed the challenged town to begin town operations, the town might have achieved de facto status and then only quo warranto could be used to challenge the town's existence. But by acting promptly once the challenged election

48. *Id.* at 178, 180, 113 S.E.2d at 279, 281.

had been held, the plaintiffs brought their challenge before de facto status had been reached. Similarly, plaintiffs challenging an annexation must act before the city has exercised sufficient corporate power for the annexation to achieve de facto status.[49]

Section 7.05. Standing: Another City

There are several contexts in which one city has standing to challenge another's pending or just-completed annexation, most importantly when there is a dispute over prior jurisdiction.

[a] A city that seeks to annex some or all of the same property

The North Carolina appellate courts have a long-time practice of allowing declaratory judgment actions between two cities seeking to annex some or all of the same property. Although the most recent of these cases focused on the question of whether the issue was ripe when the action was brought, there was no dispute between the litigants or, apparently, among the judges and justices, as to whether the plaintiff city had standing to bring its action; and there was no such dispute in any of the other declaratory judgment actions in this series. Here, chronologically arranged, are these reported appellate cases.

- *Town of Hudson v. City of Lenoir*[50] Hudson had begun an involuntary annexation of an area when Lenoir received petitions for annexation of some of the same property. Before Lenoir could hold a public hearing on the voluntary annexation, Hudson brought suit to declare the Lenoir proceeding invalid and to enjoin its continuation.
- *Conover v. Newton*[51] Conover had begun an involuntary annexation of an area when Newton received petitions for

49. *See* Scarry v. Lewis, 30 N.E. 411 (Ind. 1892) (when property owner has paid taxes, received services, voted, and held office over multiyear period, it would be "inequitable and unjust" to allow him to then attack the annexation that brought his property into the city). The North Carolina courts have used the concept of laches to bar other sorts of actions under the Declaratory Judgment Act; *e.g.*, Taylor v. City of Raleigh, 290 N.C. 608, 227 S.E.2d 576 (1976) (challenge to rezoning); and Capps v. City of Raleigh, 35 N.C. App. 290, 241 S.E.2d 527 (1978) (challenge to rezoning).

50. 279 N.C. 156, 181 S.E.2d 443 (1971).

51. 297 N.C. 506, 256 S.E.2d 216 (1979).

annexation of some of the same property. After both cities had adopted annexation ordinances, Conover brought suit to declare the Newton annexation void.

- *City of Burlington v. Town of Elon College*[52] Burlington had begun an involuntary annexation of an area when Elon College received petitions for annexation of some of the same property. After both cities had adopted annexation ordinances, Burlington brought suit to declare the Elon College annexation void and to enjoin it from taking effect and Elon College counterclaimed to declare the Burlington annexation void.
- *Town of Hazelwood v. Town of Waynesville*[53] After Hazelwood had adopted a resolution of *consideration* under the involuntary annexation statute, Waynesville received petitions to annex some of the property included within the area of Hazelwood's resolution. During the time Waynesville was proceeding with the annexation, Hazelwood brought suit to have Waynesville's annexation declared invalid.
- *City of Kannapolis v. City of Concord*[54] After Concord received a petition to annex land lying between the city and Lake Concord (a city-owned lake), but before adoption of an ordinance annexing the property, Concord adopted a resolution of intent to voluntarily annex its lake, which would become contiguous once the first annexation was complete. After a hearing on both annexations, the city adopted ordinances annexing the petition properties and the lake. After these ordinances were adopted, but before they became effective, Kannapolis began an involuntary annexation that included the lake property. After Kannapolis completed its annexation, it brought suit to declare Concord's annexation of the lake invalid, and Concord counterclaimed for a declaration that Kannapolis's annexation was improperly begun and therefore invalid.
- *Town of Spencer v. Town of East Spencer*[55] After both cities had adopted resolutions of intent to involuntarily annex some of the same properties, Spencer brought suit to have East

52. 310 N.C. 723, 314 S.E.2d 534 (1984).
53. 320 N.C. 89, 357 S.E.2d 686 (1987).
54. 326 N.C. 512, 391 S.E.2d 493 (1990).
55. 351 N.C. 124, 522 S.E.2d 297 (1999).

Spencer's resolution declared invalid, thus depriving East Spencer of prior jurisdiction to annex.

Only in the *Spencer* case did an appellate court address the appropriateness of the action. And in that case the issue was not whether the cause of action was appropriate or whether the plaintiff town had standing, but rather whether the action was brought prematurely. The defendant city argued that the action should not have been brought until that city had adopted its annexation ordinance, but neither party argued that the plaintiff city was without standing. In the end, the court held that when two cities are attempting to annex the same area, a declaratory judgment action may be brought to challenge the validity of the resolution of intent without waiting for the annexation proceeding to be concluded, because whether the resolution is valid is determinative of which city has prior jurisdiction.

Therefore, based on long practice and on the holding in *Spencer*, a city that is seeking to annex the same territory as another may bring an action pursuant to the Declaratory Judgment Act to determine which city has prior jurisdiction to annex. So understood, this line of cases doesn't really fit within the framework established by the *Gaskill–Taylor* rule. The exception to the basic rule that best fits these cases is the one that permits a person or entity with a sufficient personal interest to challenge a void annexation. Clearly, a city that is attempting to annex the same property as another has an interest sufficient to provide standing, but that plaintiff city is not really claiming that the other city's annexation is void, nor does it need to. Rather, it is claiming that the first mandatory step in the defendant city's annexation process was sufficiently flawed to deny that city prior jurisdiction to annex. In the *Spencer* case, for example, the plaintiff city successfully claimed that the defendant city's resolution of intent was flawed because the proposed annexation area included territory already within the plaintiff city (as discussed in chapter 3). If, however, the plaintiff city had not begun its own annexation and thereafter brought suit, and if the defendant city had corrected the property description by the time it adopted the annexation ordinance, it is unlikely that a court would have invalidated the resulting annexation in a suit brought by property owners.[56] That is, the initial error made by the defendant city did not thereby render the

56. The substantive requirement in G.S. 160A-36, that no part of the annexation area be within another city, would then be met; and if the city's initial error was considered merely procedural, what material injury would any petitioners have suffered?

annexation invalid but only cost the city its prior jurisdiction. Thus, the right of one city to challenge another's prior jurisdiction to annex exists somewhat outside the framework of the *Gaskill–Taylor* rule.

Permissible arguments. One unanswered question about this sort of suit is whether the plaintiff city is limited to challenging the initial step in the defendant city's annexation—the crucial step in determining whether the other city has prior jurisdiction—or whether the plaintiff city can also challenge the annexation generally, and by invalidating the final product gain the right to complete its own annexation. For example, assume that the plaintiff city believes that the defendant city's involuntary annexation is invalid because the annexation area did not meet the statutory standards of urban development. Such an argument could not be made simply as an attack on the resolution of intent, because compliance with the statutory standard is not required at the time the resolution is adopted.[57] May the plaintiff city nevertheless argue that, although the resolution of intent might have been legally adequate (allowing the defendant city to achieve prior jurisdiction), the completed annexation was invalid, so that the plaintiff's annexation should now be given priority?

Cities have attempted to make that sort of argument in at least two of the North Carolina lawsuits involving prior jurisdiction. In *Conover v. Newton*, both cities had completed their annexation procedures when the suit was brought. One of Newton's answers to Conover's complaint asserted that Conover's annexation was invalid because that city had not correctly followed the involuntary annexation procedures and because the annexation area did not meet the statutory standards for urban development.[58] In response, Conover's motion for summary judgment asserted that as several property owners had removed their names from Newton's voluntary petition, the latter's annexation was invalid.[59] Both cities, that is, presented arguments that went beyond whether prior jurisdiction had attached and addressed the validity of the annexations themselves. Similarly, in *Hazelwood v. Waynesville*, the plaintiff city, which claimed prior jurisdiction because of its resolution of consideration, argued that the voluntary petitions received by Waynesville were invalid because in several instances both spouses had not signed for parcels that were jointly owned.[60] Although in neither case did the

57. See the discussion of this point in section 3.03[b].
58. 297 N.C. 506, 256 S.E.2d 216 (1979) (R. at 19–20).
59. *Id.* (R. at 23–26).
60. 320 N.C. 89, 357 S.E.2d 686 (1987), Plaintiff-Appellant's brief at 5–6.

supreme court specifically address whether plaintiff cities had standing to make these kinds of arguments, its treatment of the arguments is suggestive.

In *Conover*, the reported decision actually involved three separate lawsuits, the other two being actions brought by persons whose property was annexed against one or the other of the annexing cities. As those two actions raised the same arguments about the validity of the annexations as the cities' suits, the court could have dealt substantively with the arguments without deciding whether the cities themselves were entitled to raise the arguments. Nevertheless, both the trial court and the supreme court did allow Conover to raise the issue of whether Newton's annexation was invalid because some signers had withdrawn their signatures before the annexation ordinance was adopted. The trial court granted summary judgment to plaintiffs in *both* actions on this ground, and the supreme court upheld those judgments in both actions.[61] In *Hazelwood*, moreover, the supreme court, after ruling that Hazelwood's resolution of consideration did not give it prior jurisdiction over Waynesville, mentioned Hazelwood's attack on Waynesville's annexation, though it refused to address the issue—but not because Hazelwood lacked standing. Rather, it noted that Hazelwood had not raised this issue in the complaint, nor did it enter objections or exceptions into the trial record; as Hazelwood raised the issue only on appeal, the court refused to decide it. These two decisions suggest the court's willingness to hear any arguments raised by a competing city against the other city's annexation, not just arguments against the initial mandatory step. And that seems a reasonable outcome. If a competing annexation gives a city sufficient interest to challenge the validity of the other city's first mandatory step in that city's own annexation effort, why shouldn't it also be a sufficient interest to allow the competing city to argue that the other city's completed annexation is invalid?

[b] A city that is party to an annexation agreement with the annexing city

Sections 3.11 through 3.17 describe and discuss annexation agreements between cities, which are entered into pursuant to G.S. 160A-58.21

61. 297 N.C. at 520, 256 S.E.2d at 225 ("The grant of summary judgment in favor of plaintiffs in *Allman v. Newton* and the grant of summary judgment in favor of plaintiff in *Conover v. Newton* declaring the entire Newton annexation ordinance to be void are affirmed.").

through 160A-58.28. Under such an agreement, the cities delineate one or more areas into which one or more of them *may not* annex. Once an agreement becomes effective, G.S. 160A-58.25 prohibits a city from adopting an annexation ordinance that violates the agreement. If one of the cities adopts an ordinance that another participating city believes violates the agreement, G.S. 160A-58.27 permits the second city to file a petition in superior court within thirty days after adoption of the annexation ordinance, seeking review of the ordinance. Thus, this statute specifically creates a remedy against a limited class of annexations, thereby fitting into the framework of the *Gaskill–Taylor* rule. If a city files a petition pursuant to G.S. 160A-58.25, the issue before the court is whether the annexation ordinance and the annexing city's annexation proceeding violate either the annexation agreement statute or a particular annexation agreement.

[c] A city whose territory is apparently being annexed by another city

In *Town of Spencer v. Town of East Spencer*,[62] Spencer brought suit because both cities were seeking to annex some of the same land, and the supreme court recognized that Spencer's own annexation attempt was a sufficient interest to justify its action. Even if Spencer had not had annexation plans, however, and East Spencer had proceeded with the annexation, continuing to include in its annexation area a small amount of land already within Spencer, Spencer surely would have had standing to challenge the completed annexation on that account. By including part of another city within an annexation area, a city violates one of the standards of the annexation law; therefore its annexation is void within the meaning of that term, as explained above. Moreover, a city whose territory is purportedly being annexed by another city certainly has the requisite special interest that justifies its standing to challenge the annexation on that account. Again, such a right to sue fits easily within the *Gaskill–Taylor* framework.

[d] Other interests

Other interests that might be put forward by a neighboring city to challenge an annexation do not carry the weight of those set out above. In its brief to the court of appeals in *Seven Devils*, the town of Seven

62. 351 N.C. 124, 522 S.E.2d 297 (1999).

Devils suggested a number of interests that, it argued, justified its standing to challenge the annexation by Sugar Mountain. They included the effect on its extraterritorial land-use jurisdiction, which would be reduced by the annexation; the loss of its own future ability to annex property within the annexation area; the possibility that Sugar Mountain might open an ABC store within the annexation area in competition with Seven Devils' store; and the possibility that Sugar Mountain's regulations in the annexation might be inconsistent with regulations in Seven Devils territory just across the street.[63] (It might also have added the possible diminution of its share of various state-distributed revenues, because of the additional territory added to another town in the same county.[64]) The court of appeals was unpersuaded by any of these suggested interests, and it refused standing to Seven Devils. Similarly, in *Ayden,* the plaintiff city argued that Winterville's annexation caused a possible loss in Ayden's extraterritorial land-use jurisdiction; but here, too, the court of appeals found this interest insufficient to confer standing. The same outcome seems likely for other, comparable interests that might be suggested by cities seeking to block an annexation by a neighboring city. Such an outcome is in accord with the majority of similar decisions in other states.[65]

One further, special interest to consider is that of a city that believes itself to be closer to a satellite annexation area than the city attempting to annex that area. In *Seven Devils*, the plaintiff city argued that the annexation under attack was a disguised satellite annexation and was therefore illegal, because it was closer to the plaintiff city than to the defendant city.[66] The city's argument for standing to make the attack was based on the idea that the provision in the satellite annexation statute prohibiting annexation of a satellite area closer to another city than to the annexing city was intended to protect the other city.

If that were true, it might well be adequate grounds to confer standing, but is the statement in fact true? G.S. 160A-58.1 sets out

63. 125 N.C. App. 692, 482 S.E.2d 39 (1997), Plaintiff-Appellant's brief at 5–6.

64. For example, the addition of territory to one city will usually marginally affect the amount of local government sales and use tax received by the county and each other city in that county.

65. Fort Collins–Loveland Water Dist. v. City of Fort Collins, 482 P.2d 986 (1971) (nearby city without standing to challenge annexation); People *ex rel.* Brooks v. Village of Lisle, 321 N.E.2d 65 (Ill. Ct. App. 1974) (city claiming loss of extraterritorial land-use regulatory authority without standing to challenge annexation); Sanitary and Improvement Dist. No. 57 of Douglas County v. City of Elkhorn, 536 N.W.2d 56 (Neb. 1995) (special district without standing to challenge annexation).

66. 125 N.C. App. 692 at 694, 482 S.E.2d 39 at 40.

several standards that must be met before a satellite area may be annexed: it must be within three miles of the annexing city, it may not be closer to any other city than the annexing city, the annexing city must be able to provide city services to the area, if the proposed area is a subdivision all the subdivision must be annexed, and the annexation may not cause the total area of satellite areas to exceed 10 percent of the area of the main body of the city. When seen in this context, it becomes plain that the standard concerning relative closeness to another city is not intended as special protection to neighboring cities but rather is one of a number of policy-based standards. An alleged violation of that single standard ought not to confer standing on a neighboring city any more than an alleged violation of the standard limiting the total area of satellite areas confers standing on residents of the main body of the annexing city.

Section 7.06. Standing: Other Possible Plaintiffs

It is possible that the above discussion exhausts the list of possible plaintiffs who have standing to challenge an annexation. There are no North Carolina cases that grant standing to other persons or entities, but there are several that deny standing to other persons or entities. We must recognize, however, the power of facts to drive doctrine. If a court were presented with a blatantly void annexation[67] and no likely plaintiff identified in the above discussion appeared to challenge it, the court might be strongly inclined to stretch doctrine in order to allow for some kind of judicial review of the annexation.

67. Two sorts of examples come to mind. First, the voluntary contiguous annexation statute defines contiguity to include the situation where the city is separated from the annexation area by a creek or river. Although this clearly intends that the annexation area be *across* the river, cities have very occasionally annexed areas some distance *along* a river, claiming the annexation as contiguous. Second, the voluntary satellite annexation statute includes a number of conditions that any annexation area must meet, including that it be no more than three miles from the annexing city. Suppose a city purported to annex an area four or five miles away? *See* State *ex rel.* Earhart v. City of Bristol, 970 S.W.2d 948 (Tenn. 1998), in which the court seemed to relax standing rules when faced with a purported annexation of street rights-of-way only.

[a] Residents of the annexing city

The court of appeals has held that residents of the annexing city do not have the requisite interest to bring an action challenging an annexation,[68] an outcome mirrored by decisions in other states.[69]

[b] Non-city residents living near the annexation area

The supreme court and court of appeals have held that persons owning property near an annexation area (but outside the annexing city) do not have the requisite interest to bring an action challenging an annexation,[70] an outcome mirrored by decisions in other states.[71]

[c] The county

A county within which an annexation occurs has a number of potential interests that are affected by the annexation. The county may lose land-use authority over the annexation area and will lose authority to exercise its police power. Its revenues from shared taxes will probably be adversely affected, although in most instances the effect will be quite small. Depending on agreements it might have with the annexing city, its utility systems might lose customers and, therefore, revenues. All these effects are comparable to those suffered by a city situated near an annexation area, effects that have not been held sufficient to give such a

68. Joyner v. Town of Weaverville, 94 N.C. App. 588, 380 S.E.2d 536 (1989).

69. *E.g.*, Fort Collins–Loveland Water Dist. v. City of Fort Collins, 42 P.2d 96 (Colo. 1971); White v. City of Columbia, 461 S.W.2d 806 (Mo. 1970). ***But see*** King v. Corbin, 535 S.W.2d 85 (Ky. 1976) (residents of annexing city have standing to challenge annexation, but only if "personally, substantially and adversely affected by the annexation" by special damage different from damage suffered by public generally; merely being resident insufficient).

70. Taylor v. City of Raleigh, 290 N.C. 608, 227 S.E.2d 576 (1976) (satellite annexation); Davis v. City of Archdale, 81 N.C. App. 505, 344 S.E.2d 369 (1986) (voluntary contiguous annexation).

71. *E.g.*, Marshall County Concerned Citizens v. City of Guntersville, 598 So.2d 1331 (Ala. 1992); City of Tallahassee v. Kovach, 733 So.2d 576 (Fla. Ct. App. 1999); Sanitary and Improvement Dist. No. 57 of Douglas County v. City of Elkhorn, 536 N.W.2d 56 (Neb. 1995); Quinn v. City of Columbia, 401 S.E.2d 165 (S.C. 1991). ***Contra***, Martee v. City of Kennett, 784 S.W.2d 621 (Mo. Ct. App. 1990) (person whose property is substantially enveloped by voluntary annexation has standing to challenge the annexation because such property would become more susceptible to involuntary annexation).

city standing.[72] They are probably also insufficient to give standing to the county.[73]

[d] Existing service providers

A public or private entity currently providing services in the annexation area may well be adversely affected by the annexation, but the courts have not, by and large, seen that effect as sufficient to give such an entity standing.[74]

72. Town of Seven Devils v. Village of Sugar Mountain, 125 N.C. App. 692, 482 S.E.2d 39 (1997).

73. St. Louis County v. Village of Peerless Park, 726 S.W.2d 405 (Mo. Ct. App. 1987) (Loss of revenues not sufficient to give county standing.). *But see* Yandle v. Mecklenburg County, 85 N.C. App. 382, 355 S.E.2d 216 (1987), in which the court held a challenge to a voluntary annexation by a county that had brought an eminent domain action to acquire the property for which annexation was being sought. This case is discussed in the text above in section 7.04[b].

74. *E.g.*, O'Donell Fire Service and Equipment Co. v. City of Billings, 711 P.2d 822 (Mont. 1985) (company providing fire protection in annexation area without standing to challenge annexation). *Contra*, St. Andrews Public Service Dist. v. City Council of City of Charleston, 529 S.E.2d 64 (S.C. Ct. App. 2000) (displaced public service district may challenge annexation alleged to be void).

8

The Effect of Annexation on Existing Services, Service Providers, and Regulations

8

The Effect of Annexation on Existing Services, Service Providers, and Regulations

Section 8.01. Introduction

This chapter and the four that follow address the effects of annexation on county regulations and the public services provided by both government and private entities. This chapter addresses the subject in a general way, while the four succeeding chapters discuss annexation's effect on four specific types of services for which there are special legislative regimes: fire protection, solid waste collection, electric and natural gas services, and water or sewer services financed by outstanding federal debt.

Section 8.02. The Effect on County Ordinances

[a] In general

In North Carolina, unless a city has consented to a broader application of a particular ordinance, county ordinances apply only outside city boundaries.[1] As a result, unless modified by statute, the effective date of an annexation marks the end of county regulatory authority and of the application of county ordinances in the annexation area. This basic rule is illustrated by *Taylor v. Bowen*.[2] In 1957 the General Assembly adopted a local act permitting Cumberland County to zone a specified area of its unincorporated territory. The plaintiff owned property in the

1. N.C. GEN. STAT. § 153A-122 (hereinafter G.S.). However, under G.S. 130A-39(c), rules adopted by a county board of health apply throughout the county and are therefore unaffected by annexation.

2. 272 N.C. 726, 158 S.E.2d 837(1968).

area, and the county zoned the property residential. In 1961 the city of Fayetteville annexed the plaintiffs' property and continued the residential zoning. In 1966 the county purported to rezone the property as commercial and the plaintiff then sought a permit from the city to build a commercial building. The city refused the permit, and the plaintiff brought an action for mandamus. The supreme court held that the county's authority over the property had terminated upon annexation and that, therefore, its 1966 attempt at rezoning was without effect.[3]

Not only does county regulatory authority end upon annexation, but persons, property owners, and businesses in the annexation area retain no automatic, constitutionally protected vested rights in existing county regulations. This point was made graphically in *Stillings v. City of Winston-Salem*,[4] which involves the county's authority to grant and maintain franchises. Forsyth County had granted the plaintiffs in this action a solid waste collection franchise for an unincorporated area that was soon thereafter annexed by the city of Winston-Salem. When the annexation became effective, the city began tax-supported solid waste collection in the annexation area, in direct competition with the plaintiff's fee-supported service. The plaintiffs brought suit, arguing that the city's actions had taken their property rights in the franchise. The North Carolina supreme court rejected their arguments, holding that as the county's franchising power terminated upon annexation the plaintiffs had no continuing property rights to lose.[5]

Similarly, if a newly applicable city ordinance prohibits existing conduct or property uses within the annexation area, no constitutional rule grandfathers the existing conduct or property use. A federal court of appeals decision illustrates this point. In *Davidson v. City of Clinton, Miss.*,[6] the plaintiff owned a night club at which he sold beer; the club was located about 475 feet from a local school. When the property was annexed, it became subject to a city ordinance prohibiting the sale of beer within 3,000 feet of a school, and the plaintiff was

3. *Accord*, Rosehill Cemetery Co. v. City of Chicago, 185 N.E.170 (Ill. 1933) (when Chicago annexed a smaller city, the ordinances of the smaller city lost all effect).

4. 311 N.C. 689, 319 S.E.2d 233 (1984).

5. *Accord*, Schneider v. Lazarov, 390 S.W.2d 197 (Tenn. 1965) (property owner had no vested rights in building permit issued under county zoning ordinance, and therefore annexation terminated his rights under the permit). The rule articulated in *Stillings* has been modified somewhat by statute, as described in Chapter 10.

Although a property owner does not have a vested right in county regulations, he or she may have such rights in a particular development project under the common law and in certain statutory systems, as discussed below in section 8.02[b].

6. 826 F.2d 1430 (5th Cir. 1987).

ordered to stop selling beer. He brought suit in federal court, but the U.S. Court of Appeals upheld the city order. It held that there was no constitutional right to continue a nonconforming use and that the plaintiff's beer license created no vested rights under state law.[7]

[b] The effect on county land-use regulations

The basic rule described above has been modified somewhat by statute with respect to the sorts of regulations that cities adopt pursuant to G.S. Chapter 160A, Article 19: zoning, subdivision control, housing code enforcement, and other development matters. These statutory modifications provide for a transitional period between the effective date of annexation and the termination of county authority; they also establish a system that sometimes vests development rights a property owner holds under the county ordinances. (As noted in footnote 5, a property owner can also obtain vested development rights pursuant to the common law.)

The transition to city regulation. If the county has been regulating land use and development in an annexation area, G.S. 160A-360(f) provides that its regulations and powers of enforcement—pursuant to G.S. Chapter 160A, Article 19 and G.S. Chapter 153A, Article 18[8] — remain in effect until the city extends its own ordinances and regulations to the area or until sixty days after the effective date of the annexation, whichever occurs first.

If the city does not adopt its own ordinances and regulations by the end of the sixty-day period, the area will be unregulated until it does so. In the case of most regulations, this deadline creates no problems. The city's subdivision and minimum housing ordinances apply throughout the city's jurisdiction, and no special action is necessary to extend them to an annexation area. Zoning is a different matter, however. The city will have to decide how properties within the annexation area will be zoned under the city's zoning ordinance. Because the basic procedures many cities use to adopt and amend zoning ordinances take more than sixty days to complete, a city may have to take special steps to ensure

7. *Accord*, Louder v. Texas Liquor Control Board, 214 S.W.2d 336 (Tex. Ct. Civ. App. 1948) (upholding application of ordinance limiting areas in which liquor could be sold after property including package store is annexed by city, thereby prohibiting continued operation of package store).

8. These two sets of statutes contain a county's statutory authority to adopt zoning ordinances, including the zoning of historic properties and districts; adopt subdivision regulations; enforce the state building code; and adopt a minimum housing code.

that some kind of zoning remains in place after the sixty-day period. There are two possible methods a city might use to do so. First, it can simply adopt the county's existing zoning for the area, thereby giving itself breathing room to devise a zoning map for the annexation area. If a city decides to take this route, it must still follow the basic procedures for amending a zoning ordinance—review by the planning board, public notice, and a public hearing. Alternatively, a city might initiate the procedures leading to zoning the area before the annexation becomes effective—indeed, even before the annexation ordinance has been adopted. G.S. 160A-360(f) specifically permits a city to hold public hearings and take other necessary procedural steps during the sixty-day period, but this explicit statement probably does not bar it from beginning even earlier.[9] As long as there is proper public notice and property owners in the annexation area have a full opportunity to participate in the process, there seems to be no strong policy prohibiting a city from starting the process before the annexation ordinance is adopted. Although there is no North Carolina case law on this issue, such an early start has been upheld elsewhere.[10] If a city follows this route, it may wish to wait until after the effective date of the annexation ordinance to adopt the new zoning; and it certainly may not make the new zoning effective until after that date.

Extraterritorial jurisdiction. If a city has an existing extraterritorial jurisdictional area (ETJ) for land-use regulations, as permitted by G.S. 160A-360, it may already be exercising authority over land use and development in the annexation area. In such a case, it need not take any special steps with respect to those regulations; they stay in effect after annexation.

The annexation may, however, give the city an opportunity to expand its ETJ. G.S. 160A-360(e) provides that if the county is exercising zoning power, subdivision regulation, and building-code enforcement in an area, a city may not expand its ETJ into that area without the county commissioners' approval. If the county is not exercising all three powers within the area, however, a city is entitled to an ETJ of up to one mile from its current boundaries (and further, with county approval, for

9. Some annexed areas have no zoning at all. In order to have zoning in place on the effective date of annexation, a city must be able to begin the process before that date. This very practical reality also argues in favor of starting early when the goal is to replace existing county zoning.

10. Schanz v. City of Billings, 597 P.2d 67 (Mont. 1979) (city planning commission may hold public hearings on zoning of annexation area before adoption of annexation ordinance).

larger cities). Expansion of the city's ETJ is not automatic. The city council must adopt an ordinance expanding the ETJ, following all the procedures applicable to Article 19 ordinances; a map or written description of the expanded ETJ must be maintained in the city clerk's office and recorded in the office of the register of deeds.

Vested development rights.[11] There are three methods by which a property owner may obtain vested rights to undertake or complete a development project pursuant to county regulation. Vesting entitles the property owner to exercise those development rights after the property has been annexed by a city.[12] First, if a property owner has made substantial expenditures in good faith reliance on a specific approval of a project, the common law accords that owner a vested right to continue and complete the project, even if the zoning regulating the property has changed.[13] Second, if a property owner has obtained a building permit for a project pursuant to the State Building Code, his or her right to use the permit may not be invalidated by changing the zoning regulations applicable to the property until after the permit has been used or has expired. (A permit expires after six months if not used.) Third, G.S. 153A-344.1 creates a statutory vested right when a county has given approval to a site-specific development plan or a phased development plan; depending on the county's ordinance, such a vested right is good for at least two years and may be good for as long as five years.[14]

11. Chapter 5 of David W. Owens, *Legislative Zoning Decisions: Legal Aspects,* 2d ed. (Chapel Hill, N.C.: Institute of Government, 1999) is a full discussion of how a property owner gains vested rights in a development project.

12. G.S. 160A-360(i) specifically entitles any person who has gained vested rights to utilize those rights even if the government with regulatory jurisdiction over the property is changed.

13. Godfrey v. Zoning Board of Adjustment, 317 N.C. 51, 344 S.E.2d 272 (1986).

14. G.S. 160A-385.1 provides an identical system for vested rights pursuant to city government approvals. G.S. 160A-31(h), for voluntary contiguous annexations, and 160A-58.1(d), for voluntary satellite annexations, permit a city to adopt an ordinance requiring persons petitioning for voluntary annexation to sign a statement declaring whether there are vested rights applicable to their property under either G.S. 153A-344.1 or 160A-385.1; if none is claimed, any existing in fact are thereby terminated. This statement is discussed further in Volume 2 of this series.

Section 8.03. The Effect on Existing Government Services

The discussion in this part assumes that the annexing city plans to provide one or more services currently being provided to the annexation area by another local government. If the annexing city does not provide such a service, presumably the existing service provider will continue to do so.

[a] Water and sewer services

If the county owns and operates water distribution or sewage collection lines in an annexation area, it may have a standing agreement with the city governing the effect of annexation on those lines. For example, an agreement might provide that upon annexation the city automatically assumes ownership and operation of the lines. If there is an agreement, its provisions govern the effect of annexation of the affected utility systems. (A city might also have a similar agreement with another kind of local government entity that operates utility lines—perhaps a sanitary district or a water and sewer authority. But as a practical matter, utility agreements between cities and these other kinds of entities are much less common than those between counties and cities.)

In the absence of any agreement or special legislative treatment of the matter, utility lines in an annexation area belonging to some other government remain that government's property after annexation.[15] In addition, and, again in the absence of an agreement or specific legislation, a city may install new water or sewer lines in the area that run parallel to existing lines, thus competing with the existing service provider.[16] For the reasons discussed below in section 8.04[a], competition of this sort does not give rise to an obligation to compensate the existing service provider for lost business.

County water and sewer district lines. One statute mandates a somewhat different treatment when the existing lines are owned by a

15. State *ex rel.* East Lenoir Sanitary Dist. v. City of Lenoir, 249 N.C. 96, 105 S.E.2d 411 (1958) (annexation of area including sanitary district lines does not transfer ownership of such lines to annexing city).

16. If the existing governmental lines were financed by a loan from the U.S. Department of Agriculture Rural Development (formerly, Farmers' Home Administration), federal law may prohibit an annexing city from running parallel lines or otherwise interfering with the operations of the existing government. This possibility is discussed in detail in Chapter 12.

county water and sewer district. G.S. 162A-93 establishes the following rules, which apply when a city annexes territory within a county water or sewer district.

1. Unless the district's governing board (that is, the board of county commissioners) consents, the city may not install or operate utility lines that duplicate those of the district nor require property owners in the annexed area to connect to city-owned lines. In these circumstances, the district's system satisfies the city's legal responsibility for providing that utility service.
2. If the district's system does not, however, operate with sufficient pressure to provide adequate fire flow, the first principle does not apply. The city may install parallel water lines, and apparently may require property owners to connect to the lines.[17] Before authorizing these steps, the city council must hold a public hearing on whether the district's lines do in fact provide adequate fire flow, after mailing notice of the hearing to each affected customer and publishing it in a newspaper with general circulation in the affected area. These notices must be mailed and published at least ten days before the hearing. After the hearing, the city council must make a formal finding that the district lines do not provide adequate fire flow to support city fire protection in the affected area.
3. If the district's system does provide adequate fire flow, the statute entitles the city to install and use fire hydrants on the district's water lines under arrangements with the district and at the city's cost. The arrangements with the district concern such matters as timing, cost, and the like; the statute does not permit the district to refuse to allow installation of the hydrants.
4. If the city annexes parts of the district where the district does not operate water or sewer lines, the city remains responsible for providing the service in those areas and may install the necessary lines.

17. The prohibition on mandating connection appears in G.S. 162A-93(a), and the exception for providing adequate fire flow expressly exempts a city from all the provisions of that subsection.

[b] Street maintenance

If the state is maintaining residential streets in the annexation area, the General Statutes contemplate that these streets will be transferred to city control by agreement with the state Department of Transportation.[18] Often a member of the city's staff, such as the engineer or planner, and the department's district engineer meet to determine which streets in the annexation area will be transferred to city responsibility and which will continue to be maintained by the state. Once this has been decided, the city council adopts a resolution listing the streets the city will maintain and stating its intention to assume that responsibility on the effective date of the annexation. Such a resolution should give the street's state number, any locally adopted name, and the length of the particular portion for which the city is assuming responsibility. Once adopted, the resolution is sent to the Department of Transportation and placed on the agenda of the Board of Transportation. When that board has concurred in the city's resolution, the street transfer is complete.

Sometimes one or more state-maintained streets in the annexation area will not meet current city standards. They may be unpaved, too narrow, underconstructed, or the like. If a developer offered to dedicate them to the city, the city would probably reject them. Does the city nevertheless have an obligation to assume maintenance responsibility for these streets? That may depend on circumstances that differ from city to city.

To begin with, the statutory system for street responsibility inside cities differentiates between state and city responsibilities in a way that supports a city's power to refuse to accept responsibility for a particular street.[19] The statute makes the state responsible for those major streets and highways inside cities that are necessary to move traffic through cities and to major destinations within them. It also makes each city responsible for streets and highways accepted by the city that are not part of the state highway system. The statute's use of the word *accepted* implies that the city has some choice about whether to accept an existing state-maintained street; rejecting a street because it does not meet established city standards is a reasonable exercise of that power of choice. In practice, cities do refuse to assume responsibility for streets for this reason, and the state acknowledges its continuing responsibility to maintain those streets.

18. G.S. 136-66.2.
19. G.S. 136-66.1.

Thus, as a matter of the law that specifically addresses responsibility for streets, a city is probably within its rights to refuse to accept responsibility for particular streets. Such a step may, however, be inconsistent with the city's responsibilities under the annexation statutes. The voluntary annexation statutes generally provide that property and persons annexed by a city are entitled to the same privileges and benefits as those in other parts of the city,[20] while the involuntary statutes specifically require that street maintenance be extended to the annexation area on substantially the same basis as it is provided to the rest of the city.[21] In *In re Annexation Ordinance (Jacksonville)*,[22] the city's annexation report stated that the city's policy was that new development had to meet the city's standards for paving and curbs and gutters and that the city would not accept streets that did not meet those standards. As a result, the report continued, the city would not accept responsibility for a few unpaved streets in the annexation area. Despite this existing street policy, the city did in fact maintain several unpaved streets that were already within its boundaries. Based on this fact, the supreme court held that the city did not meet its statutory responsibilities for street maintenance under the involuntary annexation statute. At the very least, it appears that the annexation statutes require the city to accept maintenance responsibility for any publicly maintained street in the annexation area that is comparable to streets the city currently maintains.

Furthermore, leaving residential streets in a city under state maintenance places them in a disadvantaged position. Because they are within a city, such streets are by definition not part of the state's secondary road system.[23] Therefore they cannot be paved with secondary roads moneys, which might affect how well the state maintains them. Even if a city is not maintaining streets that don't meet its current construction standards, it thus might have a problem under the annexation statutes. The reality of state maintenance (or lack thereof) could lead a court to hold that by refusing to accept maintenance responsibility for these streets because they don't meet city standards the city is violating the annexation laws' directive that annexed property and persons receive the same level of services as property and persons elsewhere in the city. For that reason, a city should be cautious in refusing to assume responsibility for streets

20. G.S. 160A-31(e), 160A-58.3.

21. G.S. 160A-35(3)a., 160A-47(3)a.

22. 255 N.C. 633, 122 S.E.2d 690 (1961).

23. 19A N.C.A.C. 2C.0101 defines the secondary road system as including only roads outside of municipal boundaries.

and roads that are currently maintained by the state. (Streets in the annexation area that are not part of the state highway system—that is, that are privately maintained—are discussed below in section 8.04.)

[c] Other services

Law enforcement. The sheriff's department normally provides law enforcement to areas outside of cities. Although the sheriff's department enjoys legal authority to enforce the law throughout the county, it usually ceases doing so within an annexation area after the effective date—if the city has its own police department.

Fire protection. Chapter 9 discusses the effect of annexation on services provided to the annexation area by a rural fire department that is supported by county fire district taxes, while Chapter 14 explains the effect of annexation on fire district taxes.

Solid waste collection. Under G.S. 153A-292(a), a county's authority to collect solid waste is limited to areas outside of cities. Therefore, if a city annexes an area in which the county itself provides such services, the county loses its authority to continue providing them. (The specific statutory system that protects private collectors of solid waste in an annexation area is described in chapter 10.)

Section 8.04. The Effect on Private Service Providers

[a] In general

The basic rule is that, in the absence of special statutory protection, private service providers have no vested right to continue providing services in an area that has been annexed by a city.[24] Nor has such a provider any constitutional protection against a city that provides a competing service, even to the extent of installing utility lines that parallel those of the private provider. These statements hold true even though the city pays no taxes on its revenues from its service and may support its service from taxes, both of which permit it to significantly underprice the private provider. The Iowa case of *Water Development Co. v. Board of Water Works*[25] illustrates these points. A privately owned water utility provided service in areas outside of Des Moines. In

24. Stillings v. City of Winston-Salem, 311 N.C. 689, 319 S.E.2d 233 (1984).
25. 488 N.W.2d 158 (Iowa 1992).

1988 the city annexed a part of the utility's service area where the utility had forty-five customers. As the city was not interested in purchasing the utility lines—largely because it thought them inadequate—it installed its own lines parallel to the utility's. When all forty-five of its customers switched to the city water system, the utility brought suit for inverse condemnation and intentional interference with a contract. The Iowa supreme court rejected the utility's suit. There was no inverse condemnation, it said, because there was no taking; the city was simply competing with the utility. And there was no tortious interference with the utility's contracts with its customers because there was nothing improper in the city's actions.[26]

This basic rule might not hold true if the city uses its police power to force customers to select its service over that of a competing private provider. For example, a city that extends its water or sewer system into an annexation area already served by a private provider might have an ordinance requiring all abutting properties to connect to the city system.[27] If the city enforces the ordinance in the annexation area, a court might find that it has taken the property of its private competitor. Similarly, a city that enforces an ordinance requiring use of its solid waste collection service might be found to have taken the business of a private collector.[28] In both cases, the city has moved beyond mere competition and *required* people to use its system rather than its competitor's. When state courts in other states have been faced with these kinds of situations, they have found that enforcement of such a connection or use requirement constitutes a taking.[29]

26. *See* Carolina Water Service, Inc. v. Town of Atlantic Beach, 121 N.C. App. 23, 464 S.E.2d 349 (1995), in which the town, after an annexation, built water lines that paralleled those of the plaintiff utility. The court of appeals held that the plaintiff's complaint did not support an action for tortious interference with contract or for unfair competition.

Other cases holding that duplicating a service is not a taking include Knoxville Water Co. v. Knoxville, 200 U.S. 222 (1906) (water); Avery v. Marengo County Comm'n, 646 So.2d 1347 (Ala. 1994) (water); City of Tucson v. Polar Water Co., 259 P.2d 561 (Ariz. 1953) (water); Laidlaw Waste Systems, Inc. v. City of Phoenix, 815 P.2d 932 (Ariz. Ct. App. 1991) (solid waste collection); Amos Plumbing & Elec. Co. v. Barnett, 411 S.E.2d 490 (Ga. 1992) (water); Citizens Utilities Co. v. Metropolitan Sanitary Dist., 322 N.E.2d 857 (Ill. Ct. App. 1974) (sewage treatment); Bagford v. Ephraim City, 914 P.2d 1095 (Utah 1995).

27. Such an ordinance is authorized by G.S. 160A-317(a).

28. Such an ordinance is authorized by G.S. 160A-317(b)(4).

29. Clare v. Florissant Water and Sanitation Dist., 879 P.2d 471 (Colo. Ct. App. 1994) (ordinance requiring connection to district water system is taking of plaintiff's

Finally, a city that annexes an area served by a private service provider has no legal obligation to take over private facilities or lines and to compensate the owner or operator. For example, if there are privately maintained streets within the annexation area, annexation does not itself cause those streets to become public responsibilities. The city can leave private facilities or lines in place and rely upon the private entity to continue providing the service or maintaining the facility; or it can provide a competing service; or it can enter into negotiations with the private owner or operator to cooperate with or acquire the private lines or facilities.[30]

[b] Special situations

State and federal laws provide special protections for four, or perhaps five, kinds of private service providers: rural fire departments, private solid waste collectors, investor-owned electric utilities and electric membership corporations, investor-owned natural gas utilities, and water and sewer systems that have outstanding debt owed to U.S. Department of Agriculture Rural Development. The next four chapters describe these special protections.

---

private system); Coeur d'Alene Garbage Service v. City of Coeur d'Alene, 759 P.2d 829 (Idaho 1988) (ordinance requiring use of city's designated garbage service is taking of plaintiff's competing service). In Carolina Water Service, Inc. v. Town of Atlantic Beach, 121 N.C. App. 23, 464 S.E.2d 349 (1995), where the court held that duplicating water lines did not constitute tortious interference with a private utility's contracts with its customers, the court emphasized that the city did not have a mandatory connection ordinance. The implication is that such an ordinance might have changed the outcome of the case.

30. The North Carolina supreme court decided a number of cases from 1933 through 1960 that raised the issue of whether a city that provided water or sewer services through privately owned utility lines had to compensate the owner of those lines when the city annexed the lines. (Today a city is likely to require the dedication of the lines to the city before it provides water or sewer service through the lines, and the issues raised by these cases is therefore unlikely to recur.) Basically, the rule that emerges from these cases is that if the city had been providing water or sewer service through the lines and maintaining the lines before annexation, and continued to do so after annexation, there was no taking and no duty of compensation. Farr v. City of Asheville, 205 N.C. 82, 170 S.E. 82 (1933). The city's position was even stronger if it had a written policy or ordinance specifying that such lines became city property upon annexation. Spaugh v. City of Winston-Salem, 234 N.C. 708, 68 S.E.2d 838 (1952); Honey Properties, Inc. v. City of Gastonia, 252 N.C. 567, 114 S.E.2d 344 (1960). If the city did not, however, exercise control over the lines before annexation but began doing so only afterwards, it would be required to compensate the lines' owner. Jackson v. City of Gastonia, 246 N.C. 404, 98 S.E.2d 444 (1957). *See also* Styers v. City of Gastonia, 252 N.C. 572, 114 S.E.2d 348 (1960).

9

Protections for Rural Fire Departments

9

Protections for Rural Fire Departments

Section 9.01. Introduction and Summary

Rural fire departments have often opposed city annexation. Sometimes their opposition reflects the fact that the residential property of some of their members is being annexed, and these members oppose the annexation. Often, though, departments have opposed annexation because of its effect on the department's service area and its resource base. When a city annexes an area that is currently being served by a rural fire department, the annexation area ceases being part of the department's territory and becomes part of the city's. If the department is supported by a county tax district, the annexation takes territory from the district, thereby reducing the tax base that supports the rural department. Frequently the department is not realistically able to reduce its costs, and higher rates of property tax become necessary to maintain the same level of service.

In 1983 (and, further, in 1989), the General Assembly acknowledged these concerns of rural fire departments and enacted a set of statutes that offer them and their employees some transitional protections when a city annexes territory they serve. The protections take three forms. First, in involuntary annexations, the annexing city must offer to contract with the rural department to continue to provide fire protection within the annexation area for up to five years. Second, also in involuntary annexations, the annexing city must offer employment to any full-time employee of a rural department who has lost employment because of the annexation. Third, in both voluntary and involuntary annexations, the city must assume responsibility for payment of a proportionate share of the rural department's indebtedness. (Note that not all of these protections extend to all statutory annexations and that none of them extend to legislative annexations.) This chapter details the requirements of each of these statutory protections.

The statutes extend their protections to *rural fire departments*, as defined in G.S. 160A-1. Such a department is any nonmunicipal fire department with an Insurance Services Office (I.S.O.) rating of at least 9 that owns at least $5,000 in apparatus and equipment. In almost all cases, a rural fire department is a private, nonprofit, incorporated fire department staffed wholly or largely by volunteers.

Section 9.02. Service Contracts with Rural Fire Departments

[a] General summary

The service contract requirement is set out in G.S. 160A-37.1 and 160A-49.1, identical statutes applicable to involuntary annexations by, respectively, cities under 5,000 population and cities of 5,000 or larger. (The requirement does not apply to voluntary annexations, nor to legislative annexations unless the legislation so specifies.) In summary, the statutes require that if an area described in a resolution of intent to annex includes part of a fire tax district or a fire insurance district, and that district is served by a rural fire department, the city must make a good faith offer to negotiate with that department a five-year contract to continue providing fire service to the annexation area.[1] To qualify as a good faith offer, the city's offer must compensate the department for the loss of tax base attributable to the annexation, unless the city offers a contract for first-responder service only. (*First responder service* is defined below, in notes 4–6 and accompanying text.) If the offer is for first responder service, the city must offer to compensate the department for only half the loss of its tax base. If a rural fire department believes that an annexing city has not made a good faith offer as required by the statute, it may appeal to the Local Government Commission, which may delay the annexation's effective date until such an offer

1. Subsection (f) of each statute provides that the section does not require a city or a rural fire department to enter into a service contract. This provision does not mean, however, that a city complies with the statute by making a good faith offer but then not entering into the contract if the department accepts the offer. If the city refuses to meet its own offer, as defined in the statutes, that offer cannot be defined as good faith. What the statutory provision means, first, is that the rural department has no duty to agree to the city's offer, even if it does meet the statutory definition of a good faith offer; and, second, that the city has no duty to enter into a contract if the department refuses to accept the city's offer and makes a counteroffer, assuming that the city's original offer meets the statutory definition.

is made. Under G.S. 160A-35 and 160A-47, a contract with a rural fire department meets the city's responsibility to provide fire protection in the annexation area on substantially the same basis as it does elsewhere within the city.

Many smaller annexing cities do not have their own fire departments and are in fact already served by the rural fire department that serves the annexation area. Even then, the rural department is entitled to a good faith offer to continue service in the annexation area for five years, although reaching agreement with the department ought not to be difficult.

The next several subsections detail the various elements of this statutory requirement and the procedures that a rural fire department must follow to assert its rights.

[b] County tax and insurance districts

To qualify for the protections of G.S. 160A-37.1 and 160A-49.1, the rural fire department must be providing fire protection to a county tax district or county insurance district on the date the city adopts its resolution of intent to annex. There are two types of county *fire tax districts*: the first is a county *rural fire protection district*, established pursuant to G.S. 69-25.1 through 69-25.17; the second is a county *fire service district*, established pursuant to G.S. 153A-300 through 153A-310. The essential difference between the two types of tax districts is that the rural fire protection district requires voter approval to be established, while the county fire service district does not. Both types of district are supported through an annual property tax levied by the board of county commissioners. Most often, the commissioners then contract with a rural fire department to provide fire protection within the district.[2]

An *insurance district* is an area served by a rural fire department but not supported by a specific district tax. The department might not receive any government support at all; or it may receive support from the county's general fund, which draws on countywide resources; or it may be part of a fire tax district that includes the entire unincorporated area of the county and therefore supports several rural departments.

2. The commissioners could also provide fire protection through an arrangement with a municipal department or by a county department, although the latter is quite uncommon.

G.S. 153A-233 permits the board of county commissioners to "designate fire districts or parts of existing districts and prescribe the boundaries thereof for insurance grading purposes."

If an annexation area is not part of either a tax district or an insurance district, the service contract requirement does not apply, although any area near a city is likely to be organized as one sort of district or the other.

[c] Good faith offer

The statutes contemplate two sorts of good faith offers by the annexing city (although, as noted below, practice has diverged somewhat from the statutory system). The first kind offers the rural fire department either primary or significant responsibility for fire protection in the annexation area. The second offers a contract for only first responder service to the annexation area. Although it is legally possible for the parties to negotiate something quite different from these statutorily defined good faith offers, in practice city contracts with rural fire departments almost always follow the statutory patterns.

Good faith offer—generally. The statutory requirement of a good faith offer from a city to a rural fire department is intended to compensate the rural department for five years of revenue losses arising from the annexation. In G.S. 160A-37.1(d) and 160A-47.1(d), the statute defines one form of good faith offer as any offer "which would compensate the rural fire department for revenue loss directly attributable to the annexation by paying such amount annually for five years." That is, if the city and rural department can agree on a dollar amount of the department's revenue loss, the city can simply agree to make that amount of payment to the department, thereby satisfying the statute. In practice, though, cities and departments are much more likely to accept the more specific statutory definitions of good faith offers than to try to reach agreement on some other dollar amount. Therefore, it is appropriate to turn to those more specific statutory definitions.

Good faith offer—tax districts. If the annexation area is part of a rural fire protection district or a county fire service district, the statutes define a good faith offer in a way that generally seeks to hold the department harmless from the loss of tax base resulting from the annexation. The department is entitled to an annual sum calculated as follows: the fire district tax rate in effect at the time the city adopts the resolution of intent is multiplied by the valuation of the taxable property in the annexation area on January 1 for each year for which the contract is in effect.

Assume, for example, that the fire district tax rate in effect on the date of the resolution of intent is 5 cents per $100 of valuation. Assume also that the total valuation of property in the fire district is $150 million and that of property in the annexation area is $10 million. Thus, the gross tax levy in the tax district is $75,000, and the gross tax levy in the annexation area is $5,000. Thus, in the first year of the five-year contract, the city would pay the rural fire department $5,000; in each succeeding year the city would pay the department the amount that would have been produced by levying a 5-cent tax against the then-current valuation within the annexation area. Thus, if there is new construction in the annexation area that would have become part of the district's tax base, the department receives the benefit of that increase in the tax base for the duration of the contract.

The purpose of the good faith offer requirement is to assure to the department the same revenues from the annexation area that it would have received in the absence of annexation. In fact, however, the statutory mechanisms accomplish this goal in a somewhat imprecise way and can sometimes result in significant differences between what the city actually pays and what the department would have received in tax revenues in the absence of the annexation.

First, the department is entitled to whatever the tax district's gross tax levy would have produced from property within the annexation area. If there had been no annexation, however, the district might not have received the gross tax levy but only the net levy—that is, the gross levy reduced by collection costs and by the percentage of uncollected taxes in the annexation area. In this respect, then, the department might be marginally better off under the contract than it would have been without the annexation.

Second, if the county raises the property tax rate within the district during the term of the contract, the department does not receive the benefit of that increase with respect to property in the annexation area. The city's payment obligation under the contract is calculated by multiplying the value of property within the annexation area by the tax rate "in effect on the date of adoption of the resolution of intent." Although the district will benefit from increases in valuation within the annexation area, it will not benefit from increases in the tax rate within the district. In this respect the department is marginally worse off under the contract than it would have been without the annexation.

Third, and similarly, if the county lowers the tax rate within the district during the term of the contract, the reduction will not be reflected in the city's payment to the department. Again, the department is entitled to the amount generated by multiplying the current valuation in the district by the tax rate in effect when the annexation began. Such a scenario is most likely to happen when a revaluation takes effect in the county. A revaluation typically results in significant increases in property valuations; as a result, the county is likely to reduce various tax rates, including fire district tax rates. The city, however, is required to continue to calculate its payment to the department on the basis of the tax rate in effect when the city adopted the resolution of intent. In this case, the department could receive a significant bonus over the amount it would have received if the annexation had not occurred.

There is one other situation in which the amount paid to the department might not accurately reflect the amount of revenue it would otherwise receive from the fire district tax. In at least two counties, the commissioners have replaced a multitude of fire tax districts, each supporting a separate fire department, with a single tax district covering the entire unincorporated area of the county. The county then contracts with several fire departments to provide fire service to different parts of the district; the amount the county pays any single department, however, does not necessarily reflect the taxes raised from the properties in the department's service area. Consequently, when a city contracts to make payments to the department based on the county's fire district tax rate multiplied by the tax valuation of the annexation area, the city's payments may not reflect the change, if any, in the amount the county pays to the department under its own contract with the department.[3]

Good faith offer—insurance districts. If the annexation area is part of an insurance district but not part of a fire tax district, there is no county fire tax rate that can be used to calculate the amount of the city's payment under its contract with the rural department. In that case, the statutes' good faith offer requires that the amount of the city's payment be based on the city's own general fund expenditures for fire protection. The city calculates the percentage of its general fund budget appropriated for fire protection, and multiplies that percentage against the city's general tax rate. The result is a putative fire protection tax rate, which is then multiplied by the valuation of property within the annexation area. This final result is the amount of the city's annual

3. This situation creates a more difficult problem for a department with respect to the city's payment of a share of the rural department's debt service. See the discussion below in section 9.04 at note 11.

payment to the rural fire department. (The statutes limit the fire protection tax rate calculated for this purpose to a maximum of 15 cents per $100 of value.)

Assume, for example, that 12 percent of the city's general fund appropriations are for the fire department and that the city has a tax rate of 60 cents per $100 of value. Multiplying the 60 cents by 12 percent produces a putative fire protection tax rate of 7.2 cents per $100. If the tax valuation in the annexation area is $10 million, the annual payment to the rural department is $7,200.

Note that all these calculations are made each year the contract is in effect. If the city changes the percentage of its general fund appropriated for fire protection, or if it changes its tax rate, these changes will affect the amount of its payment obligation to the rural department. Similarly, any changes in the valuation of property within the annexation area will change the amount paid to the department.

Note, finally, that these calculations are based on a considerable simplification of the city's actual methods of supporting its own fire protection services. The statutory formula appears to assume that the property tax is the only source of revenue to the general fund, and that therefore property taxpayers are paying a determinable amount of their taxes for fire protection. But the typical city, of course, has a broad range of revenues that go into the general fund, and these other revenues also help pay for fire protection. Therefore, the percentage of any property owner's tax payments that actually supports the fire department will be less than the putative fire protection tax rate used to calculate the payment obligation to the rural department.

Good faith offer—first responder service. If the amount of a good faith offer is calculated as set out above, the city has one further option. As mentioned above, it may offer to contract only for "first responder service" and, in that case, to offer only half the amount otherwise required. Although the phrase *first responder* has a fairly accepted meaning in some fields of emergency services,[4] there does not appear to be an accepted meaning in the field of basic fire protection. There is probably a maximum level of service that a rural department might accept as first responder service, but in practice the term has often come to mean considerably less than the maximum. The kind of service a city expects under a first responder contract is discussed in the next paragraphs.

4. In the context of dealing with hazardous materials, "first responder" refers to a level of training. In emergency medical services, it refers to the stabilizing care given a person in need of medical care until trained medical personnel arrive.

Contract practice. If a city and a rural fire department enter into a contract under which the city makes the full amount of payment required by the statute, the statute seems to contemplate that the rural department will be the department primarily responsible for providing fire protection in the annexation area for the term of the contract. G.S. 160A-35 and 160A-47 each provide that a contract with a rural fire department meets the city's responsibility to provide fire protection in the annexation area on substantially the same basis as it does elsewhere within the city; this implies that the city itself need not provide fire service to the annexation area. When a city has a municipal fire department, however, the contract with a rural department does not normally cede all or even primary fire protection responsibility to the rural department. The reasons for this are not so much legal as political. In many cases the I.S.O., or fire insurance, rating for the city's fire department will be stronger than the rating for the rural department. The city's rating, for example, might be a 4 or a 5 or even better, while the rural department's might be 6/9S. The city is more likely to employ full-time firefighters, while the rural department is more likely to rely on volunteers, so that the city's response time may be shorter; the city might also have newer or more extensive equipment; and so on. If the city leaves fire protection in the annexation area solely in the hands of a rural department that does not enjoy as strong a rating as the city department, fire insurance rates for the annexation area will be higher, especially for commercial or industrial property. Usually the city will not be willing to have property owners in the annexation area pay higher prices for casualty insurance than owners of comparable property elsewhere in the city.

As a result, it is common practice for the city's contract with a rural department to provide that both the municipal department and the rural department will respond to fires in the annexation area. If the municipal department arrives first, it might find that it can call the rural department and wave off the latter's response. If the rural department arrives first, the city will normally come as well, at least for structure fires. (In fact, the city needs to actually respond to a structure fire in order to maintain its I.S.O. rating.) Once the municipal department arrives, it will assume command of fire-suppression activities.[5]

5. This is the sort of contract set out in the North Carolina League of Municipalities (NCLM) publication, CONTRACTING FOR FIRE SERVICE WHERE ANNEXATIONS HAVE OCCURRED (1991 revision). This publication was first published in 1983, just after the statutes under discussion were enacted.

To someone not in the fire service, the contract described in the preceding paragraph might appear to involve first responder service; indeed, the parties to a first responder contract could certainly define the service in just that way. Often, however, they define it to mean something less. In common practice, when a city enters into a first responder contract with a rural department, it is most often asking only that the rural department respond to a fire if called upon to do so by the city. That is, such a contract is little more than a mutual aid agreement.[6]

These contracts also typically include provisions regarding city and department liabilities, requirements for training of firefighters and maintenance of equipment, and, perhaps, a statement about the effect of the contract on emergency medical services (if both departments provide such service).

[d] Required procedures

The annexation statutes set out procedures that the city and the rural department must follow in order for the requirement of a good faith offer for service to arise. The statutes do not expressly require the city to notify the rural department of the planned annexation, but other provisions in the statutes make it very likely the city will in fact do so before adoption of the resolution of intent. G.S. 160A-35(4) and 160A-47(4) both require that the annexation report include a statement on the impact of the annexation on any rural fire department serving the annexation area. The statutory provisions also require any affected department to give the city the information necessary to prepare such a statement within thirty days of the city's request. In order to include the information in the report, the city will obviously need to receive the information some time before it adopts the report. Because the report must be adopted within twenty-five days after adoption of the resolution of intent,[7] the city is almost certain to request the information from the

6. This is the sort of first responder contract set out in the NCLM publication cited in ibid. In the spring of 2000 the city of Morganton made such an offer for first responder service to a volunteer fire department, and the department appealed the matter to the Local Government Commission. Although the LGC determined that it was without jurisdiction, because the appeal was untimely, it noted that "the Commission staff has reviewed the offer and has determined that the City made a good faith offer in accordance with 160A-49.1." Local Government Commission Agenda, July 6, 2000, copy on file at the Commission's offices.

7. N.C. Gen. Stat. § 160A-37(c) and 160A-49(c) (hereinafter G.S.) require the city to adopt the report at least thirty days before the public informational meeting.

rural department, thereby giving the department notice of the proposed annexation before the council adopts the resolution of intent.

The department must make a written request for a good faith offer from the city. The request must be signed by the chief officer of the rural department and delivered to the city clerk no later than fifteen days before the public hearing on the annexation. (The hearing must be held between sixty and ninety days after adoption of the resolution of intent.) If the department does not request a good faith offer as required by the statute, the city has no obligation to offer one or to seek to contract with the rural department. Similarly, the city has no obligation to offer or otherwise seek a contract if the department does not provide, within forty-five days of receiving the request, the information needed to prepare the statement of impact mentioned above. (For this forfeiture of rights to apply, the city's request must give the department notice of this possibility.[8])

Appeal by the department. If the rural department believes that the city has not made a good faith offer for a fire service contract, the statutes permit it to appeal to the Local Government Commission (LGC). Such an appeal must be made within thirty days after the city adopts the annexation ordinance; if the rural department does not act within that thirty days, it appears that the LGC is without jurisdiction to respond to the appeal.[9] In making its appeal, the rural department may ask the LGC to stay the effective date of the annexation ordinance until the commission has completed its review of the matter. The LGC has authority to grant such a stay and, if some portions of the annexation area are unaffected by the rural department's appeal, to allow those portions to become effective in the meantime. As a practical matter, the LGC has only rarely received an appeal, and it has never had to stay the effective date of an annexation.

If the LGC finds that the city has made a good faith offer, it affirms the ordinance, allowing the annexation to go forward. If, however, it

---

Subsection (a) of each statute requires that the public informational meeting be held between forty-five and fifty-five days after the day the council adopts the resolution of intent. Simple subtraction shows that the report must therefore be adopted no later than fifteen to twenty-five days after adoption of the resolution of intent, depending on the date of the informational meeting.

8. Forms for the required notice are included in the NCLM handbooks, MECHANICS OF ANNEXATION UNDER 5,000 POPULATION and 5,000 OR MORE POPULATION, available from NCLM, PO Box 3069, Raleigh, NC. 27602 or through its Web site: http://www.nclm.org/Pubs/pub-link.html (last visited May 16, 2002).

9. This was the LGC's conclusion in the appeal brought against the city of Morganton reported in note 6 above.

finds that the city has not made a good faith offer, it must remand the ordinance to the city for further proceedings. If the ordinance is remanded, the annexation may not become effective until the LGC finds that a good faith offer has been made. As a practical matter, when an appeal is filed, the LGC will seek to have the parties reach their own agreement; as a last resort it will require that the city make precisely the offer set out in the statute.

Section 9.03. Employment of Full-Time Employees of Rural Fire Departments

If a city annexes territory pursuant to either of the involuntary annexation statutes, and if as a result of the annexation a rural fire department must terminate a full-time employee, G.S. 160A-294 requires the city to take one of three steps as a means of protecting that employee. (The statute does not apply to voluntary annexations or to annexations by legislative act.) To qualify for the statute's protection, the person must have been employed by the rural department for at least two years at the time the city adopts its resolution of intent. Which of the three steps to take is at the option of the city, although normally a city would discuss the matter with the affected employee.

1. *Employment with the city fire department.* The city may offer the person employment with the city's fire department. There must be no loss of salary nor any loss of seniority because of the transfer into the city's department, and the city must place the person in a position "as near as possible in type to the position that was held in the rural fire department." If the city has minimum requirements for fire department employees, such as specific physical tests, that the person cannot pass, the statute does not seem to require the city to waive compliance with its requirements. Rather, the city should use one of the other two options for protecting the rural department's employee.

2. *Employment with the city in some other department.* The city may offer the person employment with the city, but in a department other than the fire department. The new position must be "comparable" in pay and seniority to the person's job with the rural department. Although the statute does not say so, presumably the city should seek a match between the person's skills and whatever position is offered to him or her.

3. *Severance pay.* The city may pay the person the equivalent of a year's salary as severance pay. This payment is calculated by first

determining his or her base salary as follows. If the city adopts a resolution of consideration that includes the annexation area, the person's base salary is his or her total salary for the twelve-month period ending on the last pay period before adoption of the resolution. If the city does not adopt a resolution of consideration for the annexation area, the employee's base salary is his or her total salary for the twelve-month period ending on the last pay period before the city council adopted the resolution of intent. Once the base salary is determined, any reasonable cost-of-living increases are added, as well as any increases attributable to bona fide promotions. The result is the year's salary that the city must pay.

It seems clear that the person's salary is not affected by any withholdings, nor by any fringe benefits paid for by the rural department.

Section 9.04. Payment of Rural Fire Department Debt

If a city annexes territory served by a rural fire department, either voluntarily or involuntarily, and the territory is within a fire tax district or a fire insurance district, the city must eventually pay a proportionate share of any debt, including interest, owed by the rural department at the time the annexation proceeding began. This requirement is set out in G.S. 160A-37.2 and 160A-49.2 for involuntary annexations, in G.S. 160A-31.1 for voluntary contiguous annexations, and in G.S. 160A-58.2A for voluntary noncontiguous annexations. (The requirement does not apply to legislative annexations, unless the legislation so specifies.) There are some differences between the involuntary and voluntary statutes, as noted in the discussion below.

When does the city's payment obligation begin? If a city has made an involuntary annexation and has entered into a service contract with the rural fire department, whether for full service or first responder service, the city's obligation to assist with debt service payments begins when the contract terminates. In all other involuntary annexations and in all voluntary annexations, the city's obligation begins on the effective date of the annexation.

Gathering information from the rural fire department. The voluntary statutes set out a simple set of steps to be followed if the rural department is to qualify for debt payment assistance. First, the city must request information concerning the debt from the department. (The NCLM annexation publications include sample forms the city can send for the department to fill out.) The most important information that is under the exclusive control of the department is the amount of its outstanding debt on apparatus and facilities, the amount to be paid annually, and the scheduled debt-retirement date. The statutes direct the department to respond to the city within thirty days, although there is no penalty for missing that deadline by a few days. If the department does not respond within forty-five days, however, it forfeits its rights to have the city assist in making payments on its debt. For the forfeiture to apply, the city's request for information must state that failure to respond in forty-five days will result in forfeiture, and it must cite the appropriate statute.[10]

The involuntary annexation statutes are similar, but not identical, on these points. The city normally makes a written request to the department for the information necessary to prepare the statement on annexation's impact on the department—a required part of the annexation report.[11] If the department does not respond to this request within forty-five days, the city's obligation to pay debt service ends. (As in voluntary annexations, the city's request for information must state that a failure to respond in forty-five days will result in forfeiture of the department's rights, and it must cite the appropriate statute.)

For what departmental debt is the city responsible? For an involuntary annexation, the city is responsible for paying its share of debt service on any departmental debt outstanding when the city adopted its resolution of intent. For a voluntary annexation, the city is responsible for paying its share of debt outstanding when the city received the petition for annexation. The city is not responsible for assisting in the payment of any debt incurred after those dates. Similarly, if an otherwise qualifying departmental debt is paid off before the city's payment obligation begins—that is, before the service contract ends or before the annexation becomes effective—the city has no obligation for that debt. If the department refinances existing debt, the city's obligation presumably continues for the refinanced debt, although it should share in any cost savings effected by the refinancing.

Calculating the city's payment obligation. The amount of the city's obligation is calculated in the same way, regardless of whether the annexation area is in a fire tax district or in an insurance district. The city determines, as of the effective date of annexation, what percentage of the assessed valuation of the entire district is constituted by the

10. Forms for the request statements for voluntary and involuntary annexations are included in the NCLM publications cited in note 8 above.)

11. See the discussion of this point in section 9.02[d] above.

assessed valuation of the property being annexed. That percentage is then applied to the total amount of each annual debt payment the rural department is required to make to derive the city's payment obligation.[12]

Assume, for example, that the total assessed valuation of the fire district served by the rural department is $150 million, and that the assessed valuation of the property being annexed by the city is $7.5 million. Therefore the annexation area constitutes 5 percent of the fire district's assessed valuation. Assume then that the department's annual debt service obligation on qualifying debt is $90,000 a year for four years. This amount is multiplied by 5 percent, with the result that the city's annual obligation on this debt is $4,500.

The discussion in section 9.02[c][13] notes that in a few counties the commissioners have replaced a multitude of fire tax districts, each supporting a separate fire department, with a single tax district comprised of the entire unincorporated area of the county. The county then contracts with several fire departments to provide fire service to different parts of the district. When that sort of system is used, the percentage of the total district's tax base represented by any single annexation is likely to be very small, and it may not accurately reflect the department's loss in support for its debt. If in such a county the board of commissioners also designates insurance districts, it would better serve the statutory goals if a city annexing a rural department's service area based its payments of the department's debt service on the insurance district rather than the tax district.

A number of cities prefer to make a lump-sum payment to the department at the time of annexation rather than make annual payments. Typically, the amount is the projected total of annual debt service payments discounted to its present value. If the department agrees, such an arrangement can be entered into. The Local Government Commission routinely approves this sort of payment arrangement.

12. G.S. 160A-31.1(b) and 160A-58.2A(b) set out a method by which the city's payment obligation is to be determined. Subdivision (1) of each cited subsection directs the rural fire department to "certify to the city each year" the amount of its required debt service on qualifying debt. The quoted language can be read to mean that the department is to make this certification annually while debt remains outstanding. Later provisions in the cited sections, however, make it clear that the city and the rural department are to agree upon a complete schedule of payments before any payments are made, making an annual certification of the amount due unnecessary. What the statutes apparently intend is that the rural department make that certification once, before any payments are made, *for* each year there will be debt service obligations.

13. See the text discussion following note 2, above.

Tax-exempt property. If some or all of the property being annexed is exempt from property taxation, the city has no payment obligation with respect to that property. The statute casts the city's obligation in terms of the assessed valuation of the district and the annexation area. If property is exempt from taxation, it is not part of that assessed valuation. The theory implicit in the annexation statute is that as such property is not now supporting the rural department's debt service, the department has suffered no loss because of the property's annexation.[14]

The de minimis exception. The two voluntary annexation statutes relieve the city from assisting with debt service payments when the amounts to be paid are quite small. (There is no comparable exception in the involuntary statute.) This de minimis exception reads as follows:

> This section does not apply in any year as to any annexed area(s) for which the payment calculated under this section as to all annexation ordinances adopted under this Part by a city during a particular calendar year does not exceed one hundred dollars ($100.00).[15]

The statutory language is perhaps confusing, but its meaning is as follows: In any calendar year, the city determines the amount of its debt service obligations arising from each voluntary contiguous and from each voluntary noncontiguous annexation. (The city makes separate calculations for contiguous and for noncontiguous annexations.) For each annexation, the city makes this calculation for each year in which there is outstanding rural fire department debt that qualifies for city assistance. If the total amount of such obligations for any year for contiguous annexations or for noncontiguous annexations is less than $100, the city need not make those payments for that year. It should be noted that the $100 applies to the total amount of payments the city is required to make in any single year; it does not refer to the amount the city must pay on behalf of any single rural department. If the city has a $2 obligation to one department and a $99 obligation to another, the total is more than $100 and the city is required to pay both amounts.

14. This theory is not always supported by fact. The State of North Carolina makes payments in lieu of taxation to both municipal and rural fire departments to support provision of fire service to property owned by the state; and sometimes owners of other tax-exempt property make comparable payments. Annexation of such property will in fact cause a revenue loss to the benefiting rural department, but the statute does not obligate an annexing city to assist in making debt service payments in such a situation.

15. G.S. 160A-31.1(c) and 160A-58.2A(c).

Local Government Commission approval. Once the rural department has provided the city with the information necessary for the city to calculate its debt service obligations and the city and department have agreed upon the resulting schedule of payments, the two entities are to present that payment schedule to the Local Government Commission (LGC) for its approval. Until the commission gives its approval, the city may not make any of the required payments. The statute contemplates that the LGC will arbitrate any disagreements between the city and the rural department as to the amount of the city's required payments.

10

Protections for Private Solid Waste Collection Firms

10

Protections for Private Solid Waste Collection Firms

Section 10.01. Introduction

Section 8.02[a] summarizes the case of *Stillings v. City of Winston-Salem*,[1] in which the North Carolina supreme court held that a private solid waste collection firm's franchise from the county terminated when its service area was annexed by a city. Thereafter, it had no right to continue to collect solid waste within the annexation area. There are other ways in which a private collection firm that served the annexation area could see its business suffer. The annexing city may have a franchise ordinance that requires any entity collecting solid wastes in the city to have a franchise from the city, and the existing collection firm might not have such a franchise. Even a private solid waste collection firm that remains legally able to operate within an annexation area will frequently be at a severe competitive disadvantage. The city may collect solid wastes itself and support the service through property taxes, or it may contract with a different private collection firm and finance the contract with property taxes. In either case, a collection firm that charges customers for services is unlikely to be able to compete with a service financed through taxation.

These likely effects of annexation were recognized by the General Assembly in 1985, when it first adopted legislation providing some transitional protection for private solid waste collection firms seriously disadvantaged by certain annexations. If a collection firm qualifies for the statutory protections, the city must either enter into a contract with the firm, allowing it to continue operating within the annexation area for at least two years after the annexation becomes effective, or reimburse the firm for its "economic loss," providing, essentially, a severance payment. This chapter summarizes this statutory system of protection.

1. 311 N.C. 689, 319 S.E.2d 233 (1984).

Section 10.02. Qualifying for the Statutory Protections

[a] Annexations to which the protections apply

These statutory protections apply to involuntary annexations (G.S. 160A-37.3 and 160A-49.3) and to annexations achieved by legislative act (G.S. 160A-324). They do not apply to voluntary annexations. In 2006 the General Assembly enacted legislation protecting private solid waste collection firms that are "displaced" by certain actions of a local government.[2] That legislation, codified as G.S. 160A-327, specifically states that it does not apply when the firm is displaced "as the result of an annexation under Article 4A of Chapter 160A of the General Statutes."[3] Because the statutory reference includes the voluntary annexation statutes, a city is not required to compensate or otherwise protect a private solid waste collection firm that loses business because of a *voluntary* annexation.

[b] Qualifying private firms

The statutes set out three conditions a collection firm must meet to qualify for the statutory protections.[4]

1. *The firm has an established business in the area.* In an involuntary annexation, the firm must have been collecting solid wastes in the annexation area on the ninetieth day preceding the city council's adoption of the resolution of consideration[5] or, if there was no resolution of consideration, on the ninetieth day preceding the council's adoption of the resolution of intent. Regardless of which resolution is counted, the firm must still be providing solid waste collection services in the annexation area when the city adopts its resolution of intent for that specific annexation. In a legislative annexation, the firm must have been collecting solid wastes in the annexation area on the ninetieth day

2. S.L. 2006-193.

3. G.S. 160A-327(g).

4. These tests are set out in subsections (a) and (a1) of each statute.

5. A city's resolution of consideration is valid for two years; a city may extend the resolution by adopting a new one before the end of the two-year period. The statute's reference to the time of adoption of the resolution of consideration almost certainly refers to the most recent adoption or extension of a resolution and not to the time a resolution of consideration applicable to the annexation area was first adopted. To refer back to the first resolution of consideration applicable to the annexation area might well require that the collection firm have been in business a decade or more earlier, and that is clearly contrary to the statutory purpose.

preceding introduction of the annexation bill in the General Assembly and must still be collecting in the area on the day the bill becomes law.[6]

Note that the collection firm does not need to have a county franchise or a contract with the county. It simply needs to be operating within the annexation area at the appropriate times.

2. *The firm has lost business because of the annexation.* The annexation must cause the firm to lose either its franchise rights (if any) in the annexation area or arrangements for solid waste collection it has made with third parties. Although the application of this condition is clear in many cases, uncertainties can arise.

If the collection firm holds a county solid waste collection franchise, that franchise terminates upon the effective date of annexation.[7] Such a firm clearly meets the requirements of this second condition. So does a collection firm that provides service under contracts at will or contracts that may be terminated with a very short notice when customers terminate those contracts in order to receive service from the city or a city-financed collection firm. Even though these third-party contracts have not been terminated by law, they clearly have been terminated because of the annexation. Thus the collection firm meets the requirements of this second condition.

If the firm provides service under a longer-term contract, however, the matter is more clouded. Say the contract continues in force for eighteen months after the effective date of the annexation and the collection firm expects the customer to switch to city or city-financed service at the end of the contract. In one sense, the third-party arrangement will be terminated because of the annexation—the city or the city-financed firm would not be a competitor except for the annexation. But in another sense, it distorts reality to attribute the ultimate loss of such a customer to the annexation. After all, the collection firm will continue to serve this customer for some time after the annexation becomes effective and might, in any event, have lost the customer to a competitor at the end of the contract. The longer such a contract continues in effect

6. The statute requires the collection firm to still be operating in the annexation area on the date of enactment of the local act accomplishing the annexation. This will often be different from the effective date of the legislation. (The statute several times uses the term effective date, so its use of the different term, date of enactment, does not seem to have been inadvertent.) Because a legislative annexation is accomplished by a local act of the General Assembly, it is not subject to gubernatorial veto [N.C. Const., art. II, § 22(6)], and therefore the date of enactment is the date the act is ratified by the two presiding officers of the General Assembly.

7. Stillings v. City of Winston-Salem, 311 N.C. 689, 319 S.E.2d 233 (1984).

after the effective date of the annexation, the weaker is the argument that the ultimate termination of the arrangement is caused by the annexation. Until the statute is clarified, however, or this matter becomes the subject of appellate litigation, such a contract is likely to be discussed in negotiations between the annexing city and the collection firm.

3. *The firm must have substantial business in the county in which the annexation takes place.* Until 2007 the statutes did not protect a firm unless it had a substantial amount of business in the annexation area.[8] Under statutory changes that took effect on January 1, 2007, however, that is no longer true. The firm must have substantial business in the *county* within which the annexation takes place—at least fifty customers at the time the firm makes a formal request to contract with the annexing city. If the firm meets that qualification, it is eligible for protection—even if it has only a single customer in the specific annexation area.

Although the statutes do not deal specifically with this possibility, if collection firm A qualifies for the statutory protections and then is sold to firm B, it seems appropriate that firm B will succeed to the entitlements of firm A under the statutes.

Section 10.03. Statutory Procedures

The three statutes providing transitional protection for collection firms set out the following procedures for determining the rights of firms collecting solid waste in an annexation area.

1. Firms that provide solid waste collection services to areas outside cities must file a notice of that fact with the clerk of each city located within its "collection area" or within five miles of that area. This requirement was inserted into the statute in 2006 and is evidently a response to the difficulties that some cities have had in determining what firms actually provide services within an annexation area.[9]

8. The statutes required that the firm either have at least fifty residential customers in the annexation area or have average monthly revenue of at least $500 from nonresidential customers in the annexation area.

9. *See In re* Blanton v. North Carolina Local Government Commission, No. 9027SC888, decided by the court of appeals 2 July 1991. The city did not notify plaintiff firm of an annexation because it could find neither an address nor a telephone number for the firm. Because the firm learned of the annexation, however, and attended the public hearing, and because the city did successfully notify all other collection firms

2. At least four weeks before the public informational meeting on an involuntary annexation, the city must give written notice of adoption of the resolution of intent to each private firm that has provided notice according to paragraph (1) above that it serves customers in the annexation area. In a legislative annexation, the city must provide a copy of the ratified act to each affected firm at least thirty days before the effective date of the legislation. In each case, the notice must be sent by certified mail, return receipt requested.[10]
3. At least ten days before the public hearing on an involuntary annexation, a collection firm that believes it qualifies for the benefits of the statutes and that wishes to receive those benefits must make a written request for a contract with the city. In a legislative annexation, a comparable request must be made at least ten days before the effective date of the annexation. In either case, this request must be signed by an officer or owner of the firm and delivered to the city clerk. The request must also include a certification that the firm has at that time at least fifty customers in the county in which the annexation area is located.
4. Either before this time or afterward, the city may make a written request for information to each firm that has submitted a request for a contract or to each firm that the city believes is eligible to make such a request. The city's request must be sent to each firm by certified mail, return receipt requested. The request may seek "all information in [the firm's] possession or control, including but not limited to operational, financial and budgetary information, necessary for the city to determine if the firm qualifies for the benefits of this section and to determine the nature and scope of the potential contract and/or economic loss."[11]

operating in the annexation area, the court held that the city had satisfied the statute's requirement that it make a good faith effort to reach each affected firm.

10. Appropriate forms for transmitting these documents are included in the North Carolina League of Municipalities (NCLM) handbooks, Mechanics of Annexation under 5,000 Population and Mechanics of Annexation 5,000 or More Population, available from NCLM, PO Box 3069, Raleigh, NC. 27602 or through its Web site: http://www.nclm.org/Publications/pubs.htm (last visited November 1, 2006).

11. G.S. 160A-37.3(h); 160A-49.3(h); and 160A-324(h) The NCLM annexation handbooks include a form for seeking this information from eligible collection firms.

5. In both an involuntary and a legislative annexation, the firm must respond to the city's request for information within thirty business days. If it does not do so, and if the city's request makes it clear that failure to respond will cause a forfeiture of rights and cites the appropriate statute, the firm forfeits its rights under the statute.[12]

Section 10.04. What the City Is Required to Do

As noted, if a firm qualifies for the benefits of these statutes, the city must either enter into a service contract with the firm or compensate the firm for its statutory economic loss.

[a] Service contract with the collection firm

If the city decides to offer a contract, the statutes set out a rough formula for determining the amount to be paid to the firm under the contract.[13] If the firm will be providing services that are substantially the same as those it provided before annexation, the statutes direct the city to pay the firm at least 90 percent of the amount paid or required under the firm's preannexation arrangements. If, for example, the firm charged $10 a month per household for residential collection before annexation, the city must pay it at least $9 a month for comparable service under the contract.[14] If the firm's services will differ from what it provided before annexation, the amount paid by the city must be increased or decreased from the 90 percent starting point. For example, the firm may have to meet different city standards for collection, or serve a different number of customers, or change the frequency of collection; its disposal costs may have changed, or it may have to meet new requirements for storage capacity (i.e., by purchasing new dumpsters or carts). If the city and

12. The NCLM handbooks include a form for notifying the firm of the possibility of forfeiture.

13. The formula is set out in subsection (d) of each statute.

14. In one example the firm charged extraterritorial customers $11 a month for residential service. This same firm had an existing contract with the city to provide residential service within the city for $5.50 a month. When the city contracted with the firm to provide residential service within the annexation area, the statute required that the city pay the firm 90 percent of the $11 charge, rather than the existing $5.50 charge. (Presumably this result could be avoided by provisions in the master contract for collection services within the city.)

the firm cannot reach agreement on the amount to be paid under the contract, the parties may take the matter to the Local Government Commission, which is authorized to decide the issue.

The statutes set out a number of provisions that the city may, at its discretion, include in the contract.[15] These provisions are quite flexible, giving the city a variety of options for integrating a collection firm's services into the city's existing services.

1. The city may require the firm to post a performance bond.
2. The city may require the firm to carry public liability insurance.
3. The city may require the firm to serve customers in the annexation area that it did not serve before annexation. Alternatively, it may limit the firm to serving only those customers it served before annexation, reserving the remaining customers for itself.
4. The city may divide the annexation area among qualifying collection firms, or among one or more firms and the city's own service.
5. The city may establish performance standards as long as those standards were in place when the city published notice that it had adopted the resolution of intent. (In a legislative annexation, the standards must have been in place when the notice of annexation was sent to the private firm.) In this regard, the contract will need to describe carefully the service the firm is expected to provide: whether residential and/or commercial, backyard or curbside, once or twice a week or (for commercial) more often, required hours of collection, holiday schedule, kinds of waste accepted, eligible containers, and so on. It might also impose various requirements regarding the firm's employees, such as whether they must wear uniforms, what kind of training they must have, and the like.
6. The city may provide for the cancellation of the contract if performance standards are not met or if there are other substantial violations of the terms of the contract. Before the city may cancel the contract, however, the Local Government Commission must find that substantial violations of its standards or other provisions have occurred. In addition, the firm

15. These potential provisions are set out in subsection (c) of each statute.

must be given thirty days in which to cure any violation. (If the city believes the firm has substantially violated health laws, it may suspend the contract for up to thirty days without prior approval from the Local Government Commission.)

7. The city may provide for monetary damages if the company violates any performance standards or other provisions of the contract.

In addition, the contract will need to specify the frequency and timing of the city's payment obligations, and might include provisions for increasing the payment made to the firm because of inflationary factors.

[b] Payment for economic loss

As an alternative to contracting with a collection firm, the city may pay the firm for its *economic loss*, as defined in the statutes.[16] In an involuntary annexation, this amount is determined by the firm's revenues in the annexation area during the three months immediately preceding the city's adoption of the resolution of consideration that included the annexation area; if the city did not adopt a resolution of consideration, the base period is the three months immediately preceding the city's adoption of the resolution of intent. In a legislative annexation, the amount of the payment is based on the firm's revenues in the annexation area during the three months immediately preceding introduction of the annexation bill in the General Assembly. The statutes refer here to the *three months* preceding adoption of the appropriate resolution or introduction of the annexation bill, rather than to the *ninety days* preceding, the terminology used elsewhere in the statutes. This difference may reflect the reality that, as most collection firms bill on a monthly or quarterly basis, it would be easier to calculate revenues from the preceding three months' bills (or single quarterly bill) than from the billing for the exactly preceding ninety days. The firm's economic loss is defined as fifteen times its average monthly revenue from solid waste collections in the annexation area during the relevant three-month period.[17]

16. The economic-loss provision is found in subsection (i) of each statute.

17. From original enactment of these statutes until 2007, the economic loss was defined as *twelve* times a firm's average monthly revenue.

There are several general points to note about the statutory calculation of economic loss. First, it is based on the firm's *revenues* in the annexation area, not on its profits. Second, it is unaffected by changes in the firm's operations in the annexation area after the relevant ninety-day period. Third, it is based on the firm's revenue from customers in the annexation area that are lost because of the annexation. Thus, if a firm provides both residential and commercial collection services in the annexation area but loses only residential customers because of an annexation, then its economic-loss calculations may include only revenues from residential but not commercial customers.

Section 10.05. Appeal to the Local Government Commission

The preceding discussion has already mentioned two situations in which the statutes permit or require an appeal to the Local Government Commission (LGC). First, if the parties cannot agree on the amount the city will pay the collection firm under a service contract, subsection (d) of each statute permits them to appeal to the LGC, which is empowered to decide the issue. Second, if the city seeks to terminate the contract because of an alleged substantial violation of the contract's provisions by the collection firm, it cannot do so until the LGC has itself found that there was a substantial violation. The statutes also permit appeal to the LGC in a third situation: when the collection firm alleges that the city has made no contract offer (and apparently has also not agreed to make an economic-loss payment).[18]

In an involuntary annexation, the collection firm must make its appeal to the LGC within thirty days after the city adopts the annexation ordinance. In a legislative annexation, the firm must make its appeal within sixty days following the effective date of the annexation. (The firm must give the city at least thirty days following the effective date to make an appropriate offer.)

In an involuntary annexation, the firm may request the LGC to stay the effectiveness of the annexation, and the commission has discretion to do so or not. If the LGC then finds that the city has not complied with

18. These provisions are found in subsection (g) of each statute. Both speak only to a situation in which the city has allegedly made no offer to the private firm and are silent about whether the city has offered an economic-loss payment to the firm. If the city has made a satisfactory payment, however, it has satisfied the statutes and the firm has no grounds for seeking a service contract.

the statute, it must remand the annexation ordinance to the city for further proceedings. The ordinance may not then take effect until the LGC finds that the city has come into compliance.

In a legislative annexation, the statute does not give the LGC the power to stay the annexation, which will, after all, already be in effect when the firm makes its appeal. Rather, if the LGC finds that the city has not complied with the statute, it must order the city to pay a civil penalty to the collection firm. The amount of this penalty is the amount the city would have paid the firm under a contract that did comply with the statute; further, the city must continue to make the payments until it enters into a satisfactory contract with the firm.

11

Municipal Electric and Gas Distribution Systems

11

Municipal Electric and Gas Distribution Systems

Seventy-two North Carolina cities and towns operate electric distribution systems, and eight cities[1] operate natural gas distribution systems. The cities with electric distribution systems are often characterized as *electric cities*, and those with gas systems will be characterized here as *gas cities*. This chapter discusses the rights of electric and gas cities and their competitors to extend their distribution systems into an annexation area.

Section 11.01. Electric Distribution Systems

[a] Introduction

G.S. 160A-312 authorizes an electric city to extend its electrical distribution system outside its boundaries "within reasonable limitations."[2] If a city has done so and is, as a practical matter, already the exclusive provider of electricity within an annexation area, the annexation will have no effect on its rights or responsibilities as a distributor of electric power.

If there is a competitive electric distribution system in the annexation area, however—either an investor-owned public utility or an electric membership corporation—G.S. Chapter 160A, Article 16, Part 2 grants that competitive system the right—sometimes exclusive,

1. The eight are listed in N.C. GEN. STAT. § 105-187.40(1).

2. The supreme court has decided two cases that apply this statutory language. In Domestic Electric Service, Inc. v. City of Rocky Mount, 285 N.C. 135, 203 S.E.2d 838 (1974), the court read the language fairly narrowly and denied the city's right to extend its lines to a customer just outside the city. In Lumbee River Electric Membership Corp. v. City of Fayetteville, 309 N.C. 726, 309 S.E.2d 209 (1983), the court recast the reasoning of Domestic Electric somewhat and took a broader view of the statutory language, permitting the city to serve a customer some four miles from the city's boundary. The court of appeals also took the broader view in South River Electric Membership Corp. v. City of Fayetteville, 113 N.C. App. 401, 438 S.E.2d 464 (1994), permitting the city to serve a customer some five miles from the city's boundary.

sometimes not—to serve customers within three hundred feet of its existing distribution lines. The statute characterizes a city that distributes electric power within the city as the *primary supplier*,[3] while private competitors are characterized as *secondary suppliers*.

[b] Secondary suppliers' corridor rights

When a city annexes an area, G.S. 160A-332 grants the following rights to a secondary supplier already operating a distribution line in the annexation area, or elsewhere in the city, on a date known as the *determination date* (discussed below).

1. If the secondary supplier is already serving a customer's premises on the determination date or the secondary supplier's facilities are attached to the premises as of that date, it is entitled to continue serving those premises. The secondary supplier's right is exclusive; unless it gives its consent, the city may not serve those premises.
2. If premises needing initial electric service are located wholly within three hundred feet of a secondary supplier's distribution lines as those lines existed on the determination date, and if the premises are wholly more than three hundred feet from the city's lines as they existed on the determination date, the secondary supplier has the exclusive right to serve those premises. Unless the secondary supplier gives its consent, the city may not serve those premises.
3. If premises needing initial electric service are wholly within three hundred feet of the lines of two different secondary suppliers as of the determination date and are wholly more than three hundred feet of the city's lines as they existed on that date, the customer may select either of the two secondary suppliers but may not select the city. Unless the secondary supplier chosen to provide the service gives its consent, the city may not subsequently serve those premises.
4. If premises needing initial electric service are wholly or partially within three hundred feet of a secondary supplier's

3. The statute also defines *primary supplier* to include a distribution system that operates under a current or expired franchise from the city. This chapter, however, is only concerned with the rights of a city-owned distribution system and not with contests between rival private suppliers.

lines as of the determination date and wholly or partially within three hundred feet of the lines of the city as of the same date, the customer may select either the secondary supplier or the city. After the customer chooses, another supplier may not thereafter serve those premises without the consent of the original supplier.

5. If premises needing initial electric service are only partially within three hundred feet of the lines of a secondary supplier as of the determination date and are wholly more than three hundred feet from the lines of the city as of the same date, the customer may select either the secondary supplier or the city. After the customer chooses, another supplier may not thereafter serve those premises unless it receives the consent of the original supplier.

Except as set out in the preceding five numbered paragraphs, a secondary supplier may not provide electric service within an electric city except with the city's consent.

[c] Determination date

With respect to annexed property, G.S. 160A-331(1b) defines the determination date as the effective date of annexation. This definition was the subject of the 1997 supreme court decision in *City of Concord v. Duke Power Company*.[4] In 1986 the city had annexed an area that included premises that both the city and Duke Power sought to serve. The city had a distribution line in the 1986 annexation area within three hundred feet of the premises, while Duke had no line in the annexation area or in any nearby area of the city. In 1992 the city annexed a second tract, and that tract included a distribution line belonging to Duke; this line was within three hundred feet of the contested premises annexed earlier. When the owner sought to connect to Duke's system, the city brought suit to enjoin the connection. The city argued that the determination date was the date in 1986 when the city annexed the premises in question. At that time, as Duke's line was not in the city, it had no rights pursuant to G.S. 160A-332. The supreme court disagreed. It held that the determination date was the date the competing supplier's lines were annexed by the city. Because the customer did not seek power until

4. 346 N.C. 211, 485 S.E.2d 278 (1997).

after the second annexation, Duke's line did qualify, and the company was permitted to serve the contested premises.

Although the city lost this particular case, it should be noted that if the customer had needed power before the second annexation, the city would have been the only available supplier. Although the power company's lines were in fact within three hundred feet of the premises, even before the second annexation, it could not rely on those lines for distribution rights until after the later determination date, that is, until those lines were in fact annexed to the city. Until then, there was no determination date applicable to those lines and, therefore, no rights to serve based on their existence.

[d] Service to street lights and city facilities

G.S. 160A-336 specifically permits an electric city to extend electric service to its own facilities wherever located and to extend electricity to street lights anywhere within the city, even if it may not legally extend service to premises located adjacent to the city facilities or street lights. In *Duke Power Company v. City of High Point*,[5] the court of appeals held that the city could extend power into an annexation area before the effective date of the annexation (but after adoption of the annexation ordinance) in order to light the streets in that area once the annexation became effective. Such an extension was within reasonable limitations, even though a public utility or electric membership corporation was already serving the area. By extending the distribution lines prior to the annexation, of course, the city gave itself greater rights to serve the annexation area, as it will already have distribution lines in place on the determination date.

Section 11.02. Natural Gas Distribution Systems

There are no appellate cases concerning provision of natural gas services within cities; nor has the General Assembly enacted any statutes regulating extension of natural gas service that are comparable to those for electric service. The regulatory regime for natural gas, however, is the same as that for electric service before the specific electric service statutes were enacted in 1965. Therefore, any appellate case law about

5. 69 N.C. App. 378, 317 S.E.2d 701 (1984).

electric service not centered on the electric service legislation is relevant to similar questions involving natural gas service. For that reason, the discussion below is based on North Carolina appellate cases involving electric service.

First, if an investor-owned natural gas supplier is providing natural gas in an annexation area on the effective date of annexation, it is presumably doing so under a grant of territory from the North Carolina Utilities Commission. Such a supplier may not discontinue service to an existing customer without the approval of the Utilities Commission, as the court held in, for example, *State ex rel. North Carolina Utilities Commission v. Casey*.[6] After Kinston had annexed areas served by Carolina Power and Light Company, the city and the company agreed that the latter would convey its lines within the annexation areas to the city, and the N.C. Utilities Commission approved the transfer. The court upheld the transfer *because* the Utilities Commission had approved it. It is thus clear that the parties could not have effected the transfer without the Utilities Commission's approval and that the annexing city could not have required the investor-owned company to discontinue service to its customers in the city.[7]

Second, if the annexing city does not have an ordinance that requires a franchise for providing natural gas service in the city, an existing investor-owned system would be free to compete with the city for new customers in the annexation area, assuming that those customers were within the territory assigned to it by the Utilities Commission.

Third, even if the annexing city requires a franchise and the existing investor-owned provider does not have a franchise, the city cannot force the company to give up existing customers. This is illustrated by *Duke Power Company v. City of High Point*.[8] Duke had been operating in High Point, an electric city, under a franchise first granted several decades earlier. That franchise expired in 1969, and the city chose not to renew it; then, in 1973, the city ordered Duke to cease providing service to one or more existing customers. But because Duke had also been operating in the city pursuant to the regulations of the state Utilities Commission, the court of appeals held that the city could not force the company to discontinue service within the city unless the

6. 245 N.C. 297, 96 S.E.2d 8 (1957).

7. *See also* Duke Power Co. v. City of High Point, 22 N.C. App. 91, 205 S.E.2d 774 (1974), in which the court held that the city could not force the power company to relinquish customers served within the city unless the Utilities Commission agreed.

8. *Id.*

commission also approved. In a conflict between the city's franchising power and the Utilities Commission's regulatory power, it was the city power that had to give way.

Finally, it appears that if the city requires a franchise and the investor-owned company does not hold a franchise, the company cannot *expand* its customer base within the city. The state's regulatory scheme for utility service appears to leave at least this much life to a city's authority to require and adopt franchises.

12

Rural Water or Sewer Systems

12

Rural Water or Sewer Systems

Section 12.01. Introduction

[a] Broad construction

For several decades the U.S. Department of Agriculture (U.S.D.A.) has made loans to rural water and rural sewer systems, first through the Farmers Home Administration (FmHA) and, more recently, through its successor agency, the Water and Environmental Programs of U.S.D.A. Rural Development (RD). Since 1961, a federal law has protected any rural water or sewer system with an outstanding loan from FmHA or RD from municipal or private competition; this federal law can affect a city's service plans when it annexes an area served by such a system. As of September 2006, there were 195 rural utility systems in North Carolina with outstanding FmHA or RD loans.[1] This chapter discusses how the federal courts have interpreted the protective statute[2] and how the statute might affect annexations by North Carolina cities.

The federal protections are established by 7 U.S.C. § 1926(b), which reads as follows:

> The service provided or made available through any such association shall not be curtailed or limited by inclusion of the area served by such association within the boundaries of any municipal corporation or other public body, or by the granting of any private franchise for similar service within such area during the

1. Telephone conversation with Dennis DeLong of the North Carolina office of United States Department of Agriculture Rural Development, September 6, 2006.

2. Most of the reported litigation involving the statute has been in federal court, and obviously federal interpretations of a federal statute carry more weight than state court interpretations do. Indeed, some of the state court decisions are inconsistent with the federal decisions. Compare *Comanche County Rural Water District No. 1 v. City of Lawton*, 501 P. 2d 490 (Okla. 1972), which suggests that assertion of its federal rights by the water district might violate the state constitution, with *Rural Water District. No. 3 v. Owasso Utilities Authority*, 530 F. Supp. 818 (N.D. Okla. 1979), which criticizes the state court decision and holds that there is no conflict between state and federal law.

term of such loan; nor shall the happening of any such event be the basis of requiring such association to secure any franchise, license, or permit as a condition to continuing to serve the area served by the association at the time of the occurrence of such event.

The federal courts have identified two purposes served by this statute. First, it protects the federal government's interest in having its loan repaid by the rural utility system (sometimes referred to in this chapter as a "protected association"). Second, it encourages creation of community water and sewer systems in rural areas.[3] Given those purposes, the federal courts have consistently read the statute broadly, clearly extending the protections of the statute beyond its specific terms. The statute specifically prohibits curtailment of a rural utility system's service by either municipal annexation or the granting of a private franchise. The federal courts, however, have held that the statute also prohibits curtailment of a rural utility system's service caused by a city's (1) extraterritorial extension of utility services into the rural system's area,[4] (2) sale of water at wholesale to a current wholesale customer of a protected rural system,[5] or (3) condemnation of the rural system's lines and operating certificate.[6] Furthermore, the federal courts have ignored actions taken under state law to reduce the service area of a protected association.[7] This broad understanding was established in the

3. *E.g.*, City of Madison, Miss. v. Bear Creek Water Ass'n, Inc., 816 F.2d 1057, 1060 (5th Cir. 1987) (The legislative history "indicates two congressional purposes behind §1926: 1) to encourage rural water development by expanding the number of potential users of such systems, thereby decreasing the per-user cost, and 2) to safeguard the viability and financial security of such associations (and FmHA's loans) by protecting them from the expansion of nearby cities and towns.").

4. *E.g.*, North Alamo Water Supply Corp. v. City of San Juan, Texas, 90 F.3d 910 (5th Cir. 1996); *Owasso*, 530 F. Supp. at 818.

5. *E.g.*, Adams County Reg'l Water Dist. v. Vill. of Manchester, Ohio, 226 F.3d 513 (6th Cir. 2000); Jennings Water, Inc. v. City of North Vernon, Ind., 628 F. Supp. 421 (S.D. Ind. 1988).

6. *E.g.*, *Madison*, 816 F.2d at 1057; Moore Bayou Water Ass'n, Inc. v. Town of Jonestown, Miss., 628 F. Supp. 1367 (N.D. Miss. 1986).

7. Pittsburg County Rural Water Dist. No. 7 v. City of McAlester, 358 F.3d 694 (10th Cir. 2004) (State-approved de-annexation of territory from district does not affect district's federally protected service area.). *But see Moongate Water Co., Inc. v. Dona Ana Mutual Domestic Water Consumers Corp.*, 420 F.3d 1082 (10th Cir. 2005), in which the court held that a state public regulation commission decision concluding that the protected association did not have a legal right under state law to serve the disputed area foreclosed the association's rights under federal law as well.

first reported federal decision interpreting the statute, a district court opinion from 1979. In that case, the court wrote:

> While it is true that 7 U.S.C. § 1926(b) does not *explicitly state* that "there shall be no open competition," it is clear from the legislative history . . . that the intent of Congress was to protect rural water districts [and other associations] from "competitive facilities," especially those which would be developed as a result of the expansion of neighboring municipalities.[8]

Basically, then, the statute prohibits any sort of municipal or state action that might curtail or limit the services of a protected association or any form of competition with such an association.[9]

The federal courts have also refused to consider the effect, or lack thereof, of a particular curtailment or limitation on a protected association's earnings in determining whether the curtailment or limitation violates the statute. In one case, a city accused of violating the statute noted that the protected association received only $200 a month in revenues from the customers in the disputed area; the city characterized this amount as negligible and argued that the transfer of those customers to the city would not impair the association's ability to repay FmHA. The court responded, first, that the statute on its face prohibits *any* curtailment or limitation, without regard to amount. Second, accepting the city's argument "would allow the piecemeal erosion of the area served by a rural water association to occur as long as any single attempt would not result in a finding of significant impairment," though the ultimate effect would be violation of the statute's purposes.[10]

The federal courts have also not been willing to allow a city to avoid violating the statute by purchasing some or all of the assets of the

8. *Owasso*, 530 F. Supp. at 823–24 (italics in original).

9. In *City of Madison, Miss. v. Bear Creek Water Ass'n, Inc.*, 816 F.2d 1057, 1059, the court wrote that the statutory language "indicates a congressional mandate that local governments not encroach upon the services provided by such associations, be that encroachment in the form of competing franchises, new or additional permit requirements, or similar means."

The federal courts have refused to extend the federal statute's protections to the following actions: (1) taking water from the same aquifer as a protected association, even if doing so might affect the association's ability to provide service (*Chesapeake Ranch Water Co. v. Board of Commissioners of Calvert County*, 401 F.3d 274 (4th Cir. 2005)); (2) refusing to continue to sell bulk water to a protected association (*Pittsburg County*, 358 F.3d 694).

10. *Moore Bayou*, 628 F. Supp. at 1370.

protected association when the association does not wish to sell those assets—even when the city offers to pay fair value. In one early case, the city sought to condemn assets of the association that were located inside the city, but the federal court of appeals refused to allow the condemnation. Noting that the facilities in question constituted 60 percent of the association's assets and 40 percent of its customers (the most profitable ones), the court wrote:

> Even if fair value is paid for the lost facilities, such an action would inevitably have an adverse effect on the remaining customers of [the association], in the form of lost economies of scale and resulting higher per-user costs. To allow expanding municipalities to "skim the cream" by annexing and condemning those parts of a water association with the highest population density (and thus the lowest per-user cost) would undermine Congress's purpose of facilitating inexpensive water supplies for farmers and other rural residents and protecting those associations' ability to repay their FmHA debts.[11]

[b] Statute's effect on annexations

In the event that a rural utility system meets the qualifications for protection under the federal statute (explored in detail in the following sections), what will be the effect on a North Carolina city planning to annex into the system's service area? To begin with, the statute does not prohibit a city from annexing an area currently being served by, or capable of being served by, a protected water or sewer association. If a city annexes property within a protected service area, however, it may not extend its own utility lines into the area if doing so curtails or limits the protected services of the association. This second point creates at least two potential problems for a North Carolina city.

Fire protection. The city may not be able to provide adequate fire protection by using the lines of the protected association. The federal courts have made it clear that the purpose of the federal loan program is to extend domestic water or sewer service to rural areas—not to provide for a water service adequate for fire protection. As a result, a number of reported decisions have involved associations whose lines

11. *Madison*, 816 F.2d at 1060.

did not in fact supply sufficient fire flow to provide organized fire protection.[12] If a North Carolina city were to find itself in such a situation, it would still be responsible for providing sufficient fire protection in the annexation area. Perhaps a city could meet its fire protection service responsibilities in such an annexation area by providing water through tankers; the North Carolina courts have allowed cities to use tankers until water lines sufficient for fire protection are installed in an annexation area; and, as section 6.04[c] of Volume 3 notes, this solution might legitimately be used for several years.[13] If a city must install water lines to provide fire protection, however, it may not use them to provide domestic water service to the area.[14]

Rate differentials. The rate structure of the rural system may cause property owners in the annexation area to pay significantly higher rates for water or sewer service than those charged by the city. (Such a rate differential is not a sufficient reason to deny the rural association the protection of the federal statute.[15]) In that case, the city will have to take steps—particularly in an involuntary annexation—to ensure that annexed property owners pay water or sewer charges comparable to those paid by its own customers.[16]

If either of the above problems affects a given annexation, the annexing city will almost certainly find it necessary to negotiate some kind of solution with the protected rural association. A city might try,

12. Rural Water Dist. No. 1, Ellsworth County, Kan. v. City of Ellsworth, Kan., 995 F. Supp. 1164 (D. Kan. 1997); Rural Water Sys. No. 1 v. City of Sioux Center, 29 F. Supp. 2d 975 (N.D. Iowa 1998).

13. E.g., Dunn v. City of Charlotte, 284 N.C. 542, 201 S.E.2d 873 (1974) (city to purchase and use two new tankers); *In re* Annexation Ordinance (Winston-Salem), 303 N.C. 220, 278 S.E.2d 224 (1981) (city to continue use of existing tankers and continue practice of contracting with rural fire departments that also have tankers); *In re* Durham Annexation Ordinance, 69 N.C. App. 77, 316 S.E.2d 649 (1984) (city to continue use of tankers).

14. *See* Water Works Dist. No. II of Tangipahoa Parish v. City of Hammond, No. 86-0187, 1989 U.S. Dist. LEXIS 11752 (E.D. La. 1989).

As noted in section 12.02(a) below, over fifty of the protected associations in North Carolina are county water and sewer districts. G.S. 162A-93 protects such districts from competition from cities when territory within a district is annexed by a city, but the statute provides that the protection does not apply if the city is unable to provide fire protection through the city's lines. An annexing city must remember, however, that even if it is permitted to run parallel lines pursuant to this North Carolina statute, the federal statute discussed in this chapter may still prohibit the city from providing domestic water service through those lines.

15. *Rural Water v. Ellsworth*, 995 F. Supp. at 1164.

16. See the discussion of differential utility rates and their effect in an involuntary annexation in Volume 3, section 6.02(i).

for example, to work out an arrangement under which the association waives its rights to particular customers; or a city may attempt to purchase some or all of the association's assets. If these negotiations are unsuccessful, the city may ultimately need to run its own water lines into the area to provide adequate fire flow or find some way to subsidize the rural association's water and sewer rates so that all customers in the city receive utility service at comparable rates.

Section 12.02. What Is a Qualifying Association?

For a rural utility association to qualify for the protections of the federal statute, it must meet three tests, which are considered in the next three subsections.

1. It must be an association within the meaning of the statute.
2. It must have outstanding obligations on loans from FmHA or RD.
3. It must have provided service or made service available to the customers or area in dispute.

[a] Defining an association within the meaning of the statute

Although the language of the statute might lead one to think otherwise, any entity that has been loaned money by FmHA or RD for a water or sewer system meets the first test: it is an association within the meaning of the statute. The potential confusion arises from 7 U.S.C. § 1926(a)(1), the basic authorization to make the federal loans. That subsection authorizes the secretary of agriculture to make rural water or sewer system loans to "associations, including corporations not operated for profit, Indian tribes on Federal and State reservations and other federally recognized Indian tribes, and public and quasi-public agencies." The quoted language can be read as authorizing loans to three types of entities: associations (including nonprofit corporations), Indian tribes, and public and quasi-public agencies. Such a reading is supported by other parts of the statute that differentiate between *associations* and these other types of entities.[17] Under this reading, because Section 1926(b) refers only to *associations*, one might conclude that the protected associations are some subset of those entities to which the

17. For example, 7 U.S.C. Sec. 1926(a)(19)(a) authorizes grants to "associations, units of general local government, nonprofit corporations, and federally recognized Indian tribes."

Department of Agriculture has made water or sewer loans pursuant to Section 1926(a). For example, a reader might conclude that the statute protects private associations but not cities, districts, or other public entities that have borrowed from the department.

The federal courts, however, have not read the statute that way. Rather, they appear to read all the quoted language after the word "including" as modifying the word *association*. That is, nonprofit corporations, Indian tribes, and public agencies are each an example of an association. In *Lexington–South Elkhorn Water District v. City of Wilmore, Kentucky*,[18] both the plaintiff water district and the defendant city had outstanding loans from Farmers' Home. Accordingly, the court held that both entities—each of which was a public agency—were protected associations under the federal statute. This holding accords with the practice of the federal courts generally. Without any discussion of the matter, various federal courts have held that an incorporated village,[19] a variety of public water or sewer districts,[20] and even a county[21] are associations within the meaning of Section 1926(b).

Therefore, if an entity meets the second test—that is, if it has outstanding obligations on a loan made to it by FmHA or RD—it necessarily meets the first test.

As of August 2001, almost one hundred of the North Carolina entities with outstanding FmHA or RD loans were cities or towns. Over fifty were county water and sewer districts, and over thirty were some other form of public agency, such as sanitary districts, metropolitan sewerage districts, metropolitan water districts, or counties. Only about thirty of the entities with outstanding loans were private water or sewer associations or corporations. It is unlikely that the mix of public agencies and private entities has changed dramatically since then.

[b] An outstanding federal loan

The federal statute does not provide permanent protection to protected associations. Several federal courts have made it plain that it protects them only while they remain obligated on any loan made by FmHA or

18. 93 F.3d 230 (6th Cir. 1996).

19. Wayne v. Vill. of Sebring, 36 F.3d 517 (6th Cir. 1994).

20. *E.g.*, Glenpool Util. Serv. Auth. v. Creek County Rural Water Dist. No. 2, 861 F.2d 1211 (10th Cir. 1988); Adams County Reg'l Water Dist. v. Vill. of Manchester, Ohio, 226 F.3d 513 (6th Cir. 2000).

21. Pinehurst Enter., Inc. v. Town of Southern Pines, 690 F. Supp. 444 (M.D. N.C. 1988).

RD.[22] Most federal decisions, although not all, also make it clear that obtaining a federal loan does not allow a protected association to displace a competing service provider whose lines are already in place. This subsection discusses these points and other issues concerned with whether a protected association meets this second test.

U.S.D.A. loans have been retired. Once all such loans are retired, the statutory protection ends and an association is susceptible to competition from a city or other water or sewer utility.[23] (If an association receives a new loan from RD, however, the federal statute again becomes applicable, and the association is protected from competition from the date the new loan is made.[24]) Several federal court decisions have defined the circumstances under which a loan remains protected.

During the mid-1980s Congress directed the Department of Agriculture to sell loans it held from protected associations to third parties. The question then arose: Do the statutory protections remain in place after the loans have been sold? At the time, Congress instructed the department to give the associations the first right to purchase those loans themselves. Concurrently, it directed that Section 1926(b) "shall be applicable to all notes or other obligations sold or intended to be sold" pursuant to the congressional directions.[25] Although the issues arising from these loan sales have been more or less settled and the practical effect of the loan repurchases is almost certainly behind us, Congress might repeat its directions to the department at some future date. It is therefore appropriate to summarize the effect of any loan sale on an association's status under Section 1926(b).

First, if the department sells the loan to a third party, the association remains protected by the statute as long as the loan remains outstanding, even though the federal agency no longer holds it.[26] The courts have agreed that this is the outcome intended by the federal statute quoted above and have noted the policy reasons supporting such an outcome. If the loans are to be attractive to third-party buyers, the statutory protections need to remain in effect. If rural utility systems

22. "Title 7 U.S.C. § 1926(b) is an Act of Congress prohibiting certain activities during the life of loans made pursuant to the Agricultural Act of 1961." Rural Water Dist. No. 3 v. Owasso Util. Auth., 530 F. Supp. 818, 825 (N.D. Okla. 1979) (emphasis added).

23. *E.g.*, Sequoyah County Rural Water Dist. No. 2 v. Town of Muldrow, 191 F.3d 1192 (10th Cir. 1999).

24. *E.g.*, *id.*

25. Agricultural Credit Act of 1981, Pub. L. No. 100–233, § 803(g).

26. Wayne v. Vill. of Sebring, 36 F.3d 517 (6th Cir. 1994); Moongate Water Co., Inc. v. Butterfield Park Mut. Domestic Water Ass'n, 291 F.3d 1262 (10th Cir. 2002).

become susceptible to municipal or private competition once the loans are in third-party hands, potential buyers might be scared off, or might demand such deep discounts from the Department of Agriculture that the loan sale program would fail to reach the deficit-reduction goals Congress intended.[27]

Second, if the department sells the loan to the indebted association and the loan is cancelled, the statutory protections end. This is true even if the association has borrowed money from private sources to finance purchase of the loan. The reasoning behind this conclusion is complicated, but the Fourth Circuit is among the courts that have accepted it, so this is the law in North Carolina.[28]

Applicability of Section 1926 protections to existing facilities of competing entities. Most of the federal courts that have considered the issue have held that Section 1926 does not permit a protected association to displace competing lines that were in place when the U.S.D.A. loan was made. For example, in *Northern Ohio Rural Water v. Erie County Board of County Commissioners*, the county had installed lines in the disputed service area before the protected association obtained its U.S.D.A. loan. The court held that therefore the county was entitled to provide service from those lines even though the U.S.D.A. loan proceeds were to be used to provide service in the same service area.[29] This seems a sensible result, but one federal court of appeals decision appears inconsistent with it. In *Pittsburg County Rural Water District No. 7 v. City of McAlester*, the district had outstanding U.S.D.A. loans from 1967 until 1989 and then again from 1994 on.[30] During the

27. *Sequoyah*, 191 F.3d at 1192.

28. Bell Arthur Water Corp. v. Greenville Util. Comm'n, 173 F.3d 517 (4th Cir. 1999). Other decisions accepting this reasoning are *Scioto County Reg'l Water Dist. No. 1, Auth. v. Scioto Water Inc.*, 103 F.3d 38 (6th Cir. 1996); *Sequoyah*, 191 F.3d at 1192; and *Rural Water Sys. No. 1 v. City of Sioux Center*, 967 F. Supp. 1483 (N.D. Iowa 1997). The one decision that might be thought to be inconsistent with the statement in the text is *City of Grand Junction v. Ute Water Conservancy Dist.*, 900 P.2d 81 (Colo. 1995), which continued the statutory protections even after the district purchased its own debt from FmHA. In that case, however, the loan was not cancelled, and the federal courts each distinguished the case on that basis.

29. *Northern Ohio*, 347 F. Supp. 2d 511 (N.D. Ohio 2004). The court held that it was the county's construction of the lines, and not its subsequent solicitation of customers, that gave it priority. *See also Sioux Center*, 967 F. Supp. 1483 (Association has no rights vis-à-vis areas annexed by city while association had no outstanding FmHA loans.); Vill. of Grifton v. Rural Lorain Co. Water Auth., 419 F.3d 562 (6th Cir. 2005) (Village must install lines in the disputed area to avoid being subjected to statute's protections; merely annexing the area was insufficient.).

30. 358 F.3d 694 (10th Cir. 2004).

intervening period, when the district had no outstanding U.S.D.A. loans, the city extended service to a number of customers within the district. The district court held that the district had no rights under Section 1926 to those customers, but the court of appeals disagreed. Relying on an earlier decision from the same circuit,[31] the court wrote that the "fact that a municipality had provided service to those properties prior to the FMHA loan was no bar in [the earlier case] to claims arising out of a city's service during the period of indebtedness."[32] As noted below, the Fourth Circuit has been unwilling to allow a protected association to use Section 1926 offensively;[33] therefore it may well be that the *Pittsburg County* decision will not be followed in this circuit.

Loans that have been assumed. The protections apply regardless of whether the loan was made directly to the indebted association or to a predecessor association and then assumed by the indebted association. In *CSL Utilities, Inc. v. Jennings Water, Inc.*,[34] Jennings had been formed by the merger of two private water associations, one of which carried an outstanding FmHA loan. Jennings assumed the loan, which remained outstanding at the time of the litigation. The Seventh Circuit panel held that Jennings's protection under the statute dated back to the original loan made to its predecessor association.

Protections apply to entire system. The protections apply to the entire system of the protected association, without regard to which part of the system was constructed or improved with the proceeds of the outstanding loan. In *Bell Arthur Water Corp. v. Greenville Utilities Commission*,[35] Bell Arthur had borrowed money from FmHA in 1993 to extend service to an area not involved in the corporation's litigation with the Greenville Utilities Commission. The utilities commission argued that the statutory protections should extend only to the area serviced through the improvements financed by the 1993 loan and not to the corporation's entire service area. The Fourth Circuit panel rejected that argument, finding no warrant for it in the statute and noting that such an outcome would allow the utilities commission to offer service in areas not covered by the most recent loan to Bell Arthur, thereby skimming off the cream of the corporation's customer base.

31. Sequoyah County Rural Water Dist. No. 2 v. Town of Muldrow, 191 F.3d 1192 (10th Cir. 1999).

32. *Pittsburg County*, 358 F.3d at 712.

33. See section 12.02(c) below, the text following note 60.

34. 16 F.3d 130 (7th Cir. 1993).

35. 173 F.3d 517 (4th Cir. 1999).

Protections only extend to indebted entity. The protections only apply to an entity that is directly indebted to the Department of Agriculture; they do not apply to other entities that may be part of the ultimate security for the debt. In *Pinehurst Enterprises, Inc. v. Town of Southern Pines*,[36] Farmers Home had loaned money to Moore County for a sewage treatment plant. The county had then entered into contracts with a number of collection systems in the county, including Pinehurst Enterprises, intending to use the payments under those contracts to repay the federal loan. When a dispute arose between Pinehurst and the town of Southern Pines over sewer service to a new development, the federal district court held that the statutory protections did not extend to Pinehurst Enterprises. The county was the protected association, and although Pinehurst was a partial source of the money the county would use to repay the loan, it was not itself indebted to the Department of Agriculture.

[c] Providing or making service available

With respect to the first two tests that a rural utilities association must meet to qualify for the protections of Section 1926(b), the federal courts have been clear and consistent. With respect to the third test, however, not all federal circuits agree on the basic standards.[37] Nonetheless, the Fourth Circuit has explicitly chosen among the competing standards, as elaborated in the following passage.

The third test requires that the rural utilities system must have provided service or made service available to the properties or area at issue. If the association currently serves a property, clearly it has provided service to that property.[38] The difficult question involves properties that the association currently does not serve: Has the association

36. 690 F. Supp. 444 (M.D. N.C. 1988).

37. Two courts of appeal have attempted to set out the different standards and show which circuits have embraced which standards. The two attempts, however, show slightly different results. *Compare* Le-Ax Water Dist. v. City of Athens, Ohio, 346 F.3d 701 (6th Cir. 2003) *with* Chesapeake Ranch Water Co. v. Bd. of Comm'rs of Calvert County, 401 F.3d 274 (4th Cir. 2005).

38. In *Moongate Water Co., Inc. v. Butterfield Park Mutual Domestic Water Ass'n*, 291 F.3d 1262 (10th Cir. 2002), the new owner of property refused to pay the fees necessary to join the association and receive service; as a result, the association terminated service to the property. The court held that terminating existing service for nonpayment has no effect on whether the association had made service available to the property; it had.

made service available to such a property or properties? In *Chesapeake Ranch Water Co. v. Board of Commissioners of Calvert County*, the court announced the test to be followed within the Fourth Circuit:

> The test articulated by the Sixth Circuit in *Le-Ax* [*Water District v. City of Athens, Ohio*[39]] is the most stringent, requiring a water association to demonstrate that (1) it is physically capable of serving the area, (2) it has the legal right under state law to do so, and (3) the disputed area is already within the geographic boundaries of the association's franchise area.
>
> We are persuaded that the three-part test articulated by the Sixth Circuit in *Le-Ax* best effectuates Congress' intent in passing § 1926.[40]

The remainder of this subsection discusses this three-part test in detail.

1. *The protected association is physically capable of serving the area.* The federal courts have generally agreed that this standard is met if the protected association has lines close enough to the disputed property or area to extend service to the property or area within a reasonable time. (A number of courts refer to this as the *pipes-in-the-ground* standard.) Obviously, such a standard is very much fact-based, and it is not clear that the federal courts have been consistent with each other in applying it.

First, a number of courts have defined fairly narrowly the requirement that the association's lines be close enough to the disputed property to allow service to be extended to it within a reasonable time. For example, a panel in the Sixth Circuit has written:

> [A number of earlier] cases teach that whether an association has made service available is determined based on the existence of facilities on, or in the proximity of, the location to be served. If an association does not already have service in existence, water lines must either be within or adjacent to the property claimed to be protected by Section 1926(b).[41]

39. 346 F.3d 701 (6th Cir. 2003).
40. *Chesapeake Ranch*, 401 F.3d at 279.
41. Lexington–South Elkhorn Water Dist. v. City of Wilmore, Ky., 93 F.3d 230, 237 (6th Cir. 1996).

In this case, the association seeking statutory protection had lines as close as 150 feet from one disputed property and 500 to 2,000 feet from other disputed properties. The court held that the lines did not meet the pipes-in-the-ground standard and that the association therefore had not made service available to the disputed properties.

The Tenth Circuit, on the other hand, has suggested in one case that lines within 200 feet were close enough to qualify for the standard;[42] and in another case, a panel from that circuit found that lines between 2,200 and 4,400 feet from the disputed property adequately met the test of service availability.[43] In addition, the Fifth Circuit has held that a water corporation whose lines served a subdivision adjacent to a disputed subdivision had made service available to the disputed subdivision.[44]

These two circuits seemed more interested in the time it would take to extend service to a particular property from the association's existing lines than in the lines' linear distance from the property. The association whose existing lines were 2,200 to 4,400 feet from the disputed property already had the necessary easements to extend its lines and had informed the court that the work could be done in three to seven days.[45] The court thought that a reasonable amount of time. An approach that pays more attention to the time an association seeking protection needs to extend service to a particular property seems more sympathetic to the purposes of Section 1926(b) than one that looks solely at the distance of existing lines from the property; and it appears that the Fourth Circuit takes this more sympathetic approach. In *Bell Arthur Water Corp. v. Greenville Utilities Commission*, the water corporation already had a six-inch water main running through the proposed development that was in dispute; but it acknowledged that a fourteen-inch line was necessary to serve the development adequately. Although the court seemed willing to give the corporation several

42. Sequoyah County Rural Water Dist. No. 2 v. Town of Muldrow, 191 F.3d 1192 (10th Cir. 1999).

43. Rural Water Dist. No. 1, Ellsworth County, Kan. v. City of Wilson, Kan., 243 F.3d 1263 (10th Cir. 2001).

44. North Alamo Water Supply Corp. v. City of San Juan, Texas, 90 F.3d 910 (5th Cir. 1996). In addition, in *North Shelby Water Co. v. Shelbyville Municipal Water and Sewer Commission*, 803 F. Supp. 15 (E.D. Ky. 1992), the court held that when the water company had lines across the road from the disputed property, it had made service available.

45. *See* Rural Water Dist. No. 1, Ellsworth County, Kansas, v. City of Wilson, Kansas, 29 F. Supp. 2d 1238 (D. Kan. 1998).

months to get the permits and financing necessary to extend the larger line, the corporation's complete inaction caused it to forfeit whatever rights it might have had.[46]

A second issue is whether the service made available by the protected association is adequate for the needs of the disputed customer. As noted just above, an association's six-inch line through a disputed property did not itself meet the third test because the property required a twelve- or fourteen-inch line. The association was therefore required to provide the necessary level of service within a reasonable time.[47] It is clear, however, that the mere fact that an association does not have an adequate line in place at present does not mean it has not made service available. The Fourth Circuit was willing to give the water corporation in *Bell Arthur* some months to construct the necessary line, and the Tenth Circuit has made the same accommodation.[48]

If the association provides adequate water for domestic purposes, however, its failure to provide sufficient fire flow for fire protection is irrelevant. As noted earlier, the federal program is intended to provide rural communities with domestic water, not fire protection; an association's failure to provide sufficient fire flow for fire protection does not cause it to lose the protections of Section 1926(b).[49]

46. "We hold that Bell Arthur's inadequate six-inch pipe in the ground coupled with only a general, unfulfilled intent to provide the necessary fourteen-inch pipe sometime in the future does not amount to 'service provided or made available.'" *Bell Arthur*, 173 F.3d 517, 526 (4th Cir. 1999).

47. *But see* Adams County Reg'l Water Dist. v. Vill. of Manchester, Ohio, 226 F.3d 513 (6th Cir. 2000). In that case, the water district supplied water to an incorporated village but was having supply problems. Therefore it had advised the village to suspend adding any new customers to the system, a prohibition that lasted two years. In response, the village contracted to buy wholesale water from another municipality, and the Sixth Circuit held that such a transaction violated the federal statute. The court stated that the apparent lack of capacity of the water district might be a breach of the district's contract with its wholesale customer, but that did not justify that customer's seeking an alternative source of supply.

48. In *Pittsburg County Rural Water Dist. No. 7 v. City of McAlester*, 211 F.3d 1279, 2000 WL 525942 (10th Cir. 2000) (unpublished), the district court had held against the association seeking protection because it did not, at the time the dispute arose, have lines in place adequate to serve the industrial park at issue. The court of appeals reversed, holding this was an incorrect standard. If the district could have extended the necessary lines within a reasonable time, as determined by the trial court, it would meet the lines-in-the-ground test.

49. Rural Water Dist. No. 1, Ellsworth County, Kan., v. City of Ellsworth, Kan., 995 F. Supp. 1164 (D. Kan. 1997); Rural Water Sys. No. 1 v. City of Sioux Center, 29 F. Supp. 2d 975 (N.D. Iowa 1998).

Third, any differential in rates between the protected association and a potential competitor is irrelevant. A number of cases have involved associations that charged higher rates than the competing city, and the courts have consistently refused to allow that fact to undermine the association's position under Section 1926(b).[50] It may be, however, that outrageously excessive connection or extension costs imposed by a protected association would cause it to lose the statute's protection. In *Rural Water District No. 1, Ellsworth County, Kansas v. City of Wilson, Kansas*,[51] the water district was prepared to extend its lines to the disputed property within three to seven days, even though its existing lines were from 2,200 to 4,400 feet away. The district court (and the court of appeals) thought the district's timing was reasonable, but the trial court balked at the district's proposal to impose the entire $32,000 cost of the extension onto the property owner. (The competing city already had a line at the property.) Although the district's rates were not relevant to whether it had made service available to the property, it could not "charge unreasonably high rates or fees while claiming the statute's protection."[52] The federal court of appeals agreed that the cost of the extension was relevant in determining whether the district had made service available, but the court was unwilling to affirm the district court's conclusion that $32,000 was excessive. It remanded the case, directing the trial court to be more specific about why the amount was excessive, using factors developed by the Kansas courts for that purpose.[53] On remand, the trial court examined the service the district would provide in exchange for the $32,000 cost—extension of service to two duplexes—and the practices followed in other districts in Kansas; these would have either allowed property owners to recoup most of the extension cost as other customers connected to the line or released the properties to the competing city, which was much closer. The court concluded that the extension cost was in fact unreasonable

50. *E.g.*, *Rural Water v. Ellsworth*, 995 F. Supp. at 1164; Jennings Water, Inc. v. City of North Vernon, Ind., 682 F. Supp. 421 (S.D. Ind. 1988).

51. 29 F. Supp. 2d 1238 (D. Kan. 1998).

52. *Id.* at 1247.

53. Rural Water Dist. No. 1, Ellsworth County, Kan., v. City of Wilson, 243 F.3d 1263 (10th Cir. 2001). *See also Pittsburg*, 211 F.3d 1279, 2000 WL 525942, at *n 7 (in which the court noted that "[w]hile certainly a relevant factor for determining the District's ability to provide service in a reasonable time, requiring the customer to foot the bill for basic utility infrastructure is not entirely unheard of, at least in regard to new developments, nor is it per se unreasonable.").

and therefore denied the statutory protections to the district.[54] There do not appear to be any North Carolina cases a federal court could use to determine whether an allegedly excessive connection charge was unreasonable in this state, but the Kansas litigation does suggest that such an allegation might help a competitor deprive an association of the protection of Section 1926(b).[55]

Finally, as the cases on rates (and several other cases) indicate, an individual customer's preferences are irrelevant to whether a protected association is entitled to serve that customer.[56]

2. *The protected association is legally capable of serving the area.* This second standard should rarely, if ever, disqualify a protected association in North Carolina. In fact, it was adopted in both the Sixth and Fourth Circuits in lieu of a more stringent test requiring that the protected association be under a *legal duty* to serve the disputed property or area. The court in *Chesapeake Ranch* explicitly rejected use of this legal-duty standard in the Fourth Circuit.

In North Carolina associations that have borrowed from U.S.D.A. have included cities and towns, counties, various sorts of special districts, water and sewer authorities, and nonprofit water or sewer corporations. Cities and towns, as well as counties, have express legisla-

54. Rural Water Dist. No. 1, Ellsworth County, Kan. v. City of Wilson, Kan., 211 F. Supp. 2d 1324 (D. Kan. 2002).

The Tenth Circuit reaffirmed the approach taken in *Wilson* in *Pittsburg County*:

> We reaffirm this approach today. This manner of factoring in cost, in addition to being binding circuit law, is a sensible rule as a policy matter. We mitigate the tendency of monopolists to price exorbitantly by conditioning the right to earn the governmentally sanctioned monopolist status on the water association's employing prices that, even if high, are not prohibitive. The doctrine's aim is to help avoid the unattractive scenario of water remaining unavailable as a practical matter due to excessively high monopolistic pricing without legal recourse for consumers and with no additional market entry by a supplier in sight.

358 F.3d at 719.

55. *See also* Moongate Water Co., Inc. v. Butterfield Park Mut. Domestic Water Ass'n, 125 F. Supp. 2d 1304 (D. N.M. 2000) (association's requirement that customer give association easement for eight-inch water line not sufficiently onerous to hold that association had not made service available).

56. *E.g.*, Adams County Reg'l Water Dist. v. Vill. of Manchester, Ohio, 226 F.3d 513 (6th Cir. 2000) (wholesale customer not allowed to connect with alternative supplier); Jennings Water, Inc. v. City of North Vernon, Ind., 682 F. Supp. 421 (S.D. Ind. 1988) (wholesale customer not allowed to connect with alternative supplier); Rural Water Dist. No. 1, Ellsworth County, Kan., v. City of Ellsworth, Kan., 995 F. Supp. 1164 (D. Kan. 1997) (that district is more expensive and customer would prefer city is irrelevant to district's protection under federal statute).

tive authority to provide service both inside and outside their borders,[57] as do the various sorts of special districts.[58] Water and sewer authorities do not have defined territorial service areas;[59] and nonprofit corporations, which are not subject to North Carolina Utilities Commission regulation, may serve customers wherever they please unless limited by their charters or by-laws.[60]

3. *The disputed property or area is within the boundaries of the protected association's franchise area.* In *Le-Ax* the district—the protected association—was attempting to serve an extraterritorial area that was adjacent to one of its existing lines. The Sixth Circuit held that the federal statute's purpose was to offer a protected association a defense against another entity's invasion of its service area and attempting to steal customers. In *Le-Ax*, however, the district was attempting to use the statute offensively, that is, to win a competition for customers outside its borders in an area not yet served by any utility provider. The court held the statute was not intended to permit such a use. Similarly, in *Chesapeake Ranch* the association was asserting the exclusive right to serve an area that was just outside its franchised service area. (In Maryland, counties grant specific franchise areas to rural water companies.) The Fourth Circuit expressly followed the Sixth Circuit's lead, holding that this was an attempt to use the federal statute offensively and was therefore not permitted.

How might this third standard play out in North Carolina? It apparently means that a city or town, county, or special district—all of which have territorial boundaries—will generally not be able to use the federal statute to win control of extraterritorial customers. It is less clear, though, how the standard might apply to water and sewer authorities or nonprofit corporations. As noted above, these sorts of entities do not have statutorily defined service areas; thus it is not apparent how a court would distinguish between an offensive and a defensive use of the federal statute.

57. N.C. Gen. Stat. § 160A-312(a), for cities, and 153A-275(a), for counties (hereinafter G.S.).

58. G.S. 130A-55(8b.) (sanitary districts); G.S. 162A-87.3 (county water and sewer districts); G.S. 162A-69(5) (metropolitan sewerage districts); and G.S. 162A-36(a)(5) (metropolitan water districts).

59. G.S. 162A-6(a)(5).

60. Bell Arthur Water Corp. v. Greenville Util. Comm'n, 173 F.3d 517, 526 (4th Cir. 1999).

Section 12.03. Remedial Issues

It is clear from the foregoing discussion that Section 1926(b) can create difficulties for a city undertaking an annexation, especially an involuntary annexation. If the city recognizes its limits under the federal statute and does not extend service to an area it has annexed because that area is served by a protected association, owners of annexed property may argue that the city has not extended utility service to them on the same basis as it is provided to residents in the city; or they may argue that the city has not extended fire protection to the annexed property on the same basis as that provided in the city. As suggested in section 12.01[b], the federal protections extended to associations with outstanding loans may require a city to negotiate with the protected association for acquisition of its lines. If those negotiations are unsuccessful, the city may have to make other arrangement to ensure that the association's customers within the annexation area do not pay utility rates substantially higher than those paid by other city residents. In a worst-case scenario, the city may have to lay parallel lines to provide adequate fire flow for fire protection but be unable to use those lines to provide domestic water.

If a city reacts to these difficulties by improperly extending, or attempting to extend, service to a customer of a protected association, the association has several remedies.[61] First, it can obtain a court order directing the city to disconnect service from any customer that rightly belongs to the association.[62] Second, if the lines serving a customer were constructed by the customer (or the customer's predecessor in title) and then dedicated to the city, a court might direct that the city transfer title to the lines to the protected association.[63] Third, some

61. A protected association would sue to enforce Section 1926 pursuant to 42 U.S.C. § 1983. *See* Pittsburg County Rural Water Dist. No. 7 v. City of McAlester, 358 F.3d 694 (10th Cir. 2004). In North Carolina the statute of limitations for such a suit is three years. *See, e.g.*, Lugo v. City of Charlotte, 577 F. Supp. 988 (W.D.N.C. 1984).

62. *See e.g.*, North Alamo Water Supply Corp. v. City of San Juan, Tex., 90 F.3d 910 (5th Cir. 1996); Rural Water Sys. No. 1 v. City of Sioux Center, 29 F. Supp. 2d 975 (N.D. Iowa 1998).

63. *See e.g.*, *North Alamo*, 90 F.3d at 910. The court also noted that if the city had spent its own funds to construct the lines, the protected association would have to compensate the city. In *Glenpool Util. Serv. Auth. v. Creek County Rural Water Dist. No. 2*, 956 F.2d 277, 1992 U.S. App. LEXIS 3369 (10th Cir. 1992) (unpublished), the court refused the water district's request to impose a constructive trust on a city water line constructed into the district's service area. The court noted that the city itself had been

courts have suggested the possibility of money damages, should the association be able to show a loss in revenues from the city's improper service.[64] Again, the end result of these remedies will be to force the city to negotiate some kind of settlement with the association.

an FmHA borrower when the line was constructed and that it needed the line for fire protection. Even so, the court characterized the issue as a "close question" (*id.* at *10).

64. Sequoyah County Rural Water Dist. No. 2 v. Town of Muldrow, 191 F.3d 1192 (10th Cir. 1999).

13

Annexation and Election Issues

13

Annexation and Election Issues

Section 13.01. The Voting Rights Act

Cities in forty North Carolina counties must seek the approval of the U.S. Department of Justice before their annexations can become fully effective. This section discusses and summarizes that requirement.[1]

[a] The preclearance requirement

Section 5 of the federal Voting Rights Act of 1965 provides that when a local government covered by Section 5 enacts or seeks to administer a change in "any voting qualification or prerequisite to voting, or standard, practice, or procedure with respect to voting," the change must be precleared by the Attorney General of the United States *before* it can be put into effect; alternatively, it may be approved in advance by the United States District Court for the District of Columbia.[2] To be approved, the change must meet the following standard: it will have neither the purpose nor the effect of denying or abridging any person's right to vote on account of race or color.[3]

The U.S. Supreme Court has held that an annexation is a change that triggers this preclearance requirement,[4] and therefore any annexation undertaken by a city located in a county covered by Section 5 must be precleared by the U.S. Attorney General or approved by the District

1. The League of Municipalities' annexation handbooks include an excellent chapter on preclearance by DeWitt McCarley, city attorney in Charlotte. This chapter is intended to complement that discussion and by no means replaces it, especially the very useful details on submissions to the federal Department of Justice. See League of Municipalities (NCLM), MECHANICS OF ANNEXATION (UNDER 5,000 POPULATION and 5,000 OR MORE POPULATION), available from NCLM, PO Box 3069, Raleigh, NC 27602 or through its Web site: http://www.nclm.org/Pubs/pub-link.html (last visited May 16, 2002).

2. 42 U.S.C. § 1973c.

3. *Id.*; 28 C.F.R. § 51.52 (2001).

4. "[C]hanging boundary lines by annexations which enlarge the city's number of eligible voters also constitutes a change of a 'standard, practice, or procedure with respect to voting.'" Perkins v. Matthews, 400 U.S. 379, 388 (1971).

Court for the District of Columbia before residents of the annexation area can participate in city elections. Section 5 of the Voting Rights Act applies to the forty counties in North Carolina listed in Table 13.1.[5]

[b] Preclearance and annexation

In *Perkins v. Matthews* the U.S. Supreme Court identified at least two ways in which an annexation can affect voting: first, an annexation determines who may vote in city elections (and who may not); second, an annexation dilutes the votes of persons who already live within the city's boundaries.[6] For example, in a city in which voting has historically been polarized by race, annexation may dilute minority voting power. If the city takes no steps to neutralize, to the extent possible, any adverse effects on its minority citizens, the Attorney General will object to the annexation and the District Court will refuse to approve the annexation. This occurred in *City of Petersburg v. United States*[7] when the Virginia city annexed fourteen square miles, bringing in approximately seven thousand new city residents, nearly all of them white. Before the annexation, the city's population was 56 percent black and 44 percent white; after the annexation it was 47 percent black and 53 percent white. Furthermore, the court's analysis of past elections "clearly indicates that almost total bloc voting by race has been the well established pattern in Petersburg. . . . [T]he vote in precincts which are racially identifiable as being almost completely black or white has been overwhelmingly along racial lines."[8] When the city initially refused to make any change in its governing board structure to neutralize the adverse effects on its black voters, the Attorney General objected to the annexation. The city responded by bringing an action before the District Court for the District of Columbia, which held that the city had failed to meet the burden of showing that the annexation did not have the effect of denying the right to vote on account of race.

What is such a city to do to achieve federal approval of its annexation? Basically, it must examine, and if possible adopt, changes in the structure of its governing board that will maximize the ability of

5. The covered counties are listed in Appendix to PART 51–JURISDICTIONS COVERED UNDER SECTION 4(B) OF THE VOTING RIGHTS ACT, AS AMENDED, 28 C.F.R. Ch. 1 (July 1, 2000 edition).

6. *Perkins*, 400 U.S. at 388.

7. 354 F. Supp. 1021 (D.D.C. 1972), *aff'd* [by memorandum decision] 410 U.S. 962, 412 U.S. 901 (1973).

8. *Id.*, at 1025.

Table 13.1

North Carolina Counties Covered by Section 5 of the Voting Rights Act of 1965

Anson	Edgecombe	Hoke	Person
Beaufort	Franklin	Jackson	Pitt
Bertie	Gaston	Lee	Robeson
Bladen	Gates	Lenoir	Rockingham
Camden	Granville	Martin	Scotland
Caswell	Greene	Nash	Union
Chowan	Guilford	Northampton	Vance
Cleveland	Halifax	Onslow	Washington
Craven	Harnett	Pasquotank	Wayne
Cumberland	Hertford	Perquimans	Wilson

minority voters to elect minority members to the governing board in a proportion roughly equal to their representation in the city's population. Most often, this has meant that cities with at-large election systems have had to shift to some kind of district election system. It might also cause a city with some combination of district and at-large representation on its council to reduce or eliminate the at-large representation. Indeed, because the Voting Rights Act has been in existence for more than thirty-five years, and has been clearly applicable to annexations for more than thirty years, many of these shifts have already taken place.

It is important to stress that the voting system changes made to secure preclearance need not result in retaining for minority voters the same proportion of governing board representation that they held *before* the annexation. Such a requirement might make it impossible for a city to ever complete an annexation of a predominantly white area. Rather, the city is responsible for devising a voting system that gives its minority population a realistic opportunity to elect members to the governing board in numbers roughly proportional to their population percentage in the city *after* the annexation. The U.S. Supreme Court made this point explicitly in a decision involving the city of Richmond, Virginia.

> We cannot accept the position that such a single-member ward system would nevertheless have the effect of denying or abridging the right to vote because Negroes would constitute a lesser proportion of the population after the annexation than before and, given racial bloc voting, would have fewer seats on

> the city council. If a city having a ward system for the election of a nine-man council annexes a largely white area, the wards are fairly redrawn, and as a result Negroes have only two rather than the four seats they had before, these facts alone do not demonstrate that the annexation has the defect of denying or abridging the right to vote. As long as the ward system fairly reflects the strength of the Negro community as it exists after the annexation, we cannot hold, without more specific legislative directions, that such an annexation is nevertheless barred by § 5. It is true that the black community, if there is racial bloc voting, will command fewer seats on the city council; and the annexation will have effected a decline in the Negroes' relative influence in the city. But a different city council and an enlarged city are involved after the annexation. Furthermore, Negro power in the new city is not undervalued, and Negroes will not be underrepresented on the council.[9]

If a city completes an annexation pursuant to state law but then cannot achieve federal approval of the annexation, that failure does not invalidate the annexation. Rather, the annexation stands, in the sense that the properties annexed are entitled to city services and become responsible for paying city taxes. But residents of the annexation area are barred from any participation in city elections, either voting or running for city office.[10] (The same exclusion applies if an annexation is pending before the Attorney General or the District Court at the time of a city election.[11]) Until the annexation is precleared by the Attorney General or approved by the court, the city is required to use its preannexation boundaries as the basis for city elections. This is obviously an untenable situation in the long term; and therefore the city, as a practical matter, will have to make the modifications in its governing board election system needed to achieve federal approval.

9. City of Richmond v. United States, 422 U.S. 358, 370–71 (1975).

10. Dotson v. City of Indianola, 514 F. Supp. 397 (N.D. Miss. 1981) (Because a series of annexations had not received preclearance, the court ordered that all city elections be conducted on the basis of preannexation boundaries until preclearance is achieved.). *See* McDowell v. Edmisten, 523 F. Supp. 416 (E.D.N.C. 1981) (After Justice Department refused to grant preclearance to 1979 and 1980 annexations, rendering residents of annexation area ineligible to vote in city elections, the court refused to enjoin 1981 municipal election.).

11. Moore v. Swinson, 58 N.C. App. 714, 294 S.E.2d 381 (1982) (residents of annexation area not allowed to vote in city bond referendum because annexation not yet precleared, even though annexation otherwise effective).

The preclearance requirement applies to all annexations in the covered counties, regardless of the procedure used to effect the annexation, including legislative annexations. But what if the land in an annexation is vacant, or is used solely for industrial or commercial purposes? If the city gains no new residents from the annexation, is preclearance still required? For vacant land, the answer is frequently yes, while in annexations of commercial or industrial property the city may wish to seek preclearance even though it is not required. Federal Department of Justice regulations require preclearance whenever an annexation alters or is "calculated to alter the composition of a jurisdiction's electorate."[12] Even annexation of currently uninhabited property might be calculated to alter the composition of the city's electorate if the property is likely to be developed in the reasonably foreseeable future. Even if an annexation area is used entirely for industrial, commercial, or other nonresidential purposes or includes vacant property that will be developed exclusively for nonresidential use, the city may wish to seek preclearance in order to be protected against future challenge. The Department of Justice permits a city to submit a short preclearance form for just such annexations.[13]

[c] Preclearance procedures

The North Carolina League of Municipalities annexation handbooks describe in detail the material to be included in a preclearance submission to the Department of Justice, and so we will not repeat that discussion here, except to make two points.

First, although federal regulations permit the submission to be made by "the chief legal officer or other appropriate official" of the submitting city, G.S. 120-30.9F directs that in North Carolina the city attorney make submissions on behalf of the city.

Second, because a failure to achieve preclearance will affect the voting rights of residents of the annexation area, a city should submit its request in plenty of time for the Department of Justice to grant preclearance and allow new residents to vote in all city elections that occur after the effective date of the annexation. The department will not act on an annexation submission until the ordinance has been adopted, but the city should submit its materials promptly thereafter. It is not necessary to wait until the ordinance becomes effective under state law. In fact, G.S. 120-

12. 28 C.F.R. § 51.61(a) (2001).

13. The content for a short form submission is set out in the preclearance chapter in the League of Municipalities' annexation handbooks, *supra*, note 1.

30.9F requires that an annexation submission be made within the thirty days following adoption of the ordinance unless the city has one or more annexation submissions pending before the Department of Justice. The department has sixty days from the time it receives a submission to respond, but this period can in effect be doubled if the department needs further information from the city. The department's usual practice is to give preclearance at the end of the sixty-day period. A city subject to Section 5 therefore needs to set the effective date of the annexation far enough after the ordinance is adopted to allow adequate time for the Department of Justice to consider and preclear the submission.

Section 13.02. The Effect of Annexation on Electoral Districts

If a city uses electoral districts to elect some or all members of its city council, it will have to amend the boundaries of one or more districts when new areas are annexed, especially areas that include residential property or property that may be developed for residences. Occasionally an annexation, or the cumulative effect of several annexations, requires the city to undertake a general redrawing of its electoral district boundaries.

[a] Assigning annexation areas to electoral districts

Even if no redrawing of boundaries is necessary, an annexation area must be attached to one or more electoral districts so that residents of the annexation area can vote or run for city council positions allocated to districts. Some cities assign the area to a district or districts in the annexation ordinance itself. Others adopt a separate resolution. In either case, it is easiest to enact such changes when the annexation ordinance is adopted.

[b] Redistricting

A city's need and authority to undertake a general redrawing of district lines because of one or more annexations depends, first, on the kind of districts the city uses.[14] There are generally three types of city electoral

14. An excellent summary of the law of redistricting, in the context of the 2000 census, is Robert P. Joyce, *Redistricting for Local Governments after the 2000 Census*, POPULAR GOVERNMENT (Spring 2001): 2–15.

districts. In all three types, candidates for council seats are required to live in the district they wish to represent; the differences among the districts concern which residents are entitled to vote for candidates for a particular district seat. If a city uses *residence districts*, all the city's voters vote for each seat. If a city uses *single-member districts*, only those voters living in the district can vote for that seat. If a city uses *blended districts*, only voters who live in the district can vote to select district candidates in the primary election, but voters throughout the city vote for them in the general election. No matter which form of district a city uses, state law *permits* the city council to redraw district lines because of annexations. Furthermore, in a city that uses single-member or blended districts, the federal constitution may *require* a city to redraw district lines when one or more annexations cause imbalances among the existing districts that exceed constitutional tolerances. But if a city uses residence districts only, federal constitutional rules do not apply,[15] and a city may leave existing district lines unchanged, even if the population imbalance among districts becomes significant.

The federal courts have not required that the population of each electoral district be exactly equal; as the U.S. Supreme Court has written, "[m]athematical exactness or precision is hardly a workable constitutional requirement."[16] Rather, the federal courts have developed a working rule that accepts a certain degree of deviation from exact equality. First, the population of the city is divided by the number of district council seats; the result is the size of the ideal district. Next, the percentages by which the smallest and largest districts deviate from the ideal size are calculated and then added together. For example, if the ideal district has 5,000 residents and the smallest district has 4,850 residents, the latter deviates from the ideal by 150 residents or 3 percent; if the largest district has 5,200 residents, it deviates from the ideal by 200 residents or 4 percent. The resulting total deviation is 7 percent. If the total deviation is less than 10 percent, the city is "entitled to a presumption that the apportionment plan was the result of an honest and good faith effort to construct districts . . . as nearly of equal population as is practicable."[17] A total deviation of 10 percent or more, however, "establishes a *prima facie* violation of the one person, one vote principle [and] . . . the burden of proof shifts to the [city] to justify the deviations by showing a rational and legitimate [city] policy for the districts"[18] —

15. Dusch v. Davis, 387 U.S. 112 (1967).
16. Reynolds v. Sims, 377 U.S. 533, 577 (1964).
17. Daly v. Hunt, 93 F.3d 1212, 1220 (4th Cir. 1996) (quoting, in part, *id.*)
18. *Daly*, 93 F.3d at 1220.

which is very difficult to do. As a practical matter, the courts will accept a total deviation between districts up to 10 percent, but once it reaches 10 percent the city is under a federal constitutional requirement to redraw district lines.

A city's statutory authority to redraw electoral district boundaries is found in G.S. 160A-23(b). That subsection sets out a subtle set of authorizations for a city council to redraw district boundaries.

First, if district boundaries are set out in the city's charter and the charter says nothing about revising those boundaries (as most charters do not), the statute permits a council to revise district boundaries only (1) to account for territory added to the city by annexation (or removed from the city by legislative deannexation) or (2) to correct population imbalances among the districts caused by a new federal census or by one or more annexations or deannexations. Some city attorneys take the position that the district population imbalances referred to in the statute are only those that cause the districts to no longer meet the federal constitutional requirements. Therefore, they believe, the authorization to redraw district boundaries only applies if the combined deviation of the smallest and largest districts exceeds 10 percent. The statute, however, does not specifically so limit the city council's authority, and other city attorneys believe that their cities may redraw district lines when imbalances are less than 10 percent.

Second, in cities where district boundaries are not set out in the charter, the first sentence of G.S. 160A-23(b) simply gives the city the authority to revise district boundaries "from time to time." In such a city, the city council is thus not limited to revising district lines to account for new annexations or to correct population imbalances, although it may do so for those reasons. Furthermore, because the statutory language about correcting population imbalances applies only to cities whose charters set out district boundaries, the councils in this second group of cities unquestionably have the authority to correct imbalances of less than 10 percent.

Section 13.03. Voting and Running for Office

Once an annexation becomes effective and has been precleared by the U.S. Department of Justice (if preclearance is required), residents of the annexation area are city residents and are presumably eligible to vote in city elections and run for city office. If the effective date of the annexation, or the preclearance, however, falls only shortly before a particular city election, questions about the eligibility of new residents to vote or run for office may arise. This section explores those questions.

[a] Voter registration

G.S. Chapter 163 includes two sections that create three different procedures under which residents of annexation areas may be registered to vote in city elections. All three will be described here, although a county or municipal board of elections is almost certain to use only the first of the three. That method may be used at any time (rather than only just before a scheduled city election) and permits a list of registered voters to be prepared more quickly than the other two methods.

Activating voters. G.S. 163-288.1 allows a board of elections to *activate* as city voters those residents of the annexation area who are already registered to vote. Shortly after the annexation ordinance is adopted, the annexing city must deliver a map of the annexation area to the board of elections that conducts the city's elections. The board of elections must then activate as city voters each currently registered voter who is shown on the county registration books as living within the annexation area and send notice of this activation to each such voter. (Obviously, the activation process will be assisted if the city's map of the annexation area shows, to the extent possible, the numerical range of street addresses on each residential street, or part of the street, included in the annexation area.) The statute requires the annexing city to pay the costs associated with activating voters under this procedure. Because, unlike the two methods described below, activation does not require the board of elections to observe statutory timelines or provide public notice before compiling the voter lists, this is the fastest way to register newly annexed voters for city elections. Indeed, some boards of election begin the activation process before the annexation becomes effective, so that the registration lists are already current on the effective date.

Registration list. G.S. 163-288.2 sets out two additional methods by which persons resident in an annexation area become eligible to vote in city elections. *Method A*, summarized in this paragraph, assumes that the board will undertake registration pursuant to this method only in the weeks just before a city election or referendum. The appropriate board of elections first prepares a list of the currently registered voters who, to the best of its knowledge, are residents of the annexation area. The board then makes this list available for public inspection in its office for a two-week period ending exactly twenty-five days before the day of the next scheduled city election. (This time requirement demonstrates that the legislature intended the method to be used only shortly before a scheduled election.) The board must also provide at least a week's public notice that the list will be available by posting notice in the annexation area; it may also publish a notice in area newspapers. During the two-week period, any voter who resides in the annexation area may add his or her name to the board of election's list. Apparently, only people whose names are on the list when the two-week period is over are entitled to vote in the next city election. This procedure takes at least three weeks from the time the registration list is prepared and the notice is posted.

New registration. G.S. 163-288.2 also includes, as *Method B*, provision for an entirely new registration of voters in the annexation area. The statute assumes that this method, like Method A, will be used only in the weeks shortly before a city election or referendum. This special registration of voters is to take place over a two-week period ending exactly twenty-five days before the day of the next scheduled city election. The statute specifies how notice of the special registration period is to be given and where the registration records are to be located during that period. Like Method A, this method requires at least three weeks to accomplish—one week for the notice and two weeks for the registration itself.

Once a person's registration has been activated for city elections by one of these three methods, G.S. Chapter 163 permits that person to vote in city elections.

[b] Running for city office

Even if a person whose home is being annexed becomes a city resident in time to vote in a city election, that doesn't clearly settle the matter of whether he or she also qualifies to run for city office in that election. G.S. 163-294.2 prohibits a board of elections from accepting a notice of candidacy from any person not registered to vote in the city at the time the notice is filed.[19] (Regardless of the form of city elections used, the

19. N.C. GEN. STAT. § 163-294.2 applies only to city elections conducted on a nonpartisan basis. Reading G.S. 163-291, which requires cities conducting partisan elections for city council to follow the procedures applicable to electing county officials, together with G.S. 163-106(g), which applies to county elections, makes it clear that the statutory requirement of current voter registration also applies in city elections conducted on a partisan basis.

filing period for city council and mayor ends at 12:00 noon on the first Friday in August preceding the election.) Thus, even if an annexation becomes effective in time for area residents to vote in the next city election, the statute seems to require that the annexation become effective before the closing of the filing period for city office in order for any of those persons to run for city office in that election. The statute is not, however, implemented in this literal manner.

In 1992, the North Carolina supreme court held that the so-called "resign to run" law imposed an unconstitutional restriction on the right to run for office.[20] The statute in question required an officeholder who wished to file as a candidate for a different elective office to resign from his or her current office before filing for the new office; the court held this was an invalid attempt to impose qualifications for elective office additional to those set out in the state constitution. In the next year, a special deputy attorney general advised a county supervisor of elections that he interpreted the case as partially invalidating the requirement in G.S. 163-294.2 that a candidate be eligible to vote for an office at the time of filing.[21] Rather, he argued, if the person will be eligible to vote for the office on Election Day, he or she must be allowed to file as a candidate for the office during the filing period. As a result, the State Board of Elections now advises local boards of elections to accept *conditional* notices of candidacy from persons who assert that they will be eligible to vote for a city office by the time of the election.[22] If such a person is in fact eligible to vote by Election Day, his or her name will appear on the ballot. That practice clearly would cover residents of an area in which annexation (or preclearance) becomes effective in time to allow them to vote in a city election.

20. Moore v. Knightdale Board of Elections, 331 N.C. 1, 413 S.E.2d 541 (1992).

21. Letter from Charles M. Hensey to Cherie Poucher, Supervisor, Wake County Board of Elections, 24 August 1993. A copy of the letter is on file with the author.

22. Conversation of the author with Gary O. Bartlett, Executive Secretary, State Board of Elections, 9 November 2001.

14

City Revenues

14

City Revenues

This chapter addresses the question of when a city can expect to receive additional revenues because of an annexation and what steps, if any, a city should take to ensure receipt of those revenues.

Section 14.01. Property Taxes

[a] In general

Until 1975, a city received no property tax revenue from a newly annexed area until the first full fiscal year beginning after the annexation's effective date. This meant that property could be within a city, and receiving city services, for up to a year before taxes could be levied against it. In 1975 the General Assembly enacted legislation that sought to prorate the city taxes on newly annexed property; that first effort was remarkably complicated and was replaced two years later by the current law, found in G.S. 160A-58.10. This statute applies to all voluntary and involuntary annexations, but it does not apply to a legislative annexation unless the legislation so specifies (which it normally does).

Calculating the prorated tax. G.S. 160A-58.10 establishes a system under which annexed property will, in most cases, be liable for some portion of the city taxes levied for the fiscal year in which the annexation takes place. Under the statute, annexed property is liable for city taxes for all full calendar months remaining in the fiscal year on the effective date of annexation. If there are nine full calendar months left in the fiscal year on the effective date, the property is liable for nine months of tax; if there are four months left, it is liable for four months; and so on. More specifically, tax officials first calculate the amount of tax that would have been due on an annexed parcel had it been in the city for the full fiscal year. They then construct a fraction in which the denominator is twelve and the numerator is the number of full calendar months remaining in the fiscal year as of the effective date of annexation. This calculated fraction is then multiplied against the full-year tax liability; the result is the property's prorated tax liability.

Several examples may make these rules more understandable. Assume that the city taxes on a parcel of annexed property, had the property been in the city for the full fiscal year, would have been $600.

- If the effective date of the annexation is any day in July, there are eleven full months remaining in the fiscal year (August through June), and therefore the appropriate fraction is 11/12. Multiplying that fraction against the liability for the full year (11/12 X $600) results in a prorated liability of $550.
- If the effective date of the annexation is any day in November, there are seven full months remaining in the fiscal year (December through June), and therefore the appropriate fraction is 7/12. Multiplying that fraction against the liability for the full year (7/12 X $600) results in a prorated liability of $350.
- If the effective date of the annexation is any day in March, there are three full months remaining in the fiscal year (April through June), and therefore the appropriate fraction is 3/12. Multiplying that fraction against the liability for the full year (3/12 X $600) results in a prorated liability of $150.
- If the effective date of the annexation is any day in June, there are no full months remaining in the fiscal year, and therefore the appropriate fraction is 0/12. Multiplying that fraction against the liability for the full year (0/12 x $600) results in a prorated liability of $0.

Because an effective date in June leaves no prorated tax, and therefore does not require officials to explain the prorated tax system to owners of annexed property, many cities prefer to make their annexations effective during that month, particularly on June 30. Of course, if an annexation is challenged in court, the city loses control of the effective date and some prorated taxes are almost certain.

Paying prorated taxes. Although an annexed parcel is liable for a prorated share of taxes levied for the fiscal year in which the annexation takes place, in most instances the owner of that parcel does not have to pay those taxes until the succeeding fiscal year. G.S. 160A-58.10(b) sets up the following rules for when prorated taxes are due.

1. If the annexation becomes effective before September 2—that is, in July, in August, or on September 1—the prorated taxes

are due on September 1 of the fiscal year for which they are levied. (September 1 is the normal due date for property taxes, which means that a local government may not offer a discount for taxes paid on that day or later.) If the taxes are not paid before the following January 6, they will bear interest in the same way as other taxes levied for that fiscal year.

2. If the annexation becomes effective on September 2 or any later date during the fiscal year, the prorated taxes are due on September 1 in the *next* fiscal year, as much as twelve months after the effective date of the annexation. In this instance, the city will have the burden of providing services to the annexed property, but it will be some months before it receives property taxes from that property.

This set of rules for paying prorated taxes carries both advantages and disadvantages for owners of annexed property. The advantage, of course, is that the property might be in the city for a considerable number of months before owners need to pay any city taxes on the property. If, for example, a property is annexed in October, the prorated taxes are not due until the succeeding September; and, as a practical matter, they might not be paid until the following December, fourteen months after the annexation becomes effective. The disadvantage is that when the owner finally pays the taxes, he or she will have a uniquely heavy tax bill—paying at one time for both the prorated year and the current year.

Billing prorated taxes. Normally, the local government that bills and collects a city's taxes bills the prorated taxes in the year in which they become due. Therefore, if they are due during the fiscal year in which the annexation becomes effective, they will be billed with other taxes for that year. But if they do not become due until the following fiscal year, they will normally not be billed until the next year, along with the taxes levied for that year. (There is no ban, however, on sending a bill for prorated taxes during the current year, even though they are not due until the succeeding year; if that is done, the billing government should make it very clear that the prorated taxes are not due until the succeeding year.)

[b] Property taxes on motor vehicles

The proration system described just above does not apply to property taxes paid on motor vehicles. G.S. 105-330.1 classifies motor vehicles as a special class of property, and the succeeding sections of the General Statutes establish a special system for collecting these taxes. The taxation of motor vehicles is tied to the registration process; because vehicles' registrations are staggered throughout the year, so is their taxation. About one-twelfth of vehicles are registered each month, and so about one-twelfth are taxed each month. The process works like this: approximately three months after a vehicle registration is applied for or renewed, the tax assessor sends a tax bill to the owner; payment is due in approximately two weeks, and interest begins to run a month after that. The ownership, situs, and taxability of a vehicle are determined annually on the day a new registration is applied for or a current registration is renewed.

That the proration system does not apply to motor vehicle taxes is evident from both the proration statute itself and from the statutes establishing the motor vehicle tax. First, the proration statute is tied to a taxing system in which the taxability of property is determined as of January 1 of each year; taxes that fall under this system are levied for a fiscal year running from July 1 through the succeeding June 30 and are due on September 1. None of this system applies to motor vehicle taxes. The taxability of a vehicle is determined as of its registration date—not as of January 1. Because the vehicle tax year is the twelve months beginning on the registration date, there are twelve different such tax years and twelve different due dates each year. Motor vehicle taxation simply does not fit the proration statute.

Furthermore, G.S. 105-330.2(a), part of the statute establishing the motor vehicle tax system, specifies that the "ownership, situs, and taxability of a classified motor vehicle . . . shall be determined annually as of the day on which a new registration is applied for or the day on which the current vehicle registration is renewed." Because both the situs and the taxability of the vehicle are determined as of that date, if the situs is not within a city on that date, no city taxes can be levied against it for that year. Even if an annexation becomes effective before the tax is due or is paid, if the vehicle's location was outside the city on the date specified in G.S. 105-330.2(a), the city will have to wait until the next year to tax that vehicle.

[c] Notice to the county

If the county bills or collects a city's taxes, it obviously is crucial for county tax officials to know when one or more parcels have been annexed to that city. It is the city's responsibility to inform the county of each annexation; thus a report containing this information should be a regular part of the annexation process.

[d] Taxpayer confusion when annexed property is sold

When real property is sold in North Carolina, it is standard procedure to prorate the property taxes that are due or that will be due on the property as of the closing date. It is also standard procedure to prorate the taxes on the basis of the *calendar year*, even though such a proration makes no sense in relation to when taxes are levied or when local government provides the services those taxes pay for. If a parcel is sold on June 30, the property taxes for the fiscal year that begins the next day will be prorated so that the seller pays half the taxes and the buyer pays the other half. That is because each party will have owned the property for half the calendar year. But as taxes are levied for a fiscal year that begins July 1, the seller is actually paying half the taxes for a fiscal year in which he or she never has title to the property and never receives the services for which the taxes are levied.

Confusion—indeed, anger—can arise if the property in question is being annexed, especially if the annexation takes place after the property is sold. Assume, for example, that a parcel of property is included in an involuntary annexation that will take effect on June 30 and that the parcel is sold on April 30. At the closing, the seller will be asked to pay city taxes for four months—January through April of the calendar year—even though he or she is selling the property before the annexation ever takes effect and will never own the property while it is in the city. Technically, the confusion is not of the city's making—it is the result of decisions made by the parties to the property transaction or, more accurately, by their professional advisers. Nonetheless, the city will often have the burden of trying to explain the matter to a property owner perhaps already unhappy with being annexed at all. A number of cities have prepared written materials for annexed property owners explaining how their property will be taxed, but these explanations are rarely entirely successful.

Section 14.02. City Reimbursement of Fire District Taxes

Chapter 9 discusses a series of statutes that protect rural fire departments and their full-time employees when a city annexes part of a tax or insurance district served by such a department. Another set of statutes, discussed in this section, seeks to sort out the tax liabilities of annexed property that has been part of a fire tax district.

The initial problem these statutes address arises because the city collects prorated city taxes on property annexed during a fiscal year. If, for example, property is annexed in October, the property owner will be liable for prorated taxes for eight months (November through June) of the fiscal year; if the city provides fire protection through its general fund, some portion of those prorated taxes will be used to furnish fire protection. At the same time, however, if the annexed property is within a fire tax district, the property owner will also be liable for fire district taxes for the full year of the annexation, even though the property is only part of the district until the effective date of the annexation. If the legislature had made no provision for adjustment, the property owner in the example would be paying two governments for fire protection for the same eight remaining months of the fiscal year but only receiving service from one of those governments.

The statutes solve this initial problem by requiring the city to pay the taxpayer a rebate—called a *prorated fire protection payment*—in the amount of the fire district taxes he or she paid for those months of the fiscal year in which the taxpayer's property is in the city. The amount of this payment is calculated in the same way as prorated city property taxes: that is, for each parcel annexed, the amount of the fire district tax levied for the fiscal year of annexation is multiplied by a fraction in which the denominator is twelve and the numerator is the number of full months remaining in the fiscal year after the effective date of the annexation. For example, if a parcel with a fire district tax liability of $120 is annexed in October (when there are eight full months remaining in the fiscal year), the amount of the city's payment obligation to the property owner is $120 X 8/12, or $80.

This prorated fire protection payment creates equity between the city and the property owner, in that the owner avoids paying taxes to two governments for the same service. If the matter stopped here, however, the city might be disadvantaged vis-à-vis the county. That could happen if the city, as required in involuntary annexations, offers to enter into an agreement with the rural fire department whose territory it annexed. As explained in Chapter 9, under such an agreement, the rural department would continue to provide some fire protection to the annexation area. In that case, the city would pay the department for fire protection in the annexed area; but so would the county, which would retain the full year's fire district tax paid by the property owner.

To correct this situation, the statutes provide that if the city has entered into such a contract with the rural department, the county must pay the city the amount due under the contract for the prorated portion of the annexation year.

To summarize, the statutes provide for the following set of payments involving fire protection and fire district taxes for the fiscal year in which the annexation becomes effective (called the *annexation year*):

- Owner of annexed property
  1. Pays the full amount of taxes levied for the fire district for the annexation year.
  2. Pays (eventually) the prorated amount of city taxes for the annexation year.

- The city
  1. Makes a prorated fire protection payment to the owner of annexed property representing the amount of fire district taxes paid to the county for services provided through the district after the annexation is effective.
  2. Perhaps has a contract with the rural fire department for services provided to the annexation area and makes payments to the department under that contract.

- The county
  1. Pays the rural fire department with tax moneys received from annexed property owners.
  2. If the city has a contract with the rural fire department, pays the city the amount the city pays the department for services during the prorated portion of the annexation year.

Section 14.03. Privilege License Taxes

Each of the statutory annexation procedures includes a subsection setting out the effect of the annexation ordinance on taxes and other matters. Each of these subsections includes the following sentence:

> If the effective date of annexation falls between June 1 and June 30, and the effective date of the privilege license tax ordinance of the annexing municipality is June 1, then businesses in the area to be annexed shall be liable for taxes imposed in such ordinances from and after the effective date of annexation.[1]

The questions raised by the quoted language are two. First, if a city has a June 1 effective date for privilege license taxes and an annexation takes place in any month other than June, are businesses in the annexation area liable for the tax in the tax year in which the annexation takes place? Second, if—as is far more likely—a city has a July 1 effective date for privilege license taxes, in what circumstances may the city collect the tax from annexed businesses for the fiscal year in which the annexation takes effect?

In 1970 the Attorney General's office published an opinion that takes a very restrictive view of the effect of the quoted language.[2] Unless property is annexed in June and the tax is effective on June 1, the opinion argues, a city may not tax businesses in an annexation area if the annexation has not yet become effective on the date that the privilege license tax becomes effective. Under this reading of the statute, if a business is annexed in any month other than June, it is not liable for privilege license tax until the effective date of the first privilege license tax levied after the annexation. If the annexation becomes effective in July, in October, in February, or in May, the business is not liable for privilege license taxes until the succeeding June 1 or July 1, depending on which privilege license effective date is used by the annexing city.

This advice was clearly correct when the opinion was published in 1970. At the time, and until 1975, the various annexation statutes provided that the "newly annexed territory shall be subject to municipal taxes levied for the fiscal year following the effective date of annexation." Thus, annexed property and property owners and residents of

1. G.S. 160A-31(e); -37(f); -49(f); and -58.3.

2. Opinion of the Attorney General to Edwin C. Ipock, Goldsboro City Attorney, 40 N.C.A.G. 863 (24 February 1970).

the annexed property were not subject to *any* municipal taxes until the beginning of the fiscal year following the effective date of annexation. The quoted statutory language actually expanded somewhat the taxing power of a city, recognizing that some cities made their privilege license taxes effective June 1 and permitting such a city to tax a business even if the annexation was effective sometime later in June.

In 1975, however, the various annexation statutes were amended, and the sentence setting out the required treatment of municipal taxes was taken out. It was replaced with those provisions under which *property taxes* are prorated, as explained in section 14.01[b]. The result is that there are now specific provisions for prorating property taxes but no general language applicable to other taxes. Therefore, the first sentence of the various subsections should be applicable. It declares that from the effective date of annexation the annexed "territory and its citizens and property shall be subject to all . . . ordinances . . . in force in such municipality." The specific language about privilege license taxes has, in reality, become an obsolete and meaningless remnant of the former taxation system.

Therefore, it is now appropriate for a city to follow a different course than that advocated by the published Attorney General's opinion; and in fact most cities do follow this different course. A city may treat a business annexed in the middle of a fiscal year in the same way it would treat a business that began operations in the middle of the fiscal year. Under the model administrative provisions for a privilege license tax ordinance published by the Institute of Government and followed in many cities,[3] a business that begins operation during the first seven months of the year is liable for the entire year's tax; a business that begins operation during the last five months of the year is liable for half a year's tax. If a newly annexed business is treated in the same way, a business annexed during the first seven months would pay the full amount of the tax, while a business annexed later would pay half the tax. A business annexed by a city that levies privilege license taxes on the basis of gross receipts would simply pay an estimated amount based on the gross receipts it expects to receive during the remainder of the fiscal year.

3. The model administrative provisions for a privilege license ordinance are published as an Appendix to William A. Campbell, North Carolina City and County Privilege License Taxes (5th ed., 2000); these provisions are also found in earlier editions of this book. The proration provision is found in section 6 of the model ordinance.

Section 14.04. Local Government Sales and Use Taxes

Cities receive a share of the four current local government sales and use taxes. The county levies these local taxes, and the board of county commissioners determines the method by which the proceeds allocated to the county are apportioned between the county and the cities and towns in the county. The board can select either of two methods.

Per capita. Under the per capita method, sales and use tax proceeds are apportioned between the county government and each city and town on the basis of population. (The county receives credit for its entire population, both citizens living inside cities and towns and those living in unincorporated areas.) In determining the population of each unit of government, the Secretary of Revenue is directed to "use the most recent annual estimate of population certified by the State Planning Officer." (This certification is now done by the Office of State Budget and Management [State OBM].)

Each June, the State OBM mails a survey to each city in North Carolina, asking it to list all annexations that became effective during the period beginning with the preceding July 2 and ending on the upcoming July 1. For example, the surveys sent out in June 2001 asked about annexations with effective dates between July 2, 2000, and July 1, 2001. The ending date of July 1 is used because that is the date on which State OBM bases the population estimates used each year to distribute sales and use taxes, as well as other taxes distributed on a per capita basis (see, e.g., 14.05 [c], [d], [e] below). Therefore, in order to ensure that it receives the proper amount of sales tax distribution, a city that has completed an annexation simply needs to be sure that it is reported on the State OBM annual survey.

Ad valorem taxes. Under the ad valorem method, sales and use-tax proceeds are apportioned between the county government and each city and town on the basis of the total amount of ad valorem taxes levied by each government during the fiscal year preceding the sales tax distribution. Thus the distribution of sales and use-tax proceeds collected during the 2001–2002 fiscal year would be based on property tax levies for the 2000–2001 fiscal year.

Each December the Division of Tax Research of the Department of Revenue sends cities and counties a survey asking for the total amount of each unit's property tax base and the amount of property taxes billed for the current fiscal year. This report is due back to the division by the following February 1. Because the report asks for the amount of taxes billed, a city should include those prorated property taxes billed in the current fiscal year, even though they are not due until the next year. (Prorated taxes that were not billed would be included in the next year's report.) The Tax Research Division compiles this information and transmits it in late June or early July to the Sales and Use Tax Division, which uses it for the mid-August distribution of local government sales and use-tax proceeds and for all succeeding distributions until the following August.

Section 14.05. State-Shared Taxes

[a] Electric utility franchise taxes

G.S. 105-116 levies an annual state franchise tax on electric utilities in the amount of 3.22 percent of their gross receipts from the business of furnishing electric power. This tax applies to both investor-owned utilities and electric membership corporations. The state distributes most of the gross receipts collected from sales within a city to that city. Therefore, when a city annexes customers of a taxed electric utility, it is entitled to the franchise tax the utility pays the state for those customers.

G.S. 105-116 directs each electric utility liable for the franchise tax to report to the Department of Revenue the gross receipts earned from sales in each separate city or town, so that the department can determine the amount of franchise tax to which each city is entitled. For that reason, it is crucial that an annexing city make certain that each electric utility doing business in the annexation area knows about the annexation and knows which customers are now city customers. If the annexation is sizable, the best way for the city to convey the necessary information to the utility is for a city official to walk through the annexation area with a representative of the utility and point out utility customers whose properties have been annexed.

If the annexing city is an electric city (see chapter 11), it does not pay the electric utility franchise tax and therefore will not receive any state-shared taxes for electric sales within the annexation area. Sometimes, however, an electric city will annex the substation from which it purchases the power that it in turn sells at retail. As the sales at the substation are subject to the electric utility franchise tax, the city will receive distributions from those sales after annexation. The city therefore needs to be sure that the tax-paying utility that owns the substation is aware that the substation is now in the city so that it will keep careful records of sales at the substation.

[b] Piped natural gas taxes

General Statutes Chapter 105, Article 5E, levies an excise tax on the piped natural gas a gas utility delivers to its customers. G.S. 105-187.41 levies the tax on the basis of the monthly therms of natural gas received by the end-user, with the rate per therm going down as monthly usage goes up.[4] G.S. 105-187.44 directs that one-half of the taxes the utility remits because of sales to city customers be distributed to that city. Therefore, when a city annexes and takes into the city additional natural gas customers of a taxed utility, it becomes entitled to a share of the taxes the gas utility remitted to the state for those customers.

G.S. 105-187.44 directs each natural gas company that is liable for the tax to report to the Department of Revenue the amount of piped natural gas it delivers or receives in each separate city or town so that the department can determine the amount of piped natural gas tax to which each city and town is entitled. For that reason it is crucial that an annexing city make certain that each natural gas company doing business in the annexation area knows about the annexation and knows which customers are now city customers. If the annexation is sizable, the best way for the city to convey the necessary information to the utility is for a city official to walk through the annexation area with a representative of the company and point out customers whose properties have been included in the annexation area.

[c] Telecommunications taxes

G.S. 105-164.4B levies a sales and use tax of 4.5 percent on the gross receipts of companies providing telecommunications services in North Carolina. G.S. 105-164.44F provides that each quarter the Department of Revenue is to distribute 24.4 percent of the proceeds of this tax (minus $2.6 million) to cities. The method by which each city's share of these proceeds is determined depends on the date it was incorporated.

Cities incorporated before January 1, 2001. Each city incorporated before January 1, 2001, receives a set percentage of the proceeds of

4. The rate begins at $.047 per therm for the first 200 therms and declines to $.003 for each therm over 500,000.

this tax, based on the distribution of the telephone utility franchise tax that was repealed and replaced by the telecommunications tax. Annexations have no effect on this percentage or, therefore, on the amount of telecommunications tax the city receives.

Cities incorporated on or after January 1, 2001. Instead of a set percentage, each city incorporated on or after January 1, 2001, receives a per capita share of the proceeds from the telecommunications tax. The Department of Revenue determines a per capita amount of tax proceeds for all cities and then distributes their proportionate share to this small class of recently incorporated cities. To receive the proper amount of telecommunications tax distribution, therefore, a city in this group that has completed an annexation needs to be sure that the annexation is reported to State OBM on the annual survey of municipal annexations that office uses to estimate town populations. (See section 14.04 above.)

[d] State street assistance (Powell Bill monies)

Each fall, the state distributes to cities a portion of the motor fuel taxes it collects.[5] Three-quarters of the available money is distributed on a per capita basis, based on the most recent annual estimates of population made by the State OBM. The remaining one-quarter is distributed according to the number of miles of streets each city maintains.

Per capita portion. Each June, the State OBM mails a survey to each city in North Carolina, asking it to list all annexations that became effective during the period beginning with the preceding July 2 and ending on the upcoming July 1. For example, the surveys sent out in June 2001 asked about annexations with effective dates between July 2, 2000, and July 1, 2001. The ending date of July 1 is used because that is the date on which State OBM bases the population estimates used each year to distribute sales and use taxes, as well as other taxes distributed on a per capital basis. To ensure that it receives the proper amount of this distribution, therefore, a city that has recently completed annexations simply needs to be sure that they are all reported on this annual survey.

Street mileage portion. G.S. 136-41.1(a) directs each mayor to submit an annual report to the Department of Transportation setting out

5. The annual Powell Bill appropriation, set out in G.S. 136-41.1, is the equivalent of 1¾ cents per gallon of motor fuel purchased plus 6.5 percent of the net proceeds of the Highway Trust Fund.

information for determining Powell Bill eligibility and distribution amounts. In this report, due near the end of each July, the mayor certifies the mileage of streets maintained by the city as of the preceding June 30. Therefore, each year this report should be updated to reflect any new streets the city maintains as a result of annexations that have become effective since the preceding report.

[e] Beer and wine taxes

G.S. 105-113.80 levies state excise taxes on beer and wine,[6] while G.S. 105-113.82 directs that a portion of the proceeds of these taxes be distributed annually to cities and counties on a per capita basis.[7] In making the distributions, the Department of Revenue is to use the most recent annual population estimates made by State OBM.

Each June, the State OBM mails a survey to each city in North Carolina, asking it to list all annexations that became effective during the period beginning with the preceding July 2 and ending on the upcoming July 1. For example, the surveys sent out in June 2001 asked about annexations with effective dates between July 2, 2000, and July 1, 2001. The ending date of July 1 is used because that is the date on which State OBM bases the population estimates used each year to distribute sales and use taxes, as well as other taxes distributed on a per capita basis. Therefore, in order to ensure that it receives the proper amount of beer and wine tax distribution, a city that has completed an annexation in the past fiscal year simply needs to be sure that the annexation is reported to State OBM on this annual survey.

6. The rates are 53.177 cents per gallon for malt beverages, 21 cents per liter for unfortified wine, and 24 cents per liter for fortified wine.

7. Local governments receive 23.75 percent of the malt beverage tax proceeds, 62 percent of the unfortified wine tax proceeds, and 22 percent of the fortified wine tax proceeds.

15

Reversing an Annexation

15

Reversing an Annexation

This chapter considers whether—and how—a city that has adopted an annexation ordinance, and now regrets doing so, may reverse the annexation.

Section 15.01. Repeal of an Annexation Ordinance before It Becomes Effective

[a] Introduction

The North Carolina annexation statutes do not specifically mention repeal of an annexation ordinance, and no North Carolina case raises or discusses that issue directly. In general, however, cities have an inherent authority to repeal ordinances that they have adopted, at least if no private rights have vested under the ordinance between the time of adoption and the attempt to repeal.[1] The courts in several states have applied this general principle about city ordinances to annexation ordinances, either acknowledging or specifically upholding a city's ability to repeal an annexation ordinance in certain circumstances. The rule that emerges from these cases is that a city may repeal an annexation ordinance at any time before it takes effect.[2]

[b] Cases from other states

The first case is *Vesenmeir v. City of Aurora*,[3] a 1953 case from Indiana. In June of 1952 the city adopted an annexation ordinance, which was challenged in court the succeeding month. (Because of the challenge, the ordinance did not take effect.) In October 1952, the city repealed the June ordinance and adopted a new ordinance annexing a smaller area. Under Indiana law, a judicial decision adverse to the

1. 6 EUGENE MCQUILLIN, THE LAW OF MUNICIPAL CORPORATIONS § 21.10 (3d ed. 1998 rev.).
2. No cases have been found that deny a city's authority to repeal an annexation ordinance before it becomes effective.
3. 115 N.E.2d 734 (Ind. 1953).

annexation would have prohibited the city from further annexation proceedings for two years, and the city's action was intended to sidestep that result. When property owners challenged the propriety of the city's actions, the Indiana supreme court held that because the power to adopt an ordinance includes the power to repeal it, the city could repeal an annexation ordinance while a legal challenge to it was pending.

> As a general rule a municipality which has been given the power to enact ordinances has, as a necessary incident thereto and without any express authorization in the statute, the power to modify or repeal such ordinances unless the power to do so is restricted in the law conferring it. The power is subject to the limitation that the repeal or change cannot be made so as to affect any vested rights lawfully acquired under the ordinance sought to be modified or repealed.[4]

A comparable case is *Powell v. City of Campbellsburg*,[5] a 1978 Kentucky case that also involved an annexation under appeal. The day before the trial court hearing on the annexation, the city repealed the ordinance. The next day, the city moved successfully in court to dismiss the action. Under Kentucky law, too, a judgment against an annexation would have precluded making a new annexation attempt for two years—a result the city sought to avoid by seeking dismissal. Even before the trial court's order of dismissal was signed, however, the city adopted a new annexation ordinance covering much of the same area. Property owners brought suit, claiming that the repeal was unauthorized and that the original dismissal was therefore ineffective. Using the same reasoning as the Indiana court, the Kentucky court of appeals upheld the city's actions, holding that the power to adopt the ordinance includes the power to repeal it.

There are also two cases from Tennessee. The first, *City of Bluff City v. Morrell*,[6] is a 1988 decision of the Tennessee supreme court. In 1980 Bluff City had attempted an annexation that was challenged in court; while the challenge was pending, the city council voted "to kill the annexation suit." The trial court treated the city's action as a repeal of the annexation ordinance and dismissed the challenge. Five years later, the city brought a declaratory judgment action: it asserted that it

4. *Id.* at 737.
5. 563 S.W.2d 488 (Ky. Ct. App. 1978).
6. 764 S.W.2d 200 (Tenn. 1988).

had had no authority to repeal the earlier ordinance; that the challenge to the ordinance had lapsed and was now barred by the statute of limitations; and that, therefore, the area was part of the city. Despite the somewhat inequitable nature of the city's argument, the city persuaded the trial court and the Tennessee court of appeals that it was, indeed, without authority to repeal its own annexation ordinance. The Tennessee supreme court affirmed the lower court, but on the ground that the motion "to kill the annexation suit" did not, in fact, constitute repeal of the annexation ordinance. Indeed, the court went on to specifically affirm that a city has the power to repeal an annexation ordinance before it becomes effective:

> We are in agreement with the Court of Appeals that the act which repeals an ordinance must be of equal dignity with the act that established it, and must be enacted in the manner required for passing a valid ordinance. An ordinance can be repealed only by another ordinance, and not by a mere resolution, order, or motion, or by a void ordinance. An annexation ordinance once validly passed but not yet operative because of a quo warranto proceeding can be repealed when the legislative body acts with equal dignity and in full compliance with procedures required for passing a valid ordinance.[7]

The Tennessee court of appeals reiterated this point the next year in *State ex rel. Schalterbrand v. Knoxville.*[8] The city had adopted six annexation ordinances in March 1987, and court challenges to all of them were filed the next day. More than a year later, while the challenges were still pending, the city repealed the six ordinances; as a result, the trial court dismissed the challenges as moot. Because Tennessee has a statute similar to those of Indiana and Kentucky—it prohibits a city from attempting to annex an area for two years after an earlier attempt to do so is invalidated by a court—the challengers appealed the trial court's dismissal, arguing that the city was without authority to repeal the ordinances. Quoting from *Bluff City*, the court upheld the city's actions and the order of the trial court.

Two other cases merit mention. In *Mouton v. City of Lafayette*,[9] the Louisiana city had attempted a substantial annexation that was under judicial challenge. While the case was pending, however, the state

7. *Id.* at 202 (citations omitted).
8. 788 S.W.2d 812 (Tenn. Ct. App. 1989).
9. 49 So.2d 638 (La. Ct. App. 1950).

legislature annexed the same territory to the city; that action enabled the city to have the challenge to its own annexation dismissed as moot. In upholding the dismissal, the Louisiana court argued that the legislature's action was in effect a repeal of the city's ordinance, rendering a challenge to that ordinance moot. In so arguing, the court clearly believed that the city could have repealed the ordinance itself.[10] In *Mitrus v. Nichols*,[11] a new city council repealed an annexation ordinance before it became effective, and the owner of the property sought a mandamus order directing the city to proceed with the original ordinance. The trial court denied the order, holding that the power to repeal the ordinance was inherent in the power to adopt it originally. The judgment does not seem to have been appealed.

[c] North Carolina cases

A North Carolina court of appeals decision is consistent with these cases from other states, inasmuch as it appears to accept a city's authority to repeal an annexation ordinance while a judicial challenge is pending. In *Chicora Country Club, Inc. v. Town of Erwin*,[12] the city adopted an annexation ordinance; two weeks later, it readopted the ordinance, with minor modifications. Sometime later the city rescinded the first ordinance—leaving only the second ordinance subject to challenge. The petitioners had filed a timely challenge to the first ordinance, but their challenge to the second ordinance missed the thirty-day statute of limitations; consequently, the trial court dismissed both petitions. On appeal, the petitioners did not challenge the city's authority to rescind the ordinance; indeed, their brief does not even mention the rescission. Instead, they argued that the city was required to give notice of its intention to rescind the ordinance to property owners in the annexation area. They reasoned that if such notice was required as a condition of adopting the ordinance originally, it should also be required when the city wants to rescind the ordinance. The court of appeals rejected the petitioners' argument, holding that there is no such requirement in the statute. (There is, of course, no mention in the statute of any right to rescind an ordinance either.)

10. "As we view Act 13, we are of the opinion that the Act repeals Ordinance No. 401 of the City of Lafayette. The Act supercedes the action of the City of Lafayette. The situation is the same as if the City of Lafayette had repealed the Ordinance." *Id.* at 639.

11. 13 N.Y.S.2d 990 (N.Y. Sup. Ct., Spec. Term, 1939).

12. 128 N.C. App. 101, 493 S.E.2d 797 (1997).

[d] Policy considerations

The cases described above make sense as a matter of policy. If a city discovers that it has committed a fatal error in its annexation process, why not permit the city to resolve any challenge by simply repealing the faulty ordinance? By doing so, the city (as well as the challengers) avoids the cost of further legal proceedings against an ordinance that the city feels will be ultimately unsupportable.[13] Furthermore, North Carolina—unlike Indiana, Kentucky, and Tennessee—has no statute prohibiting a city, for some specified period, from attempting a new annexation after a court has declared an original annexation invalid. It is not possible, therefore, to argue that permitting repeal deprives property owners of the protection of such a statute.

Section 15.02. Repeal of an Annexation Ordinance after the Annexation Becomes Effective

None of the cases described above involved an annexation that was already effective, and no cases have been found in which such an attempt was the subject of litigation. Repealing an annexation ordinance after the ordinance has gone into effect is a deannexation, and, as noted in Section 1.03, only the General Assembly may deannex territory from a city. A city's authority to repeal an ordinance is lost once rights under the ordinance have vested; and when it becomes effective, an annexation ordinance vests certain rights in the property owners in the annexation area.[14] As a result it is possible, perhaps likely, that a city has no authority to repeal an annexation ordinance once that ordinance has taken effect.

13. The Indiana supreme court made this point in *Vesenmeir*: "The effect of sustaining appeallants' contention [that the city was without authority to repeal its ordinance] would be that if the Common Council made a mistake in the description of the property sought to be annexed or made a mistake of judgment, it could not itself correct its mistake by repealing the ordinance even though the ordinance had not yet become operative, but it must persevere in its error for the sole purpose of affording the court an opportunity to put an end to a proceeding which had already been abandoned. The law does not require such an empty ritual." Vesenmeir v. City of Aurora, 115 N.E.2d 734, 738 (1953).

14. In State *ex rel.* Schalterbrand v. Knoxville, 788 S.W.2d 812 (Tenn. Ct. App. 1989) the court emphasized that because the annexation had not yet become effective, no rights had been vested that would interfere with the city's ability to repeal the ordinance.

There is one situation, however, in which it may make sense for a city to repeal an annexation ordinance that is already effective. When they adopt voluntary annexation ordinances, most cities make them effective immediately, or within a very short period. If a city does so but discovers soon thereafter that the ordinance was invalid because of some substantive failure, repeal of the annexation ordinance offers a prompt and simple way to correct the failure. Say, for example, that a city adopts an ordinance annexing a satellite area and then discovers, a few days later, that part of the annexation area is in fact closer to another city. The annexation area was therefore not, in fact, eligible for annexation in the first place. If the city repeals the ordinance promptly, it is unlikely that anyone will have acted in reliance on the annexation, so there should be much less concern for vested rights. Furthermore, the city may be able to correct the error and undertake a substitute annexation that complies with the substantive requirements of the statute. If the city is not permitted to repeal the ordinance, the matter will have to await action by the General Assembly, which might be many months away. Therefore, because it makes sense to allow such a repeal, perhaps a city may repeal a voluntary annexation ordinance on the ground that the annexation is substantively invalid, as long as the city acts within a short time after the ordinance becomes effective.

Appendix A

Major North Carolina Statutes Discussed in Text and Footnotes

General Statute (G.S.) Section	Page
1-515	7-11
1-516	7-13–15
69-25.15	2-6, 14-8–9
69-25.15(a)	2-7
105-113.82	14-16
105-116	14-13–14
105-164.44F	14-14–15
105-164.44I	14-16–17
105-187.41 et seq.	14-14
105-330.1 et seq.	14-6
120-30.9F	13-7
130A-55(8b)	12-19n
136-41.1	14-15–16
136-66.1	8-10
136-66.2	8-10
153A-275(a)	12-19n
153A-304.1	2-6, 14-8–9
153A-304.1(a)	2-7
153A-344.1	8-7
160A-1(2)	2-4
160A-22	6-9
160A-23(b)	13-10
160A-29	1-5, 6-9–10
160A-31	3-5–6
160A-31(e)	14-10–11
160A-31.1	9-14–18
160A-36(b)(3)	3-9
160A-37(f)	14-10–11

General Statute (G.S.) Section	Page
160A-37.1	9-4–13
160A-37.2	9-14–18
160A-37.3	10-3–12
160A-37.3(h)	10-7n
160A-38(l)	4-7
160A-49(f)	2-6, 2-10–12, 14-10–11
160A-49.1	9-4–13
160A-49.2	9-14–18
160A-49.3	10-3–12
160A-49.3(h)	10-7n
160A-50(m)	4-7
160A-58.1	3-6
160A-58.1(b1)	1-9n
160A-58.2A	9-14–18
160A–58.3	14-10–11
160A-58.10	14-3–5
160A-58.21 et seq.	3-20–28
160A-58.24	3-21–25
160A-58.27	3-25–28, 7-27
160A-294	9-13–14
160A-312(a)	12-19n
160A-324	10-3–12
160A-324(h)	10-7n
160A-327	10-4
160A-327(g)	10-4n
160A, Article 4A, Part 6	1-9, 10-4
160A, Article 16, Part 2	11-3–6
160A-360(e)	8-6–7
160A-360(f)	8-5–6
160A-75	5-3–5
162A-6(a)(5)	12-19n
162A-36(a)(5)	12-19n
162A-69(5)	12-19n
162A-87.3	12-19n
162A-93	2-6, 8-9
163-288.1	1-5, 6-10, 13-11
163-288.2	13-11–12

Appendix B

North Carolina Appellate Cases Discussed or Cited in the Text or Footnotes

If a case is *discussed* in the text or in a footnote, its page number is set in **boldface** type. If the case is only *cited* in a footnote, the page number is set in regular roman type.

Index

www.ingramcontent.com/pod-product-compliance
Lightning Source LLC
LaVergne TN
LVHW052303200926
848481LV00002B/445
9781560115557